Comrie's

LIVING
DANGEROUSLY

by the same author:
Talking Blues

LIVING DANGEROUSLY

Young Offenders in Their Own Words

Roger Graef

Additional research by Harry Lansdown

HarperCollins*Publishers*

HarperCollins*Publishers*
77–85 Fulham Palace Road
Hammersmith, London W6 8JB

Published by HarperCollins*Publishers* 1992

9 8 7 6 5 4 3 2 1

A catalogue record for this book is
available from the British Library

ISBN 0 00 215967 8

Set in Linotron Sabon by
Rowland Phototypesetting Ltd,
Bury St Edmunds, Suffolk

Printed in Great Britain by
HarperCollinsManufacturing Glasgow

To young burglars and their victims.
I hope this book will help resolve their problems.

CONTENTS

ACKNOWLEDGEMENTS

This book could not have been achieved without the co-operation of Graham Smith, Head of the Inner London Probation Service, and Phillipa Drew, of the Home Office, whose understanding made this venture possible. I am most grateful to the researcher, Harry Lansdown, who joined me one year after Sherborne House but gave it his full and whole-hearted attention. His journalistic judgement and sympathetic ear bodes well for his future. Stuart Proffitt and Philip Gwyn Jones, the editors, showed great patience and sensitivity to the feelings and experiences of these young people.

But most of all I must thank the staff and group members at Sherborne House. I hope they will recognise their experience from these fragments.

INTRODUCTION

One in three British males are convicted of a non-motoring criminal offence by the time they are thirty. Read that again: *one in
every three British males will have been convicted – not just
arrested – for a non-motoring criminal offence by the age of thirty*,
according to the Home Office Cohort study of three generations.

Unpicking that figure reveals a picture quite different from the
lurid accounts of crime waves which inflame the rhetoric of leader
writers and politicians. These are neither murderers nor rapists,
nor muggers of old ladies, a calibre of criminal by no means as
common as the tabloids suggest. Violent offences make up only
six per cent of recorded crime, and the victim of a violent crime
often knows the perpetrator (domestic violence – by far the largest
sponsor of such crimes – is seldom reported). The crimes which
make up the bulk of the figures and *do* affect strangers are offences
against property: burglary and theft. The vast majority of these
crimes are committed by a small number of people: not the armed
professional gangs of television drama, but teenagers. Equally,
only a small percentage – just five per cent of offenders – commit
seventy per cent of detected property crime. Only eight per cent
commit eighty per cent. That means if we were able to find a
way of diverting this small group from their habit of persistent
offending, the crime rate would fall dramatically.

Who are these habitual criminals that feed the crime figures?
Scandals about joyriding and teenage car theft hit the media as if
they were unprecedented problems. These unruly teenagers keep
the police on the defensive about their ineffectiveness; they make
the courts and prisons to which they return with exhausting regu-
larity feel useless; they push up our insurance rates, especially in
cities; they keep old ladies, even in peaceful rural areas, imprisoned ·

by fear behind locked doors; they lead pundits and politicians to fulminate about the collapse of law and order, and sometimes of Western civilisation itself. Are they a breed apart – an enemy within – as they are stigmatised by politicians? And is there any means, any hope, of diverting them from crime?

In 1990, at the time of the riots in Strangeways Prison, I was commissioned by a newspaper to ask judges and magistrates about why they sent people to prison. I interviewed fourteen judges and magistrates about their use of prison when two-thirds of ex-prisoners were reconvicted within two years of leaving jail. (For offenders under twenty-one that figure rises to three-quarters.) Although the judges and magistrates I spoke to spanned a wide spectrum of political views, they all agreed that prison was virtually useless as a means to stop reoffending. But in despair, they admitted that for persistent offenders, especially those who had already been given cautions, probation and community service, they did not know what else to do.

At least prison signalled society's disapproval of their actions. Moreover, it kept them off the streets for the length of the sentence. One judge said, 'If only transportation were still available. I'd like nothing better than to take one of these youngsters who's reappeared for the umpteenth car theft and say, "You're a thoroughly bad sort. Off you go to Australia."' Rehabilitation was never mentioned, except as a sardonic joke. Listening to their hopelessness, I could not believe there was no satisfactory alternative.

Indeed, one London Crown Court judge was more optimistic. Judge Butler described to me the Day Centre intensive probation programme, designed for persistent offenders as their last chance before prison. It was a probation equivalent to custody. In his experience, it successfully diverted young people from crime – not always, but often enough to be worth trying. He directed me to Sherborne House near Tower Bridge, which was the only such programme for young offenders in the whole of Greater London.

Some intensive programmes had been going since the early 1980s. There are now at least one hundred around Britain – but I was astonished to discover that not even the Home Office knows exactly how many there are, or what each of them does. Only half a dozen are believed to follow the full-time, rigorously structured ten-week programme on the model established by Sherborne

House. Still more significant is the fact that almost no research has been done into their effectiveness. This is all the more surprising because the few studies that have been done – in Swansea, Hereford and Worcester, and at Sherborne House – suggest these programmes are a good deal more effective than prison at reducing both the frequency and seriousness of reoffending, at far lower cost.

One reason for their relative obscurity, even among judges, magistrates and probation officers, is that professionals in the criminal justice system have been deeply demoralised about the prospects of reducing reoffending for nearly two decades. In the 1960s, they had a more hopeful approach to dealing with criminals – especially young ones. Rehabilitation was a serious goal, and borstals were designed not just for punishment but for training and education in rural settings – on the model of a strict public school. The variable sentence (up to two years) which was introduced was not intended as cruel, but as a way of ensuring that the young people returned to society, when ready to make a successful new life. In practice, the sudden separation from home and the spartan, harsh discipline was held to damage far more people than were helped. Nevertheless, some older professionals lament the loss of borstals. Their abolition was intended to reduce the punitive approach to young offenders, but unwittingly had the opposite effect.

In 1974, a team of researchers led by American criminologist Robert Martinson studied a variety of rehabilitation programmes in Britain and North America. Their report – *What Works? Questions and Answers About Prisoners' Reform* – concluded that nothing could be proved to divert offenders from crime. Coming in the wake of the Mountbatten Report on prison escapes which led to a huge shift to investment in more secure prisons and the virtual abolition of programmes for rehabilitation, the 'nothing works' syndrome echoed through the Home Office – and penal establishments around the world. When Ronald Reagan arrived in the White House, and Mrs Thatcher at Downing Street, punishment was the focus for the new crusade for law and order: prisons were merely warehouses for inmates. In Britain, the 'short sharp shock' for young offenders became the flagship of Tory criminal justice policy.

Meanwhile, Martinson, the researcher whose conclusion that 'nothing works' became so newsworthy it reached *Time* magazine, quietly retracted his findings in an obscure professional periodical, the *Hofstra Law Journal*. In Britain, the Home Office did a study proving that 'the short, sharp shock' had failed. The report was never published, but the programme was quietly disbanded. In the vacuum, the probation service tried to keep young people out of prison. But they continued to be sent to prison in large numbers, the victims of the bench's fear and desire to punish, and of the lack of convincing alternatives to custody.

But reformers made some headway: the use of fines and Community Service in place of custody slowly began to grow. The 1982 Criminal Justice Act explicitly stated that custody should be a last resort for young offenders under twenty-one. It was widely ignored by the courts, who were *more* likely to send young males between seventeen and twenty to prison than offenders over twenty-one. But the Act also contained provisions for experiments with persistent offenders. It facilitated the establishment of intensive probation Day Centre Programmes as alternatives to custody.

At a time when the criminal justice world was dominated by the riots in Brixton, Toxteth and Broadwater Farm, amid discussions about arming the police, little was heard about these experiments. Part of the problem has been the fragmentation of the Probation Service itself. There are fifty-five different services in England and Wales, while there are only forty-three police forces by comparison. Run by a Probation Board of magistrates, local councillors and police, each probation service receives funding from the Home Office and a small portion from the appropriate local authority to signify their independence. The result of this fragmentation is that probation resources, practices and standards vary wildly. Only now, with the Criminal Justice Act of 1991 requiring probation officers to play a central role in punishment in the community, are there to be common national standards. But the amount set aside for training and recruitment looks unlikely to meet the new demands on the Cinderella service of the criminal justice system. If there is a commitment to reduce the use of custody for all but serious crimes, the government will need to provide far more arrangements and resources for the hard core of persistent offenders to be dealt with outside prison than currently exist. Simply putting them on probation, or giving them an American-style cocktail of punishments – fines, compensation orders, curfews and community service – will not suffice to make them change. Intensive probation programmes like Day Centres will have to become the centrepiece of punishment in the community.

Ironically, probation officers are best placed to have the most effect in reducing crime. Every court has a probation officer. When requested they provide a Social Inquiry Report on the offender and his background for the bench before sentencing. Under the new Act, all convicted offenders must have such a report, a requirement which, though well-intentioned, will seriously overload the system at a stroke.

Their 'clients' are ex-prisoners on parole, and those sentenced to probation orders by the court. They are supposed to see their field probation officers regularly in their local probation office as a condition of their freedom. In practice, many overworked probation officers have in some offices a minimum of thirty or forty alienated clients, who skip as many appointments as they keep. This can mean meetings spaced out over months, that last only half an hour, and deal with bread-and-butter welfare matters like housing and the dole, rather than larger questions about the future. Local standards (soon to become national under the Criminal Justice Act of 1991) set the minimum number of times people on probation must meet their probation officers. If they fail to do so they are breached and sent back to court. But because the service itself is understaffed and overworked, and will be even more so under the new Act, those clients most in need of more support will be unlikely to get it.

Prisons also have probation officers, who try vainly to buck the prevailing culture of punishment and help inmates prepare for their release.

Much as it wants to encourage rehabilitation in the field, in court, and in prison, the probation service lacks the time and resources to achieve it. It suffers worst from the lack of access to training and employment for ex-offenders. Nevertheless, the Audit Commission found that pound for pound, probation delivered far better value in terms of reducing crime than prison.

Probation officers, like the police, prison officers and the judiciary, feel isolated and undervalued by both the public and the rest of the criminal justice system, which sees probation officers as being on the side of the criminals. There is some truth in that, as nobody else in the system looks to the offenders' needs. But like the judge and the policeman, there is no typical probation officer.

The Probation Service is split by class, age, and political attitudes. Its staff range from middle-class ladies intent on doing Good Works with the underprivileged to ex-hippies and Sixties radicals. Their views are spread across the spectrum between care and control. At one end are those liberals who believe the causes of crime are social and political, and not the result of individual actions. They take a *laissez-faire* attitude towards their clients, and resist interfering in their lives or telling them what to do. They see their job as helping clients out when asked, and otherwise let them take responsibility for themselves. Other probation officers feel the clients need more direction and more discipline before they can stand on their own two feet. Now the government wants probation officers to be agents of the court, overseeing the sentences of punishment in the community – a role which many liberal probation officers strongly resist. The Day Centre, and other Intensive Probation Programmes, are therefore the subject of much debate in probation circles in the areas where they exist.

Although details vary from course to course, convicted offenders must choose to go on the programme rather than to prison, and must abide by the rules. Failure to comply is tantamount to a breach of the probation order that sent them on the programme, and leads back to court and possibly to prison. Intensive probation programmes hinge on daily groups which discuss offending behaviour. Many programmes are informal and just deal with the issues that arise in the groups. The six based on the same approach as Sherborne House are tightly structured, and revolve around a series of psychological exercises which expose the values behind group members' actions, and use group pressure to change them. The philosophy behind it is based on the idea that most crimes are choices – decisions conditioned by inverted value systems and peer pressure. The course encourages the clients' own innate sense of right and wrong to help offenders make different decisions the next time the choice is offered to them.

To support such positive choices, the courses offer training in areas ranging from literacy, photography, music, art and metalwork to what they call Life Skills – sex education, drug and alcohol abuse, and civil rights. Both familiar and unfamiliar sports and adventures are also provided as a way of giving the young offenders a sense of achievement and broadening their horizons.

Such a programme sounds like a holiday camp compared to the

rigours of prison. But the daily pressure on both staff and the group members is intense. Some outside probation officers regard the groups as a kind of brainwashing. And many young offenders prefer the anonymous security of custody to the challenge of exposing their past to others, and taking the risk of a different future. By no means all that sign up for the courses have the discipline to carry through to the end. But the staff believe the effects of the programme may not show until months later – even for those who have only been on it for a short time.

Sherborne House is the best known and most established Day Centre Course. Operating from an old community building in South London, it is a showcase of the Inner London Probation Service. Many of the offenders who go there have already been to prison. They find Sherborne House harder to take.

The building is on three storeys, with high ceilings, cold walls and cold floors. Sound bounces around the rooms making small groups seem like crowds. But it is free to the Inner London Probation Service, the gift of the Trustees of Sherborne School in the old tradition of helping the less fortunate. This is all the more telling as the bleak landscape of this part of South London is mocked by the opulence of the City just across the river. The staff augment their small budget with donated equipment that is all too scarce in other parts of the probation service – another limitation on their effectiveness. Staff have kitted out the art area with a darkroom and kiln. The music room has a range of synthesisers to create current pop fashions. The tech workshop has a fine array of metal and wood-working gear. The work young people have done there is astonishingly good.

They eat and play in 'the dining room', a large area that includes ping-pong and pool tables, as well as a makeshift kitchen and dining area. Judy, the young cook, somehow produces the best institutional food I've ever eaten. She also keeps the young people in line with the blunt humour of a riding master – her spare-time occupation. That the staff and offenders eat together seems normal in that atmosphere, but for it to happen in most other penal establishments would take a radical change of attitude.

Behind the anonymous waiting area and the door with its passcode lies not only communal dining, but an ethical assault course. At the end of it is the chance for those who have come here to change their lives, and in so doing to spare countless others the distress of being burgled or robbed.

I was the first outsider to follow the programme from beginning to end. We could have filmed it, but access to the groups would be limited. I also worried that prolonged exposure on television would label the young participants forever as criminals, leaving them no room to change their lives afterwards. So I offered myself as an observer, without even a tape recorder, just a pen and a notebook.

After spending three months observing the programme at Sherborne House, I kept track of the offenders who finished the course to see what effect it had on them as of one year later. Both the course and its effects, which lingered over the following year, tested many of my preconceptions. Despite having spent many years with the police, I still had much to learn about what makes such young men turn to crime, and, knowledge still more elusive, what might make them turn away from it.

R. G.

AUGUST 1992

LIVING
DANGEROUSLY

SHERBORNE HOUSE

'We're dealing with young men, but also with old criminals.'

On a hot July morning, I arrived to start the programme. I was scared when I first saw them all together. There were fourteen of them but it felt like many more. Eight white, six black, dressed in smart baseball jackets, trainers and jeans, T-shirts, jerseys and chinos. Some looked smart, others tatty, some were tall and muscular, others thin and tentative, but they all looked guarded and threatening. They were only waiting, lounging around the dining room. Some played snooker. Others just watched, smoking silently. Several black boys stood together, smiling and joking, more confident than the whites who were visibly tense, as if waiting for a verdict. Most of them wore the hooded-eyed expressionless mask which passes for cool on the streets.

Staff members gathered at one end, around the tea urn and kitchen area. A lively bunch of men and women, mostly white, mostly in their thirties, dressed in the summer informality of shorts and sandals reminiscent of a college campus. They cheerfully exchanged jokes in a mood far removed from the cold caution prevailing at the young men's end of the room.

I took the plunge and moved through the crowd at the snooker table to sit down next to a tall black boy with a baseball cap and a fierce expression. I stuck out my hand and introduced myself. His name was Winston, and his smile and gentle handshake melted my anxiety. It was clear he was as scared as I was. We said little to each other but the ice was dented, if not exactly broken. Just by sitting there, on their side of the room, I felt better.

Jack, the Senior Probation Officer in charge of Sherborne House, was in his mid-thirties, a lithe and wiry Northerner. Energetic, bright, careful, and smiling, he tried to address the group

*but was drowned out by the noise of the pool game until he told
them to stop:*

The rules: no racist or sexist language. No violence, no drink
or drugs. You're a danger to yourselves and others in the tech
shop if you're drunk or stoned.

If you use bad language, fail to participate, or are out of order
in a session, carry knives, or thump someone, you get a warning
that lasts for six working days, and is removed if there's no trouble
in that time.

If you get a second warning during the six days, it lasts until
the ten weeks are up. A third warning is final, in writing. A fourth
means you've breached the court order, you're off the programme
straight away and will be sent back to the judge. The last guy it
happened to went down for two years. *(Fifty per cent of those
breached by Sherborne House and returned to court get custodial
sentences, often increased by the breach on top of the original
offence.)* If you're sick, you must phone in, and produce a Doctor's
certificate. You're only allowed five certificated sick days.

Anyone who drives a car or motorbike to come here will have
to produce his licence, tax and insurance. On the road in our van,
Sherborne House rules apply. No racist language. Sexist remarks
out the window at women is out of order. We don't want it.

Not everyone's here today. Some are in court, some already
back in custody! Others are out somewhere sunning themselves in
the park – and will pay for it!

*This was serious. Despite the signed contract, the failures had
begun already.*

The door code for security is not to keep you in but to keep
others out! Now for the good news. We're all going go-karting on
Friday!

*The young men were divided into two groups to start the first
session. By coincidence, both groups were led by two women, each
of them very different but sharing a no-nonsense yet sympathetic
attitude which was increasingly impressive in the face of the mixture of reactions they met from their group each day.*

*Group work – especially in daily doses of ninety minutes –
is much more intense both emotionally and professionally than
conventional probation officers' duties – the latter only see their
clients for an hour or so when they choose to drop in. Probation
officers have to volunteer for Sherborne House, and are not*

encouraged to stay for more than two or three years lest they burn out.

Within the first week, several group members had fallen away. One white East Ender revealed himself as an active heroin addict by falling asleep in the group. I was particularly saddened by the early loss of an exceptionally bright, streetwise black boy who dominated his group with tales of his activities. By the second week, he was back inside.

The others struggled with the rigid points system which docked them for being a quarter of an hour late for the 10am start, or if they bunked off early, or were late for the start of any group. Depending on who turned up — sometimes just one or two did — the groups would be by turns intimate and relaxed, or awkward, full of static and resistance, or enlivened by joking and insults. But they were always revealing.

Both groups followed exercises derived from work by Philip Priestley and James MacGuire, which are increasingly used in prison and probation. They range from listing the hierarchy of crimes in order of seriousness, asking 'How Far Would You Go?' as a way of measuring people's morality, through sample cases in which the group produce their own sentences, to role playing on video as victims, offenders and police, and judge, defence and prosecution, to help young offenders see their criminal acts from different points of view.

The climax to five or six weeks of this work is the Hot Seat, a session in which each participant examines his criminal record case by case and discusses it in front of the group. Some of these sessions are very challenging. They expose the casual morality or false excuses or whatever rationale is used to justify their criminal behaviour to themselves.

Then each of them takes the crime that brought him to Sherborne House and draws it out in cartoon form, frame by frame, to display to themselves the moments of choice when they could have acted differently.

Initially cagey both with the leaders and one another, each group member revealed more about themselves, both consciously and, rather more often, unwittingly, as the weeks went on. There was a consensus about certain values: sex crimes were out, and those who committed them despised. So was robbing the poor and old ladies.

They had no idea of the psychological trauma caused by their burglaries and thefts. They were cynical about 'rich people' – a category that included shopkeepers. All the young men presumed that everyone they stole from was insured, and were positively pleased to have the chance to fiddle their claims. Moreover, despite their criminal careers, the group members were outraged by the suspicion with which they tended to be received when they entered most shops. Their defence of robbing the rich to give to the poor – in this case, themselves – echoed Robin Hood as well as Proudhon's notion that property is theft. During an exercise that posed the group members various familiar moral dilemmas, they were asked what would they do if they were in a shop and the owner went to the back and left the till open. Would they take the money?
Winston and Sam would do it.

Joel: You've got to take the till.
Dane: *(who always attempts to be different)* I wouldn't do it.
Marianne: *(the probation officer leading the group)* Why?
Dane: *(drawing her into it)* Why wouldn't you do it?
Marianne: *(honestly, thus avoiding Dane's ploy)* I've got too much to lose. But I'd be tempted.
Joel: *(rising to this)* That what gets me about all you probation officers. You'd do it if you wouldn't get caught!
Marianne: I wouldn't, but I'd still be tempted. But it's a small shop. It would hurt the shopkeeper badly to lose the till money.
Johnnie: *(shares with the others contempt for this naive view)* Shop owners all have businesses on the side! They're not making their money from the shop!
Dane: When you go into rich people's homes and you see things you never saw, like extra toilets to wipe your rear end after crapping –
Joel: A bidet? –
Dane: *(caught momentarily off guard by the fancy word. He's supposed to be the master of language in this company)* Who named that?
Arlene: *(the other group leader)* It's French.
Dane: *(recovering triumphantly)* That's what I mean!

They got too much unnecessary stuff. I take it and
spend the money on constructive things like food
and housing.
Johnnie and Joel: *(agreeing emphatically)* They got three
or four cars, three or four houses –
Dane: They're more crooks than we are. Like in the City.
The only difference is they're white and wear suits,
so they don't get caught!

*They were all concerned to preserve face and dignity. The two who
were still under eighteen reacted sharply to any requests or activities
which they thought juvenile, such as the games to be played in the
drama workshop. Yet many of them openly expressed a surprising
degree of insecurity and self-dislike. They were unanimous in feeling
obliged to fight anyone who challenged or insulted them, no matter
what the circumstances or consequences.*

*On one occasion, Bren, a tall and athletic 'black boy' (as they
called themselves), with a disarming smile but a record that
included mugging, described what had happened on his way home
from Sherborne House the evening before. Walking past a bus
stop, he accidentally nudged another young man.*

I said 'sorry' and kept walking. But he and his mate called after
me. They called me 'Chief' *(a street insult)*. They caught the bus
and made a sign from the window. I couldn't let them get away
with Chiefing me out cos they'd just do that to me again where I
live. So I ran after the bus for two blocks, climbed on and found
them upstairs. I beat them both up, and when the conductor called
the police, I just jumped off and went away.

*It was pointed out that Bren was on probation already at Sher-
borne House, and risked being sent straight to prison if he went
back to court. He had a two year-old child and his girlfriend as
well to think about. But Bren was adamant he'd done the only
possible thing. The group agreed.*

*(As it happened, Bren did not finish the course. Within three
months of leaving, he was caught hiding in a tree on Wandsworth
Common, and sentenced to nine months in Dover Prison for
breach of Sherborne House and attempted burglary.)*

*The street code of honour also required young men to carry
knives. But they insisted that they seldom took weapons along as
part of their criminal activities, although one explained reasonably*

that he might have to defend himself against an angry burglary victim. The knives were for self-defence against other youths on the street.

The need to save face led to a certain amount of exaggeration which was impossible to verify. The official probation service versions of their criminal records – provided by the Crown Prosecution Service and the police – were hopelessly incomplete. They were just the tip of the iceberg: all but two of the group members claimed to have committed far more offences than they were caught for.

The most extreme example was Stu, a white South Londoner who was all of twenty-one and looked down on the others as inexperienced kids. A credit card thief, he also claimed to have been involved in stealing jewellery in Switzerland since the age of fifteen during outings with his uncle. He provided enough details of Swiss jails and how his family fenced the goods to make it plausible, but the fact he was sent to Sherborne House for stealing trousers from Selfridge's made it less so.

Like several others, Stu made a continual effort to disparage Sherborne House and the group leaders. He made it continuously clear he would rather be back at work – minding the fruit stall he had bought from his jewel thefts and credit card fraud. Yet in the tenth week, in the final assessment with his group leaders, Stu admitted that he felt very insecure in himself, and had found the experience valuable. Like most, he was sad to leave.

The routine of each morning is split between the offending behaviour group and the workshops – arts, crafts, metalwork and woodwork. At first their role seemed a kind of optional extra to the core work in groups. But as the weeks went on I saw their importance in providing alienated young men with a sense of their own capacity to create things – mugs, chess men, bowls, photographs, music, silk-screened T-shirts, and metal, wood and glass furniture of a high standard. As I was observing both groups discuss their offending, I could only catch the odd glimpse of workshop activity first-hand. That neglect led the instructors to persuade me to attend the following ten-week course to see for myself what they do. I shared a sense of manual incompetence with several of the next lot of young offenders. Nevertheless under the instructors' expert tutelage I made a metal and glass table, and several glazed bowls that gave me great satisfaction.

The craft instructors have been at Sherborne House far longer than any of the probation officers, but feel they have a lower status. Although some are qualified teachers, they lack the Certificate of Qualification in Social Work needed to be probation officers. Moreover there is no career structure for them as Sherborne House and an adult Day Training Centre are the only two facilities in the whole of London that provide craft training. But the instructors' achievement in showing the young people their potential and helping them to talk about their lives at least equals the accomplishment of the groups.

The so-called Life Skills sessions were less successful. Whereas the groups relied on each participant's own experience to be tested by the exercises and the others' reactions, Life Skills were more like worthy seminars given by well-meaning, middle-class, liberal probation officers about the evils of drink and drugs, and the dangers of unprotected sex. There was much new information – especially about how quickly and seriously alcohol damages the human body and how ineffective folk remedies like coffee and a cold shower are in combating it. Yet most of the group seemed so attached to the notion of being good drinkers that I felt something much sharper would be needed to penetrate them. That alcohol is the drug that causes the most crime – yet is legal – is an irony not lost on young offenders. All of them used other drugs casually, but they were shocked by the revelation that two in the group were heroin addicts. Both left within the first fortnight.

The sessions on race and sex were the most difficult. The visit to the Family Planning Clinic to discuss relationships produced the expected giggles and wisecracks, but revealed that for all their sexual experience – several were fathers already – none of them used condoms, or knew how Aids was spread. On the strength of our conversations after Sherborne House, it appeared that the advice they had received had not changed their habits at all.

Black and white members met separately to discuss race. The white session I attended began with virtually all the group – led by Stu – complaining about the racism of this separation, and denying any prejudice of their own. As the leaders attempted to list British society's standard views, the session soon became a raucous cacophony of racist jokes and allegations.

The black session followed somewhat similar lines of incomprehension and resistance. Clearly this is an intractable area that *needs lots of attention. Whether this is the form to tackle it in is open to doubt, and the staff themselves seemed to recognise that. One problem which emerged was the deeply ingrained but unack- nowledged discrimination within the Probation Service itself. Despite the disturbingly high proportion of black people caught up in the criminal justice system as accused and convicted offenders, there are only a tiny handful of black Senior Probation Officers, and all too few probation officers from ethnic minorities, with no prospect of a new intake remedying the problem. Although I thought the Service would offer an ideal job for upwardly mobile and socially conscious black people, they do not see it that way – with some reason, it would seem.*

The cultural divide between the ethical propriety and political correctness of the probation officers and the uneducated street wisdom of the group members worried me. The leaders were relentless about stopping the use of sexist or racist words like 'poof', 'Paki' or 'cunt' which were seen as descriptive, almost value-free words in the language of the streets. The young men tolerated this censorship out of courtesy but without understand- ing. The divide also existed on a more basic level: the only black probation officer left after five weeks and was not replaced. More- over, there is at least an informal ban throughout the Probation Service on ex-offenders becoming probation officers. That one of the crafts instructors was Asian and had some trouble as a youth helped his strong rapport with the groups.

The ten weeks were not all work or introspection. Both staff and group members came together for sports, which were important in breaking down the barriers between them. The sporting events were fun, and in many cases achieved their aim of giving the participants new experiences and a sense of their own capacity to respond to them. Dry slope skiing on the Becton Alps, an oasis in the bleakest part of the East End, led several of the group to return on their own, and to plan skiing trips to Europe. On their first lesson, several group members showed their interest by breaking all the rules, and trying to catch the lift to the top and ski down. They protested loudly when stopped, and claimed afterwards to have hated the whole experience. Go-karting in a hangar in South London was an instant hit among the joyriders who showed off to each other. It also gave the staff and the groups common ground on which to compete, a very important part of the informality at

Sherborne House. The staff never asked the groups to do anything they were not willing to do themselves. This had its ups and downs during water-skiing in the Docklands, under the flight path of the City Airport. This was a new experience for all the young men, who rose to the occasion with rather more equanimity and style than some probation officers. It is hard to keep your dignity and balance on water-skis, especially for the first time: they managed both.

Riding horses in the country was even more unfamiliar territory to them. Several of the group were genuinely frightened. Judy, the cook, who kept a horse of her own, moved them around the ring with such authority that soon they were demanding to leave the ring for the excitement of galloping in the woods, as they'd seen in the movies.

Rock climbing and abseiling in Surrey brought out the best and worst in those who went. Some of the swaggerers, like Stu, refused to take part, and threw in caustic remarks while lying prostrate on the grass. Several who had hidden silently in the groups – like Bren – showed courage, athleticism, and a willingness to encourage others like me who were frightened of heights.

The set piece of the ten weeks is Project Week, in which group members spend all their time on one specific activity: music, photography, or as I did with four group members and a number of staff, a four-day sailing trip across the Channel. This was an extraordinary occasion: mixing Jack, the Senior Probation Officer, Judy, the cook, two group leaders – Lenore and Molly – me, and the four young men (all white – the black members backed away one by one as the date approached because they wanted to go as a group or not at all.) The crew comprised a white South African woman and a Captain (an ex-fraudster as it turned out) who gave a rough time to his amiable assistants and exchanged racist jokes with the woman, oblivious to the mounting dismay of the Sherborne House contingent. Encouraging the four young men to do their share of the work on the boat was a major triumph for the staff and crew. Onshore, the four went off by themselves – with me along as observer and translator. They were too few to be a gang but enough to make trouble – which, perhaps, without me they might have done. Their collective reactions to the prosperity of continental life, and the abusive language with which they expressed their approval was part of the pleasure I took in their company. 'Belgium's fucking boring!' shouted one with joy, as he leapt over a fence and onto the beach. 'I'm coming back here next week!'

Afterwards, it is hard to measure the success of any such limited programme that deals with deeply damaged young people, who have been through a succession of other institutions – including prison – but remained actively offending. One feature that interested me was the total absence of fighting among so many youths who had never previously met each other, and who spoke so frequently of having battles outside. But the ten weeks were by no means plain sailing. One group began smoothly, while the other was almost paralysed in its progress by the leadership battle between two tough black boys, one of whom was a compulsive talker. As if that were not enough, another member, Peter, was so badly damaged by drugs that from his agitation and meanderings, he seemed at times more suited for the mental hospital into which he planned to send himself to hide from the police. The two rivals soon left – both were sent back to prison shortly afterwards – leaving the group to settle down, and work around, and occasionally with, Peter.

Money was always an issue in the groups. People with some kind of job, like Stu, moaned at their loss of income; they ignored the fact that in prison their loss would be longer and greater. The DSS bureaucracy made drawing the dole for the others as difficult as possible for the pettiest of reasons – causing each of them to lose time, and occasionally points as well. The under-eighteens had more problems still. Government policy since 1988 (brought in by John Major in his time at the Department of Social Security) obliged under-eighteens to live at home or take a training place, of which there are fewer and fewer available. Despite its elaborate workshops and special situation, Sherborne House was not accepted as providing training, so group members under eighteen were not eligible even for the reduced dole given to others of the same age. The limited payments they could get under strict hardship regulations left them with £8.50 per week to cover rent, clothing and food. Several warned that this was driving them back to crime, and blamed Sherborne House, unfairly, for the difficulty.

It was not clear during the course how much criminal activity went on in the evenings and weekends, when the group members went back to the situation in which they had committed their *offences. Some sloped off at lunchtime or after four o'clock when the day's programme ended to smoke grass in a nearby park. Some minor dealing in soft drugs and stolen goods clearly went on out of hours, as it does all the time between young offenders both on the streets and in prison. Stu arranged a scam of counterfeit £20 notes which he sold at half price on the weekends. One smooth black car thief, Dane, used to arrive in different cars – which he said belonged to his cousin. Warned and then thrown off the programme for driving illegally, Dane begged his way into one more chance. He then parked up outside the building the very next day. Dane was back in Feltham Young Offenders' Institution within three months of leaving.*

For those that stayed the course, it is hard to overestimate the achievement of group members who managed to raise themselves from bed in time to cross London by public transport and reach Sherborne House by ten o'clock in the morning. Their normal routine, such as it is, involves staying up most of or all through the night, and sleeping until the afternoon. Gathering themselves together, they might go and visit someone, or sniff around looking for something to do. If they 'work', and have stolen goods to dispose of, they will do so by the end of the day at sympathetic shops that buy jewellery and antiques without asking questions, or in the evening at the pubs and clubs where the market operates. Buying clothes and music, then drink and drugs, they will enjoy themselves until tiredness overtakes them and they start again. If they do not offend, they have even less to do, apart from the occasional visit to the dole office to be hassled, or still less often to their probation or housing officer to complain about being hassled. To have broken that pattern, and sustained attendance over five days a week for most of three months showed that they had the strength of character to change their lives.

By the end of the course, less than half of the original twenty-four who signed contracts had completed the ten weeks. (This was low by comparison with subsequent groups.) Three other young men who were sent off in the ninth week had gained enough to be affected by the work.

The real test of any sentence, including the Day Centre programmes at Sherborne House, comes not in the assessment at its formal conclusion, but in the months and years afterwards, in the way the (ex-)offenders respond to new pressures and temptations.

To see how effective Sherborne House had been with the group that I observed, I went back to interview those that finished the programme one year later. This book is made up of those interviews, set beside key scenes from their experiences at Sherborne House. These provide some insights but by no means a full account of the work there.

It was a privilege to be allowed in by the people involved in this process. I was the first outsider ever to follow the programme from beginning to end. It was not easy for them to be observed. Many of the young people never understood what I was doing there and thought I must have been some kind of undercover detective. Many of the staff were equally suspicious of anyone from the media.

I had hoped to show their work in greater detail. The patience and skill they showed under trying circumstances were profoundly impressive. But the complexities of following two groups five days a week for ten weeks, involving some fourteen young people and eight staff, were beyond my powers of description. Even had they not been, the scenes themselves were so complicated, with so many individuals involved, I believe it would have been impossible for most readers to follow.

One cause for that difficulty is the reason I have written this book: on the surface, many young offenders seem identical. They share the same style and passion for music, drugs and clothes, the same peer-group pressures and temptations. By and large they commit the same offences. In groups on street corners or in a magistrates' court, they appear almost faceless, with their sullen expressions, and the tongues of their trainers sticking out as defiantly as their chins.

Coming to know the young men who attended Sherborne House allowed me to see behind the superficial uniformity of this persona, to understand more about how each of them as individuals became part of the collective social problem known as crime. I came to like most of them much more than I had expected to at the start, given the many differences between our ages, background and experience.

I have assembled verbal portraits of eight young offenders. Each one is an attempt to record as honestly as I can their thoughts and feelings about crime, and about their lives − past, present, and, hardest of all for them, future. To protect their future, and the *confidentiality of the staff as well, I have changed all names.*

It will be tempting for middle-class or middle-aged readers to distance themselves from these young people, and judge them harshly, as ethical and cultural strangers from a strange land. But as youth culture spreads, and traditional assumptions about hard work leading to assured rewards are eroded by unemployment and recession, young people of all backgrounds will no longer share the ideas of motivation and future that we, their parents, had at their age. The power of pop music, trendy clothing, and drugs cuts through all barriers: the harshness of their language speaks of short-term excitement and long-term despair, of the longing for romance, and the brevity of pleasure. Discomfiting as it may seem, the vacuum these young people inhabit is familiar to our children as well.

During their brief appearance in Crown Court, more serious intelligent minds will have focused on punishing these young men than have tried to help them at any previous point in their lives. Must they commit enough crimes to be caught before they get our attention?

CHAPTER ONE

JOHNNIE

I'm criminally minded

Johnnie is a slim, sallow Irish lad of twenty, with high cheekbones and long brown hair normally kept in a ponytail. His usual expression is sombre – he takes himself very seriously – but he is gentle and diffident around adults that he likes. Among those he mistrusts, his temper and stubbornness transform his normally passive personality, and reveal a strength of will that could be put to better use. He gets on with others his age by keeping a low profile. But he is sharp-witted and a keen observer.

His family situation is a disaster: no father, and an alcoholic mother who went off with a boyfriend when Johnnie was fourteen, leaving him to fend for himself for weeks at a time in their council flat. Although he blames it on being bored, Johnnie's schooling collapsed around that time.

He was not at an inner-city sink school, however. He went to Pimlico, one of the best state schools in London. Johnnie still keeps his school reports in a drawer along with his court and criminal records. His teachers' comments are a series of cries of anger and frustration that he won't concentrate, won't live up to his potential, and finally, won't attend school at all for months at a time. They knew Johnnie had a good mind but seemed unable to find a way to harness it to productive ends.

His friends' parents like him, think he's a 'nice boy' and want them to bring him home to dinner. Johnnie seems to like this straight side of his life. He was not happy when adults wished him luck in his court case:

I thought they didn't know about that side of me. I was angry, very angry actually that my mates had told them.

Johnnie is aware of what his better off and more settled friends have that he does not, but does not seem bitter about it. Yet he covets cars and clothes with the enthusiasm of a sports fan revering his heroes – from a distance.

Johnnie seems to have spent his years since leaving school just hanging around Pimlico, which, despite its geographic centrality in London, is actually a quiet backwater, more pleasant than many other parts of the city. He played in the gardens in front of his council estate, with different problems from those that afflicted boys who grew up in far worse conditions:

Very quiet. Too quiet. Alright if you're middle-aged.

He then moved to another Pimlico council flat near one of London's largest estates where there was more action. He fell into minor crime in the usual way. In comparison with the others at Sherborne House, the offences that sent him there are minor. But to the law, to the victims, and to Johnnie himself, he is still a criminal. Talking to me in his flat, a year after his stint at Sherborne House, Johnnie looked back on how he began.

I know stealing is wrong. I wouldn't want nobody taking my stuff. But it's money at the end of the day. I used to be an angel. When you're twelve, thirteen, you do a bit of shoplifting, say at Harrods, just for a laugh, or you smash bottles or play around with the police; well I wouldn't do any of that. Then I bumped into a certain group of friends – influenced basically – that's when I started. They were into car stereos. Obviously, what your friends do, you do.

There used to be five of us. I'd smash the window, someone else would push the window in, someone else would take it, someone else would stand by with a rucksack and bike to take it home. Everyone else went off their own way. Used walkie-talkies to keep in touch. Very easy, safe, took twenty seconds, with quick-release stereos stupid enough to be left in car. A little longer with a screwdriver for the spark plug.

At the end of the day you wouldn't get much each but there wasn't much chance of getting caught, cos once I'd done my job, I'd go to the corner and keep a look out so you know where the traffic is coming from. The person taking the stereo home has got the worst job cos mine takes one second, his takes, what, ten minutes max?

Car alarms are a little inconvenience. There's a three second delay and by then you're round the corner. But if a policeman is in the vicinity he'll pull you up.

Coppers were everywhere because it's a posh area full of Ministers. But we still used to do stereos regularly – sometimes seven a night. In those days £20 was a lot of money. If you weren't into drugs, it didn't matter. We did get away with an awful lot before we got caught. About three hundred. Four or five a night.

We used to do it about 3am. But even daytime if you see a handbag or a leather jacket in a car you have to do it there and then.

One night we did six car stereos and we found four cars unlocked, i.e. the boot left open. It's unbelievable, I could never imagine it but it's true. You walk past, try the boot, and it's open.

I got a mate who is mad, completely mad for his age – sixteen – who nicked a briefcase with eight grand in it – that was lucky. He bought himself a car with it. He is waiting until he is seventeen to get his licence – he is not quite so stupid as to drive it now, especially since he loves to fight. He was nicked for tackling four coppers and the judge threw it out because he didn't believe a juvenile would set on four coppers, but it was probably true. He was actually done for nineteen offences, and the judge threw out seventeen of them because there were too many police, but he'd done most of them. The police said as he left the court, 'wait till you're seventeen, then we'll get you.' Juveniles get away with murder. He was not even remanded for nineteen charges, imagine! I think that's stupid, I'd have remanded him straight away. Anyway he loves a scrap, he's completely mad. You'd like him, you'd think he's normal.

Most people do things wrong but they don't consider themselves criminals. They drop litter, they speed, drive over the limit, it's wrong but they still do it. Stealing is wrong. I know that it's blatantly true. People say 'well, they're too rich anyway.' But if they've got things and they've worked hard and been lucky enough to make their life the way they want it, they're welcome to it. The only way someone like me is going to get rich is some deal that produces ten grand.

Money makes the world go round. I can't explain, I'm a hypocrite. I'm criminally minded. It's not nice because you spot things that other people wouldn't. If I'm walking down the street with you, I'll spot an office open, you won't. I'll spot a car door open. It's not nice to be criminally minded. But if I'm with my crowd of people, their eyes will all be open, looking everywhere.

A 'normal day', a friend or two would pick me up in the morning and we'd 'work' around Westminster all day by going in and out of offices and launderettes, looking for bags and jackets and briefcases left unattended. If a door was left open, we all knew what to do. No words had to be said. If anyone challenged us, we'd be 'looking for a solicitor's office'. If not we took what we could. We'd throw away the credit cards – too risky – but the girls would use the cheques, or sell them at £3 a page, because they'd find the cheque card in the same bag. Men always kept them separately.

I rarely take things off people in person. If I see a bike unchained I'll be in two minds whether or not to take it. I've taken bikes off people before. People say 'don't you think of the victim?' but I don't, I think of myself first. I don't think of the person, I think 'there's £50 for me.' I don't think, 'I've stolen their bike, they're going to have trouble getting to work tomorrow.' Afterwards I feel relieved when I've got it done. There is no feeling of guilt, though if I started thinking about the person I probably would. In some cases they probably want things nicked *(for the insurance)* but that's neither here nor there.

Some things you do think of other people. I don't do robberies or muggings cos I ain't into harming no one at the end of the day. If I was I wouldn't want to do it.

I've got some friends that do. I'm not going to say to them 'you're wrong.' At the end of the day it's up to them. They do what they do. They could preach to me all day – 'you shouldn't do this, you shouldn't do that' – and I could do the same to them but at the end of the day it's not worth getting into the argument.

Like most youths who spend time on the streets, Johnnie is well known to the local police. That by his own admission he had committed hundreds of offences and not been caught does not temper his sense of injustice when they hassle him.

The police round here are not nice. If they are disrespectful to me, I will be to them, it's as simple as that. I see myself as the same as them. They may be working, I'm not, that doesn't matter to me. My house got raided a few months ago. There was a break-in nearby and they thought I'd done it. That's fair enough. But then I walked out of the house and went past where it happened, and another one came over to me and he said 'What's in your pockets?' I said 'Look, you've already searched my house, you must think I'm a fool if I'd walk past here with something in my pockets!' But he still searched me and I didn't like that.

I get my revenge: I can hot them up if they're under cover – I point them out, cos I know the unmarked cars. Or I can go down the station with my friends, and grieve them, start making false complaints. There'll be three of us at the counter but the copper'll only want to see one, so we'll say, 'Look, it was all of ours – this is my chain, his padlock, and the other one's plastic bit that covered the chain!' So we'll all talk at the same time, and while he's writing something one of us will make a sly comment and we all start taking the piss out of him – not blatantly so he can chuck us out, but with our minds, talk all intellectual and calm. Then he starts shouting at you, and you say, 'What you shouting for? No one's getting angry. What's the problem?' They don't like it.

Just the other day they pushed through the door a fine for Threatening Behaviour for something that happened in 1989 that I didn't even do! I was trying to stop a fight at 2am outside a pub in Vauxhall, but the police didn't believe me. Said I should plead guilty or they'd do me for worse. We'd been drinking but I knew what I was doing. I got fined £60 plus £23 bailiff fee for coming to collect it! I'll pay the £60 but I'm not gonna pay that. The bailiff's fee ain't nothing to do with me. It's a liberty. I'm not going down for two days or two weeks or two months. If they make me go to prison, I'll catch them back, I'll pull some sly ones on them.

After hundreds of thefts, Johnnie was finally done for criminal damage and attempted entry of a car. Another time he and his friends broke into a Portakabin on a building site. It was the workman's canteen so they started cooking. When the security guard caught them, Johnnie hid two cans of Coke he had taken in a toilet cistern in the security office. But the guard found three eggs missing which they had cooked. Johnnie was given a £50 fine, which he also found unfair.

So far Johnnie has not been to prison, but he has been skirting the edges of it – not for the offences themselves, but for his indifference to court sentences. Apart from several outstanding fines, he has been sentenced to a total of one hundred and forty hours of Community Service for fiddling fruit machines, and breaching probation and Community Service orders. The first sentence was for forty-eight hours, but he only completed forty-seven.

That's an evil job, Community Service. All you do is send people
back to court. It's a punishment. You got to do it on Saturdays
which means you can't go out Friday night. The rest of the week
is no use cos nobody goes out Monday, Tuesday, Thursday. I
didn't mind doing gardening round where I lived and could see
my mates. But I got sent up to Westbourne Green, where they've
got green-fingered guys who threaten to knife you if you break a
flower. The journey there took too long: forty-five minutes. I
jacked it in after one day.

But it's much worse than probation – they don't just let you do
it, they supervise you right down to the last hour. The first breach
I had one hour left. You can't expect me to get out of bed on a
Saturday for one hour of Community Service!

*Having breached both his probation and Community Service,
Johnnie was then convicted of stealing two mountain bikes and
receiving stolen handlebars. Despite all that he'd done that had
escaped detection, he found this punishment unfair.*

I didn't do no more than watch it going on. But the police said
I was going inside this time unless I went Guilty. It wasn't wise to
go Not Guilty against police evidence. Someone else who tried
that went down for a couple of years. I got a squeeze *(a light
sentence)*. Two years probation and Sherborne House. But even
that's a liberty for just a couple of bikes!

*Johnnie was one of half a dozen whites who appeared at Sher-
borne House to start the programme I observed. They came from
different parts of London, and all seemed rather frail and solitary
compared to the black boys who were both physically larger and
shared the instant street-smart solidarity of 'brothers'. Johnnie
adopted a kind of camouflage that suggested how he must have
been at school. Despite his concern for grooming, his standard
uniform of jeans, trainers and bomber jacket was tattier than
most of the others. For the first few weeks, he sat silent for the
most part, his face shrouded in his shoulder length hair. He
appeared sullen and slightly combative – just the sort of manner
which keeps people at bay. But this was utterly misleading, the
opposite of what he was like; it disguised what he really wanted
in the way of contact. When he did speak up, Johnnie's rapid
pronouncements of firmly held convictions took us all by surprise: he loves cars, but disapproves of joyriding. He was certain
of his moral ground as a burglar who needed money, but*

detested crimes of violence, especially those perpetrated against old people.

In an early exercise, each person had to describe himself to the group; Johnnie was reflective:

I don't like anything about myself. I got no confidence. I suppose my unusual feature is my gambling. Interests: horses, fruit machines. Physically, I'm skinny. Always need money. My ambition: to be rich. But I'm useless with money. If you haven't worked for it, you blow it in a few months.

This was to be borne out by events.

I made contact with Johnnie on the second day at Sherborne House, when we all went bowling. In the van, the boys jockeyed for seats — preferring those at the rear, as far from the staff as possible. I headed there too, sitting down next to Johnnie, who was not thrilled to see me. None of them was sure whether I was effectively just another probation officer to be wary of, an undercover copper of some kind who might grass on them, or a possible ally, or just a kind of person they had not met before — disinterestedly observing them for some obscure purpose. Johnnie fired at me straight away:

Do you know any famous robbers?

As it happens, through filming the Thames Valley Police, I do, and won a disturbing number of points by telling them so. I was in a familiar predicament — I needed their trust, but didn't want to pretend I had no negative views about what they did. (The temptation to go along on an actual job as a final measure of their trust and the success of my research loomed already.) At this point, I merely dropped the names of several famous bank-robbers turned supergrasses. I'm sure the young men hadn't heard of them, but they pretended to, and were impressed.

The ploy worked at once:

Johnnie: Good job, writing?
RG: Interesting.
Johnnie: Good money? Travel where you want?

I explained that not everyone writes best sellers . . . Jeffrey Archer was their model writer, and they knew he makes money. It was to remain a deep source of suspicion for them that I was not actually being paid by anyone to do this research, and that I hoped in due course to get it funded as a book and a semi-fictional TV series. This investment in the future was absolutely contrary to the way they see the world and live their lives. They have no future – at least nothing to look forward to – as they see it. Johnnie in particular could not imagine my choosing to be financially insecure.

We arrived at the bowling alley, and the boys disembarked with a restless, prowling energy never displayed at Sherborne House. Johnnie, who had not participated in the girl-watching the others engaged in on the journey, clocked the nice cars in the parking area – a Saab Turbo and a BMW with the same quasi-sexual excitement.

The black boys enjoyed the bowling with a show of insouciant confidence not matched by the wary whites, like Johnnie, who went about their game with exaggerated seriousness. They fought over the rules like lawyers, as though they could thus order the relationships between them that were beginning to emerge. To Johnnie, cheating was deeply offensive, and when the bowling machine itself offered some of the others an extra ball, his anger seemed to reflect the unfairness of society at large.

Johnnie showed an odd mix of selfishness and real consideration for his friends. On a subsequent van journey, he disclosed that he was a passionate Thatcherite who believed in making the most of every opportunity. As for wider social obligations, he was clear:

No one's responsible for anyone else. You've got to look after yourself. Everyone does, and it's their own fault if they can't do it.

This statement, born of his personal experience, earned him flak from the others in the group who saw him as a traitor to his class. But for all his defiant independence, he was and remains devoted to his friends to whom he is generous. I was struck by how loyal and generous they all were, despite being seriously short of money most of the time.

I lent someone £200 in tens and twenties – I gave it to him when he was working and now he's got no job. I'll get it back. I'm not worried. I know who to lend to and who not.

This willingness to trust his friends and his own judgement about money produced interesting reactions to the moral dilemmas the group leaders posed to Johnnie's group: 'If a friend asks you to join in a burglary when you're on probation, and sentenced to

*Sherborne House, and you risk going inside if you get caught,
what would you do?' (This, of course, is not an exercise at all. It
happens often to Sherborne House clients.) Johnnie responded:*

My friends know I'm stuck. I'm glad to be asked, but I'd say I
was sorry. They know.

Burglary's not serious. It's just taking someone's stuff! If you
think you're too hot, you'll get caught. It's easier shoplifting food.

*Unlike the others sprawled across several low chairs, Johnnie
sat hunched, poised and watchful. As the days went on and he
began to feel more secure in the group, Johnnie's lethargy appeared
more and more to be a disguise, a convenient way of avoiding
showing himself and taking responsibility for his actions and
views.*

*The group was offered a dilemma: two friends 'on a job' ask
you to say they were at your flat. You don't know who else has
seen them commit the crime. What would you do?*

Johnnie: *(bursting – this has touched a nerve)* But you
always see people lie in court – the police do it all
the time – and they get away with it. *(to the others)*
Have you ever covered up for your friends?

Dane: *(streetwise)* I wouldn't do it for anyone. I wouldn't
ask anyone either. You don't know if anyone else
saw them, so you're fighting police and maybe a
police witness as well.

Johnnie: Yeah, but what if they've got other friends
who'll back you up?

*Obviously Johnnie has given or would give a false alibi. This
turned out to be an important exchange. Like many young people
in his situation, with little or no family, his strongest 'family ties'
are to his friends. Johnnie's wish to be accepted came out during
another exercise when they discussed the issues 'For and Against
Crime':*

Johnnie: *(Against:)* Crime stops you getting a visa if you
got a record. And if anything happens, even if you
didn't do it, you get blamed by your family, and
your friends.
(For:) Money. Money can buy everything.
The others: Not friendship. Not love.

Johnnie didn't reply.

Midway through the programme, each of the participant's own field probation officers visited Sherborne House to hear the midway assessments of how their clients were doing.

Johnnie's probation officer, Chloe, was a cheerful ex-actress in her early forties. She was at the end of her first year as probation officer, and had inherited Johnnie a few months earlier. Because he'd been vague and she'd been busy, Chloe had only seen him twice. That meant everyone at Sherborne House, including me, knew Johnnie a good deal better than she did.

Johnnie's long hair was clean, but he looked pale in his yellow jersey, jeans and trainers. Molly, his group leader, presented Johnnie with the staff assessment. This session was his chance to hear, digest, and challenge their views of him. Molly said they found him to be more confident, less nervous than when he arrived.

Fair comment. It's true of everyone.

He was on guard, but not unfriendly, more shy than cagey. But his manner was itself a challenge to them both.

Haven't a clue what would make me more confident. It's true everywhere, not just here. Friends say I talk too fast.

Molly said the staff were worried about his gambling, but Johnnie reacted defensively and impatiently to this.

I'm in control of the gambling. It's no priority, nothing to do with my offending. I never lose on fruit machines anyway. Not a problem. I can walk past arcades for a day or a month.

This was just the territory where trouble lurked for Johnnie. He might fool himself and try to fool those trying to help him, with bad results on all sides. If they pressed too hard, he'd close down. If they didn't press at all, he might not take the issue seriously.

Molly: I just wondered about your missing the odd sessions and days, I wondered if you'd been at the arcades?

Johnnie: *(blushing)* Yes. I drop into arcades and lose track of time. But I can leave if I want to.

Molly: I saw you read an old paper and you knew it was old from the horses, not the date!

Johnnie: *(squirming)* I like the horses, true. My friends say sometimes I'm an addict. But it's not a problem.

Chloe: *(a bit stunned by this revelation)* Horses are not
    a problem?
Johnnie: *(insisting now)* I just do it for fun, not to win
    big money. Only £40–50. I do play machines in pubs
    – only the good machines, not the rubbish!

*They turned to his criminal record, about which he appeared
utterly certain.*

Johnnie: All my record is bad luck.
Chloe: You committed them or were caught for them?
Johnnie: A bit of both. I shouldn't have been there,
    shouldn't have done it, shouldn't have been caught.
Chloe: I'm surprised how well you've done in the light of
    early worries about you.
Johnnie: *(smiles thinly)* My last probation officer thought
    I'd never finish. I breached probation and
    Community Service twice! I should go down if I
    breach again.
Chloe: Your last probation officer did a good report that
    kept you out last time. Don't know if I could do it
    again if you get into trouble. But it's encouraging to
    see your progress set out on the page.
Molly: Any goals?
Johnnie: *(after a pause)* Confidence, being more assertive.
Chloe: And to finish here.
Johnnie: *(firmly)* I will finish! *(no hesitation)* Unless
    something happens outside of here – like
    something at home.

*That was an encouraging session for all of them. Johnnie, a singu-
larly silent and withdrawn boy at the start, had declared himself
determined to finish, and was clearly coming out of himself more.
But there was a postscript that emerged later. He told another
Sherborne House probation officer he had finance problems with
the DSS about his dole. He then admitted he hadn't bothered to
sign on. But he warned the probation officers:*
    I might have to resort to crime to get the money I need. It's
down to you!
    Meaning – 'Not me. It's the Establishment's fault if I turn to

crime.' Two weeks later, Johnnie's financial picture suddenly changed, as he told me in the back of the van:

This friend robbed his uncle's business after being sacked after a fight with the foreman. But it weren't fair cos the fight was in a pub, not at work. So my friend held them up – using a taxi, a gun that was blocked up, and a balaclava. He invited me to come along, but I said 'No, I'm not that stupid.' Then he arrived at my place out of breath and smiling from ear to ear. He left the cash with me before going home. He said I should keep it for him, but I could use it any way I wanted. I offered it back in case he wanted to go on the run but he decided to bluff it out. The secretary must have recognised his voice cos he was pulled *(arrested)* the next day. The Old Bill interviewed me as well but I had a solid alibi – I was playing football at Sherborne House!

Johnnie was now in charge of £400 of stolen cash, on his friend's behalf. He described it in his deadpan rapid chatter – punctuated by outbursts of anger and excitement. He likes money. It was just the sort of dilemma that Sherborne House faced them with: do you look after your friend's money, even if you're hard up yourself? Or do you spend it to ease your own problems. Or do you refuse to have anything to do with it?

Don't like the responsibility. He told me to 'see his sister was alright' but didn't say how much to give her – could have been £20 or £200. So I gave her £100. He's on remand, looking at six years! But I can't visit him cos the police'll nick anyone who shows up there. He was my best friend but I got to keep away from him in case the police show up and fit me up, know what I mean? I was screwing *(anxious)* till I got to the bank and deposited the rest in me own name.

One week later his resolve was tested. It was Project Week at Sherborne House. Johnnie was one of four boys who joined two probation officers, Molly and Lenore, plus Jack the Senior Probation Officer, Judy the cook, and me on a large boat which sailed for Belgium and France. There was also a professional crew of three. The journey was a challenge to the boys to become part of a team, to fit in with strangers, and observe precise obligations to cook meals, clean the decks, and perform the other crew tasks in the rota.

Unlike the others, who made great play of oversleeping, or objecting each time they were called on to help, Johnnie made at least an attempt to do his chores, but he gave up quickly when his lethargy returned. Depending on his mood, he liked being busy, and looked forward to the prospect of foreign adventures.

During his shift in the kitchen, Johnnie revealed a concern for germs. He regarded curry sauce with disgust as 'contamie' (contaminated), and was deeply suspicious of tins of corned beef. He insisted that at home he only ate fresh food, when possible rump and fillet steak, and fresh vegetables (a claim not borne out by my later visits there). Johnnie was also fastidious about his person: he took two showers a day at home, and washed his long hair daily, which made the three days we spent without a proper shower especially unpleasant for him.

The first night was spent in Ramsgate, the best part of it in an arcade of fruit machines. It emerged that Johnnie and his pals used to holiday on the South Coast, so they could play the fruit machines in all the major resorts.

We'd go down for three or four days to Portsmouth, Poole, Weymouth. Arcades shut at 1am, we'd sleep in trains in sidings, wake at dawn when someone comes, have breakfast on the beach with milk and cakes left outside shops. Then spend the day in the arcades.

There are fruit machines everywhere – you can't avoid them if you're looking out for them – pubs, clubs, chip shops. You get some people like me Mum who say you can't win, but fruit machines pay out sixty per cent of the time. From £5 I can make £70. You know what to play and what not to play. The only risk is getting addicted. I'm not addicted, I just like playing. Real addicts are screwing if they can't play every day.

Johnnie's lethargy disappeared as we left the boat. By the time we reached the arcade, he was wired. He attacks a fruit machine like Steve Davis playing championship snooker on speed. He is the equivalent of a pinball wizard, displaying a kind of co-ordination and intelligence I had never seen before. 'I never lose,' he said as a simple matter of fact. He patiently tried to explain how to handle the games, but I was hopelessly lost. He clearly has a phenomenal degree of both manual and mental dexterity, and yet at present has no future.

But his mind was on other things – shopping in France. Alone with the boys, I learned there was a particular Chipie jacket Johnnie had in mind – and to general astonishment, he'd brought the money to buy it. Later, the captain, a bearded cynic in his mid-forties, was less surprised. He cited tough London sixteen year-olds who'd been on previous cruises flashing wads of more than a thousand pounds. He also warned of theft from our bunks as commonplace, but somehow I trusted these lads not to steal from their own, which category I hoped now included me. It did.

The temptation to steal almost anything that moves was evident the first night abroad, as we strolled down the high street of Ostend window-shopping. Their eyes were bulging as we walked past the glass showcases in the central pedestrian areas, and bulged further as we passed the prostitutes in the side-street windows. Johnnie was the only one with money, but was more interested in clothes than sex. There was much talk of taking bikes, boots, clothes, and trainers but Jack warned the lads that any stolen goods taken on board would be seized and cast into the sea, or returned. In the face of the young men's obvious disbelief, Jack spoke of 'fish wearing trainers' from the previous voyage; the image pained them.

A day later, in Dunquerque in the daytime, with me as interpreter and guide, we hit shop after shop in search of Johnnie's 'perfect' jacket. The staff bristled noticeably as we arrived. I soon learned they had suffered a plague of young English shoplifters.

There are an astonishing number of shops in Dunquerque that sell young men's clothing at different ends of town. Having exhausted all of them, and me, Johnnie found the garment of his dreams, a shiny black puffy jacket that did indeed suit him. To the jealous approval of the other boys who had fingered the goods in every shop we stopped in, Johnnie paid hard cash for the jacket and a pair of jeans. He walked out in his new uniform, floating a foot off the ground.

Over coffee, I somewhat wickedly queried their obsession with what I saw as small distinctions in the different types of jeans and trainers. I pressed them to explain why some jeans were 'great' last year, but 'crap' now. Johnnie, the most obsessive of the lot, first said,

You wouldn't use a second-rate camera to produce first-rate pictures. It's a matter of quality.

When the precious jeans were finally on board, he sheepishly conceded there was nothing he could point to which distinguished them from any others – except the label. I felt badly at having dented his excitement, as though I'd told him there was no Father Christmas. But having spent three days in a frenzied search, being lectured about the absolute need to have this pair rather than that, I felt there was some value in hinting to them they might be fashion victims rather than connoisseurs.

Our last night was spent moored off the Isle of Sheppey, where many of our party went ashore for a drink. Johnnie adamantly refused, and went to bed claiming to be 'ill', so I stayed on board with him and Sam, with whom I played cards. Johnnie was in a strange mood, highly strung and surprisingly edgy for someone who was still very pleased with his trip so far. He suddenly blurted out that this was where he'd been done for fiddling fruit machines:

We were being kicked and beaten by eight large gypsies who owned the machines behind the arcade. My mate faced being fried on the hot dog maker when the police arrived and put us in the car. We was warned never to show our faces in Sheppey again.

Johnnie was trying to sleep, as if to put it all behind him, when the others arrived on deck above him, muddy and tipsy, from the mainland. Johnnie cursed them fiercely for having 'distressed' him. He leapt up determined to 'get his revenge'. This took the form of staying up when they finally went to bed, and turning on the light to pack his things. No amount of persuasion from Jack, the Senior Probation Officer, could make him do otherwise. He'd been 'distressed' by everyone else's noise, and was having his own back by distressing them. Jack was finally reduced to sleeping sitting up with his hand on the light switch to keep it off, while Johnnie stomped up on deck in a stubborn rage.

Much to his own and everyone else's surprise, Molly, his own group probation officer, managed to talk him down again. Later on, in his final assessment a week later, the two of them discussed his stubbornness. Johnny characteristically admitted:

I realised I was being stupid. It wasn't worth it.

But Johnnie refused Molly's suggestion he use the same common sense about his unpaid court fines, which had already increased by a third with the bailiff's fee:

That's a liberty. They should research what people can pay. I'm not paying it.

Many of the young offenders shared this acute sense of fair play, as they saw it. Johnnie's concern for the rules that he chose to respect – as he'd shown in bowling – was an obsessive way of trying to make sense of the world. On the boat, going to bed had been a nightly routine ending in silence. Johnnie's retiring early on the last night of the voyage was especially significant because of the danger to him onshore. That the others knew nothing of this, and were enjoying themselves despite the hour, seemed to reinforce his sense of vulnerability and isolation.

Johnnie later admitted to me quietly another cause of his anxiety that night was that the money with which he bought the clothes was 'borrowed' from his armed robber mate's account. 'But I'll pay him back as soon as I gets a job,' he said determinedly.

Jobs – and the lack of them – are a central reason why most young people who commit crime do so in the first place. The Department of Employment training schemes are not an attractive option at the best of times – offering only £10 per week more than the dole for a full week's work. Despite government promises that every youth should have a place, there are too few for those that apply, and no secure jobs at the end of them. A recent House of Commons report condemned the whole system of social security and training for young people, particularly the way careers and dole officers tend to be officious, suspicious and off-putting when handing out tiny sums to people like Johnnie – who are themselves used to handling large sums of money. The young men are also hampered from seeing their own real potential – such as it is – by their arrogance which hides their lack of confidence. This is the inverse of the qualities usually looked for in initial interviews – modesty and ambition.

Johnnie's problem in getting started was evident in the last week of Sherborne House, in his interview with Derek, a gruff Northerner from New Bridge, an agency to help young offenders find jobs. He talked with Johnnie in a kind but patronising manner, asking if he could read and count, and suggesting menial jobs at Tesco's or McDonald's to start with. He got an earful in rapid bursts between languid pauses:

I don't mind working as long as it's the right sort of work. I'm not going to do a dead-end job, I can do better than that I think! Did well at school till I stopped . . . I worked as a Commis chef *(an assistant chef)* for five months at Imperial College . . . Done a bit of labouring and bits and bobs.

It's only now and again that I have to work for the money. Now I've got to find a job or go to college . . . Before I had money and

I could always get money. Now I can't afford to do it because I'll go to prison basically . . . My Mum was always there before.

Johnnie told me later his job at Imperial College had ended when he'd missed several days' work because he was unable to get up in time, but was too shy to call in 'sick'. He blamed his Mum for not coming round to the flat to get him up, and then she refused to make the call for him. But he didn't mind as long as she paid the rent and gave him pocket money. He explained his need for a job to Derek, in their interview:

Johnnie: *(crossly)* Now she's got another boyfriend and she won't give me no money so I'll have to get a job: office work, anything that pays £90 a week take home. I want to be an office junior.

Derek: Any skills?

Johnnie: Got no skills. *(certain)* But office work you don't need none. Typing helps obviously but anyone can do filing. I wouldn't want to work as a chef again and I wouldn't work at Tesco's or anything like that. I can do better than that. That's a low job. Anyone can get that job.

Derek: If you were offered a hospital porter job, and on the way there a friend offered you a better paid job, but he's gone bust twice already – what would you do?

Johnnie: You can always get a job. That one would stick you: it goes nowhere. Same pay for life. *(angrily)* It's like a McDonald's job, no prospects ever! But the other job you make double the money, and might have more fun – do less work, and you get paid a lot more if it stayed alive. If he kept going you might get a Xmas bonus, shares in the future.

Derek: How about the longer term? What about learning a trade?

Johnnie: I'd like one – maybe carpentry or plumbing. But it can't be done. £30 per week YTS money! Can't be done.

Derek: What about apprenticeships?

Johnnie: *(furiously)* You earn bugger all for a couple of years just for a piece of paper . . . It's okay if you

have a stable background, your family helps you,
you need that. I'm not working for £30 a week for
nobody! I'd rather stay in bed. I'd like to take a job
with long-term prospects but I can't.
Derek: Can't or won't?
Johnnie: (firmly) Can't. I try to imagine it, but I can't.

*The interview with Derek was a tantalising occasion. Underneath
his passive resistance, Johnnie had obvious abilities – and even
ambitions – but was standing in his own way. Derek offered to
try and place him as an office junior, and made a date to see him
a week later. Derek was impressed by Johnnie's potential, but was
also aware of the way he put brakes and blinkers on himself.
Derek was hopeful of arranging something for Johnnie. He agreed
that few young people at Sherborne House had the benefit of
family connections – the normal way middle-class children would
get their first job. What Johnnie didn't tell Derek was that his
Mum had arranged a starting job for him as an office junior in her
own place of work – a building society. But when he went to
court, his mother needed to ask the manager's permission to attend
his trial and that scuppered Johnnie's chances.*

*It was also typical of his capabilities that on the last day at
Sherborne House, Johnnie won both the pool and table tennis
competitions. He had barely played at all during the ten weeks.*

*The following week, I went along to the New Bridge Office in
South London to observe the job interview. Johnnie never turned
up, nor rang. Derek had arranged a place on a carpentry training
course for him, but was not surprised that Johnnie had not
responded. 'It's rarer still when they do.'*

*Five months after finishing Sherborne House, Johnnie ended up in
court again. His probation officer Chloe was also responsible for
his mate who had committed the armed robbery. While visiting
him in prison, she learned of Johnnie's accepting the cash from
him. Neither Johnnie nor his friend had realised that Chloe was
legally obliged to report this to the police. It was the sort of
coincidence that Johnnie called his 'bad luck'.*

*Chloe explained all this to me as we waited outside the
court-room:*

I confronted Johnnie, and said he had no choice but to report
it and return the money that was left. He went red but didn't

resist. The court case for handling stolen goods has been hanging over him for three months. I know this is not an offence committed after Sherborne House – he took it while he was still there, but sadly it will appear so on his record. It will look as though he's failed.

He told me about the shopping expedition in France – the coat paid for but bought with stolen money. Also the fruit machines he's so good at – he's been done several times for fiddling them.

He's very talented, has lots to offer, he's a Rolls-Royce engine not attached to anything. Yesterday I reviewed his whole criminal history – and his life – with him. I'm dismayed and frustrated by his appalling lethargy, never seen anything like it. Makes me want to kick him – not to hurt him but to get him moving. Looking at his crimes he refuses to take any responsibility for them – it was always bad luck, or he was in the wrong place at the wrong time. He missed so much in his life by the things he hasn't done, or regretted not doing. I pointed this out and he agreed.

He started truanting at fourteen, and so missed too much school to take his GCSEs, which he now minds about. Then he registered for a course and chose his preferred subjects. But he failed to turn up for the first few days and was obliged to take other subjects. This he resented, feeling that they should have allowed him to miss those days and still keep his subjects.

He only wants to do things he likes. He didn't get a job last summer because of the weather – it was too good! He liked it, and lounged around the squares of Pimlico. He hasn't worked this winter because of the court case. He never told me about the missed appointment at New Bridge.

He was given that stolen money at a very bad time, because Sherborne House had less effect on him while he had money and didn't need a job. His Mum never makes him pay rent. She did only once, over Christmas, so he's not had to take responsibility for getting himself together. He didn't sign on for *two years*. His Mum is being evicted from the flat where he lives, so I've given him a number to call to be rehoused. He says he's worried about what's going to happen but still hasn't made the call after two months.

He still hangs out with Pimlico boys from adjoining estates, much as he did when he was younger. None of them have anything to do – or much sexual drive. Johnnie said he had some girlfriends in the past but nothing now. It's conceivable he just might be gay but doesn't know it.

I'm very fond of him, and he likes me. He also liked Sherborne House – he says now – very much. I didn't think so at the time – I felt he found it very hard. I hope he'll get a further Probation Order but he is very scared, very scared indeed that he'll go to prison. I want to tell the court he is making progress. He is, but it is hard to claim.

In court, Johnnie wore a suit jacket, white shirt and tie. He was ordered to return all of the stolen £400, pay the same amount again at £5 per week in compensation. Johnnie was not sent to prison, but given another probation order of two years. He was warned that next time the court would not be so lenient.

I had a good judge. I went in a suit cos I thought I was going down. Got another squeeze.

The Detective Sergeant came in December and was very nice. He said, 'let us wait to lift you till after Christmas.' He said 'If there are any other jobs you want to help us with we have a potful of money.' He thought I was an informer but criminals never grass. It was double hard taking the money out of the bank to give back. I didn't know how much I had left. I thought £80. In fact, it was £180.

Sitting with Chloe and me in a coffee bar around the corner from the court, Johnnie could hardly believe his luck. He resolved to stay straight. It was not clear that he ever saw using his friend's money as criminal, but he now intended to keep out of prison. He had not changed his views about low-paying jobs or training schemes but if he used his stubbornness just to keep his nose clean, we all felt he could succeed.

The challenge this represented to Johnnie was all the clearer when I visited his flat a week later. He'd forgotten his key, and scaled the wall to break into his own flat on the first floor. He slid through a small open window with the ease of a cat burglar, even though house burglary was not his method of operation.

The condition of the flat expressed his situation. It was roomy and would make a comfortable family home if there was a family to live in it. He had left the sitting room alone. It looked the way his Mum must have had it, but he had done his own small room with care. This was where his mates hung out too when they visited him. His walls had smart Vogue-style pinups, along with

*cars and rock stars, not Page Three girls. His door was covered
with football stickers. There were three Walkmans on a shelf.
Another room had been dossed in by a mate. It was suitably ironic
that the police had raided Johnnie's flat on a tip-off from someone
who'd seen him climbing into his own flat on a previous occasion.
Johnnie was outraged at being 'distressed', as he had 'given up
crime' but his habit of stealing the food off the doorsteps of news-
agents carried on:*

In this area you can get salmon or nice bread off the doorsteps
of the posh restaurants if you're out early. The fish is there at six,
six-thirty and the waiters don't arrive until seven-thirty, it's a
doddle. We eat at that hour often – after staying up all night. A
friend popped in with five TV frozen dinners to be cooked and
eaten before he went to work at seven *(am)*.

*The day was weighing him down. Like many people with mild
depression – which I suspect Johnnie had – going to bed at midnight when he wasn't out at clubs raving, and waking up at noon,
he was still tired.*

I've been trying to change. These days I get up about half nine,
I don't like to lay in these days. I don't really do much during the
day. Careers office, job centre is what I do constructively but for
the rest of the day I don't do nothing. Friends say 'a job's a job',
and my friends' Mums say that as well, but it doesn't work that
way. I'd rather sit on my arse and claim a giro than work at
Tesco's, cos you get your money but you get nothing else at the
end of it. No prospects, dead-end job. Three years and what are
you at the end of that, a manager? Assistant manager? I ain't
working there three years just to become an assistant manager.
NO way.

I can do better than that. I'm not going to be filling shelves. But
I've got no proof. What proof is there? Bits of paper saying I've
done GCSEs, that's pointless really. I know I can do better than
that. What proof do you need at the end of the day? But in order
to get there in the first place you've got to start somewhere. You
go for these jobs as an office junior and they say 'you need experience'. How are you going to get the experience if they don't give
you a chance? It's a Catch 22! I have been looking but there are
no jobs at the moment, so I've been looking at college, but there
are no places left.

Evenings, with friends, maybe dossing here, maybe get in a

friend's car, someone's house. I don't really like the week, I just wait for the weekend to go out. I'll always need money whether I'm working or not. I can't get enough of it, it's as simple as that. But I've got to learn to live with it, and without it. I live on my giro and what my friends do for me.

Johnnie's friends were his family now, as I saw in various encounters with them when I visited him. Many were in the same situation – aimless, on drugs, in and out of trouble, looking for short-term amusement to fill the vacuum of time left by the absence of jobs, training and real family. Some have more money, or a more stable family situation. Those that have more shared it freely. The food in Johnnie's flat had come from a 2am relief package lowered in a bucket from a friend's family kitchen window the night before.

I need money to live and go out. It's hard to do on £62 a fortnight. My trainers are Patrick Ewing, I got them for £40 cos I knew someone who worked in the shop. Spent my giro on them, and a win on the horses, a tiny bit. I don't go in the bookies very often. But I still like the ponies. My jacket's bought off a friend, I'm not sure where he got it from.

I can live off nothing if I have to. I have to sacrifice by not going out though sometimes friends can sort you out on that as well. I'm getting evicted soon, at the end of the month. There's no electricity in the house at the moment.

I'm being thrown out cos of rent arrears. My Mum's left the flat to me but they *(the council)* won't stick it in my name so I can't get housing benefit. Catch 22. Mum's written to them to say can they put it in my name but you can't do that apparently and if my Mum leaves the house she's making me homeless, because she's moved to her boyfriend's. That's the council's policy, if your parent leaves the house you're left homeless. I can't pay the rent, but if they'd stick it in my name I'd be able to get housing benefit, and I'd pay them £5 a week!

I'm not paying any rent or electricity. But £60 goes nowhere with me. I can spend it in a day easily, on clothes or going out. I go to raves. Money to get in. £15 or £20. £5 for drinks, travel, and then you want money for your drugs. Two Es *(Ecstasy)* £30. Acid that's trip, £5, draw, hash, pot or whatever, £15 for an eighth, which is 3.5 grams, Charlie, coke *(cocaine)*, £60 a gram. Charlie is the max. People who use H *(heroin)* are stupid. I can't go out to a rave without dropping an E and I don't like to admit that but it can't be helped.

When we left his flat we encountered another friend, tall, nice-looking, well-dressed, and floating on drugs. Johnnie observed somewhat ruefully:

He's 'gone' for the day, but harmless.

You'd be surprised what people will do to go out. A lot of my friends realise that if they're going out at the weekend from Tuesday they're trying to get the money to make ends meet. If you leave it till the last day it just doesn't happen.

They get the money any way, anywhere they can. Go into offices, go into peoples' handbags and wallets, thieving out of shops, cars, all sorts of things, robbery, burglaries. But if you break into a house you know you've got money basically. Hi-fi, videos, TVs. Maybe a bit of jewellery.

Burglaries are easy to do, it's just getting the stuff home, or wherever you want to take it that's difficult. A car would help a lot. Where I live, it's a posh area, if the police see a youth with a bag on him they're going to stop him. You tell someone they're going to get £50 to drive somewhere they'll do it.

Johnnie seemed to deal with the temptation of bad company by going along some of the time but not actually taking part in the crimes or drugs, thinking this protected him from being involved. (In the eyes of the court, this would be much less clear.) But he felt 'derailed' when he was with his friends and they were committing a crime.

I know someone who takes Astra GTEs, about five a week, drives them and then dumps them again. It's foolish but he does it. He's an idiot, it's too hot. I won't get into a stolen car, it's not worth it. This person keeps coming round with an Astra which he can get 130 mph out of. I've told people not to get into it and then they do and they get arrested, they've only got themselves to blame. He wants to be big – only Astra GTEs, and he likes the thrill of going fast. Foolish. He's been in and out all his life. I've seen him come round with £500 in his pocket offering to take you out but I won't accept that cos he always asks to have it back in a week.

I don't like drink, my Mum's an alcoholic, so I know all about drink. You get drunk, you want something to eat and then you want sleep and it'll always be in that order. Nothing more. And what sort of buzz is that? You spend all your money to do it, it's not worth it.

I was in my pub scene at one point and I spent far too much. I used to drink twelve pints, shorts, vodka and coke. I'd go through £60 a day sometimes. I was seventeen. Technically I should have spent less, but in the pub it never works out that way. And when you get drunk you get rowdy. It's a fact. I think I can take anyone on, and then you get into a fight.

In the morning I used to still be drunk sometimes. I used to look at my money and all I'd have would be a few pence and I'd think 'Oh my god, where did all my money go?' Then I'd have a wash and I'd be out again. But I had the savings so I didn't need to worry about the money. I had about £3,000.

I made my money by foiling, doing dodgy coins, wrapping them in silver foil in the arcades. The foil is hard to get – comes from lagging tape used on building sites, you can't buy it in shops. My mate nicked a box and sold it for £2. I used to make £60 to £70 a day from one in the afternoon to midnight. Foiling works in drink, cigarette, and ticket machines as well. Put in foil shaped like 50p and get the real thing in change.

Luck ran out eventually. It always happens to me, if I'm onto a good thing my luck runs out. They changed the machines to stop it at London Transport and some of the arcades. I could have gone down to the seaside but I also knew I'd get caught soon. At the time I made the money, I converted it into dollars. If I made £60 I'd buy $100 with it. I had £3000 – it was $3400 dollars at the time. I was going to America.

I was going to go to America to escape my troubles. I thought I was going to go to prison because I'd breached my Community Service. But I got a good report. I was on my way. I'd got my passport done, bought clothes, told my Mum, and then I got a letter through saying I had to go to court. I saw a probation officer, he said I might get a squeeze. So I went along and I got away with it, I got a Sherborne House order. And spent the money for the States while at Sherborne House. I had a good time, but not that good.

The probation service do a good job. I enjoyed Sherborne House in the end. It shows you how you can put your abilities to good use without turning to crime. Shows that you can do things with your hands, as in woodwork. It helps you to stop you doing them.

I didn't deserve to go down I don't think, and I'm grateful for the judge for not sending me to prison.

He had left Sherborne House a year earlier. At the end of the course, his probation officer Chloe, and Molly, his group leader, had asked how he saw his future in one, three and five years, in terms of the best and worst and most realistic options. To Johnnie, the best was a good job and a flat, which would take at least several years to arrange. But when Molly suggested he put his name down now for a new council flat, his pessimism was tangible and epitomised his view of the world.

What's the point? There's not enough places. My name might come up and they'll run out of places. Or I put my name down and get a flat I didn't like.

The worst in all three cases was prison. Prison has been Johnnie's dominant fear. He's physically frail, and with his long hair, would be vulnerable to physical and sexual abuse inside. Both women asked if there was anything he could do to keep out of prison.

Don't know. Not really. I plan to stop thieving. Get a job with prospects. Didn't need to before cos I had money. Now I got to start the rest of my life, don't I? But if in three years' time I see a briefcase in the road and nobody's around, I might take it. A spur of the moment kind of thing. Or buy something stolen. I already passed up lots of opportunities.

Johnnie had left Sherborne House in October. By Christmas he was arrested for handling his friend's stolen money. Asking him to reflect on the whole experience the following October, I gained the impression Johnnie was struggling with the idea that perhaps his 'luck' had not been that bad after all.

I really thought I was going inside this time. There are some people who stop thieving if they get sent to prison and others who won't, who go in and out all their life. Some people are just craving for money. They just want money, money, money. It's true I'm quite keen on money, but there's a limit. I don't know what prison would do to me personally. It might change my views, but I don't plan to find out.

Coming out from court with a squeeze's not as good as you think. When I got out of court I wasn't screaming up and down. I wasn't as happy as I thought I would have been because I realised I shouldn't have been in that position at all. I promised myself not to be in that position again. I should've gone to America when I had the cash. I'd still like to go but now it's harder for me to get a visa and a work permit cos I've got a record.

I've given up crime. But I'm still criminally minded, I can't walk down the street as a normal person anymore. It isn't nice. I walk down the street and see opportunities everywhere, especially when I'm in a group of mates. You just clock doors that are open, windows, cars, car stereos, you do mental sums about how much they're worth. It isn't nice. This way of thinking is much harder to get away from when you're skint. So one day I'm probably going to do something.

Looking back over Johnnie's life and criminal career, it is clear how devastating his family experiences have been. With his father absent, his mother's departure from their home to live with her boyfriend coincided with the collapse of Johnnie's promising development at school. That she maintained his allowance and paid the rent so he would not have to work was no substitute for the personal involvement he needed. Without greater moral and emotional support, such financial help on its own may have done him harm. Bright but lethargic, and cushioned from economic reality, Johnnie was indeed a 'Rolls-Royce attached to nothing', in Chloe's words. He had no need to get out of bed at all.

His fear of prison has been so intense it might have been expected to act as more of a deterrent to his falling into crime. Yet as his teenage years passed, his criminal activity escalated, carried along by peer pressure like so many others in his situation. That brought closer the likelihood of him ending up inside – until he reached Sherborne House. However many car stereos he had stolen, Johnnie was out of his depth in offending terms among the people who were there. His formal reason for being sent to Sherborne House was the theft of parts to a mountain bike and breach of a Community Service order, whereas others were in for far more serious offences. He kept his distance from them to the point where what looked like independence became more like isolation. He may well have been frightened of them.

In his work at Sherborne House, Johnnie's fierce sense of the wisdom of his own judgements sat oddly with his lack of confidence. But personal judgements are the tools Sherborne House work with to point each offender in the right direction. Wanting to be accepted, he responds to his surroundings.

Although that meant he slipped easily into handling his friend's stolen money, and happily took part in the local trawl of open cars and offices, my sense is that Sherborne House, plus just enough of the company of straight friends has shown Johnnie something that he has begun to absorb. Now some eighteen months after leaving Sherborne House, and more than a year since the court case concerning his friend's money, Johnnie has stayed out of trouble. He has kept up the repayments of the money he'd spent and to cover his fines. He now has plans to go to college this autumn. With his stubbornness put to a purpose, his new probation officer firmly believes he can keep on in that direction. He has changed.

CHAPTER TWO

STAN

No such thing as a thief-proof car

Stan is white, tall, and comfortable with himself. Two scars on his right cheek add to his saturnine good looks, making him seem older than he is. But his true age shows when he smiles. Outwardly he is slightly forbidding, so the readiness and twinkle of his smile come as a surprise.

Stan's parents split up when he was very small. Erratic traffic between his parents, his uncles, and grandparents followed. More recently, he has lived in a succession of bedsitters while on the run, and then at Sherborne House after he gave himself up. His passion since his early teens has been for cars – his own and other people's – for both pleasure and gain. He's a typical joyrider and an active thief. But his young life has already included several stretches of legitimate work in which he made a good impression. He's confident and clever, with a strong but not aggressive physical presence. One has the feeling he could do anything, straight or crooked, that he set his mind to.

His air of being comfortable about himself belies his youth and his genuine insecurity about how and where to live. Until his eighteenth birthday – six months after Sherborne House – he was surviving on £32 a fortnight, a token amount given by the DSS to footloose under-eighteens for only six weeks. It is pitched that low to drive young people back home or into a training scheme or both. For people like Stan, whose home life is deeply unstable, such pressure is more likely to lead them to crime.

My parents split up when I was two. I lived with my Dad but he wouldn't let me have no contact with my Mum. He used to come looking for me cos I wouldn't go to school. Kicked me out when I was fourteen, before I got nicked, cos I kept running away. I went to find my Mum. I hadn't seen her for ten years. I rode my

BMX *(bicycle)* all the way down the North Circular to Romford to my Nan and Grandad who I hadn't seen for years. They took me to find her in Romford.

I lived there till I was sixteen, then she'd had enough. She kicked me out. Now I live with me Aunt. Me and my Mum still don't talk to this day cos of that. She hasn't tried to get in touch and neither have I. Doesn't worry me. *(He says all this flicking his lighter with apparent indifference.)*

At Sherborne House, each group member discussed his criminal record in front of the others. Stan smiled as he began:

There's a lot missing from the records I've got. I know cos I got my record pinned to my wall at home.

I think of myself as a petty criminal. I wasn't really into any other kind of crime, a couple of burglaries here and there, but the main thing on my record is TDAs *(Taking and Driving Away)*.

I learned to drive at fourteen, when a mate told me to drive his car and I just watched what he did. Being so tall since I was young, I've been able to get away with it. Police look at you and think, 'he looks old enough to drive.' They just leave you as long as you're in a motor that looks like your motor. When you start turning up in RS Cosworths they'll think, 'Nah, that ain't his car.' My Mum tried to stop me, but she couldn't.

My worst one put me inside for three months while they did a Social Inquiry Report. It was a car chase lasting an hour and three-quarters down the wrong side of the North Circular from Rainham in an Escort 1100 Estate with four people: me, a mate who was fourteen, and two birds, one seventeen and one was twenty. We got eighty police cars out after us by the end. My mate climbed into the back as I drove and tried to light a ciggie.

We only stopped when the engine blew up. I'd killed the car completely. We had two videos, a telly and microwave in the boot, nicked from caravans in Essex. The police cut us up at the lights and blocked the motorway so we went down the other side. I wish I could do it again, cos I know a way I could have got away from the police. I know the mistakes I made. I wasn't scared.

My Mum went mad, completely mad! She's big: she does weight lifting and boxing. She beat me up in the police cells. She came to hear me give a statement and went mad: 'What if an old couple had been crossing the road?' So I said 'At 2am? Leave it out.' So she jumped on my back as we walked back to the cell. In court,

she stood up and told the judge to put me away. Got a squeeze.
Probation, community service and a ban.

When I got home, my Mum threw me out. I tried to change but
couldn't hack it. She threw me out cos she couldn't stand the Old
Bill coming round the house all the time.

I do it for the money, of course, and for the buzz. They wrote
about the chase in the paper – without my name cos I was a
juvenile. So people heard about it and came round asking me if
I'd get cars for them. So I started ringing motors – changing the
motor numbers – I mean delivering the cars to people who ring
them or sell them abroad.

Actually, most of my friends don't commit offences. It's a quiet
area. But I'd usually come round in a car – a different one each
time – but nobody cared. Now I got my own car in my brother's
name.

*At Sherborne House, Stan's performance was modest in the
groups, but he joined in most other activities legal and illegal,
with more energy. In the sessions on offending behaviour, he was
largely silent, doing the minimum that was required. He watched
from the sidelines throughout the ten weeks, appearing utterly
detached, but aware of what was going on in the room. But he
was obliged to talk about himself in some of the exercises, like
Five Things About Myself:*

Stan: Dislikes: getting caught. Unusual feature: scars.
      Physical feature: big feet. One fact about my
      offending: TDAs normally. Ambition: to get own
      greengrocer's.
Molly: I think that's realistic. You have worked in a
      greengrocers, you've been promoted. You know
      the trade.

*He's pleased to be complimented but also embarrassed by it, and
is caught between the two reactions of shrugging it off, as he
normally does, and actually acknowledging its truth. He does have
a future if he wants one.*

Molly: *(also seeing that)* How come you get caught so
      much?
Stan: I make mistakes. Also I been grassed up. Sometimes
      I been caught years later for TDAs.

Molly: Why TDAs?
Stan: *(smiling)* I like cars.
Joel: *(shrewder)* Do you do TDAs for money?
Stan: Yeah. BMWs and things.

When in a group with other youths but without adults, Stan came to life showing natural leadership and good humour. His resistance to the authority of the probation officers had a ritual air, the result of his age. He was too young to tolerate being patronised, or to enjoy the youthful antics of the drama group. He stomped out of the room on such occasions – 'I ain't gonna be treated like a kid!' – accepting the loss of points involved. This was the strongest show of emotion he displayed during the ten weeks.

Another exercise involved self-assessment, again on the basis of a questionnaire intended to expand the way the young offenders defined themselves:

Stan: *(his defiance explained)* I am: brave/ friendly/
        considerate/ kind/ shy/ sure of myself/ lazy/ anxious/
        bad-tempered/ a loner. I don't want to be
        big-headed, easily led, or boring.
Dane: *(laughs)* Who says you're boring? Is that why
        you're a loner?
Stan: *(unsmiling)* When I did jobs with others I got nicked
        but when I work alone, I don't get grassed. I always
        get more tastes when someone else is in the car.
        Alone I just go for the money.

His world weariness was sad. He was only seventeen, but spoke like a hardened villain.

In the workshop, although he seemed bored and distracted, Stan distinguished himself, making a complex and well-hewn lamp out of many kinds of wood. He also worked hard at making music in Project Week with his new friend Winston while the others went sailing. But his general demeanour in all the groups was one of disinterest and disapproval. His mind always seemed to be elsewhere.

Like all the others, Stan showed most passion when complaining about the general unfairness of the authorities. He fell out with Sherborne House staff over his assignment by them to weight lifting as his 'short course' activity on Monday afternoons. He had asked to play squash, but not enough of the others wanted it so the course was cancelled. Stan maintained belligerently each Monday for ten weeks that as he had never signed up for weight lifting, he therefore refused to do it. That he might have enjoyed weight lifting was not the issue. He was exercising the choice apparently offered him by Sherborne House. This stand cost him a loss of points and a warning that he might be sent back to court.

A more genuine grievance which troubled him during the programme was the unexplained refusal of the DSS to provide the grant to which he was entitled by his age and situation. Stan blamed Sherborne House for this as well, and warned the staff ever more fiercely that he would have to 'do something serious' if the money did not arrive soon. In the group on 'How Far Would You Go?' the subject of arson came up. Others admitted to enjoying it, and Stan chipped in that he had enjoyed it too, adding without a smile that he would seriously consider burning down Sherborne House unless his grant came through.

Stan shared the general view in the group that the police are profoundly unfair and treat them all very badly. They do not associate their own offences with this treatment and regard police misbehaviour with the same distaste as their own crimes are viewed by others.

It was an important feature of Sherborne House that the group went home each day. They had to learn to resist temptation on the street. But like many others on the programme, Stan was at risk of arrest at any time he was not actually in the building. The local police in their areas knew them well. When a crime is reported they round up the usual suspects. This sense of being unfairly victimised undermines the work of Sherborne House in the weekdays to help young offenders to take responsibility for the consequences of their actions.

The Old Bill started hassling me again for no reason. I'm being pulled three or four five times a day, daytime, night-time and searched for knives, car keys, drugs. But my eyes are sharper than theirs so when I see them coming I drop things on the floor and just pick them up later. I always got keys in my pocket, always. They're my brother's spare, but they get me into other cars too. Can't leave nothing in the house. But it don't seem right I might go down for six months cos of a key? Or a bit of hash in my pocket?

I just want them to stop bothering me. They know if they give me grief, I'll give them grief, like a smack in the mouth. They'd like that, cos they want to arrest me.

The police, they're just idiots. I got stitched up when I got arrested. They had two warrants on me. They pulled me over and said I was trying to break into a flat, when I was only walking home from a party. They strip searched me in the back of a van. I gave my brother's name, and then they went round there and checked, and of course my brother came to the door, and gave my real name! They found out I had two warrants on me, one for TDA and one for *(outstanding)* fines. Then they changed it from 'trying to do a burglary', to saying 'We saw you trying to nick that white cabriolet over there,' totally rewrote their books and everything. I got the case dropped, cos there was no evidence. That was in Stoke Newington.

Previous *(arrests)*: I wouldn't say I've been stitched up, but most of them were police that knew me anyway when I was living in Holloway. They used to treat me alright. I suppose once they get to know you.

In the groups on offending behaviour at Sherborne House, Stan was posed the same moral dilemmas that echoed in their daily lives: 'If a friend asks you to join in a burglary when you're on probation, and going to Sherborne House, you would risk going inside if you get caught. What would you do?' It happens often. The others all admitted they'd be tempted but claimed the risk was too great. Stan was unruffled.

I'd do it. Custody is a risk you always take. The only thing is if you go in with friends you have to share the proceeds. If you get a really good burglary but you can't do it yourself, you got to do it anyway to get a cut, otherwise it breaks your heart to hear they got two grand and you go off and just get another poxy video recorder.

There was nothing for the probation officers to say in the face of such clarity. It was a measure of how much work they had to do, how far they had to go.

Yet Stan also spoke with some pride about his straight job as a porter in the market. But he already had his eye on bigger things: during Sherborne House, he was busy organising a rave in the East End. In this he showed an energy and determination not otherwise visible in his contributions to the group. But it suddenly came unstuck. The contrast between the tiny sums of money he was fighting for from the DSS and the huge amounts available through other sources was striking. That Stan and the others want to make ends meet on the dole was a measure of their willingness to go straight, but not yet.

I could've made anything from £3000 to £10,000 but instead I lost a lot of money. We'd hired the decks and printed the tickets already. I had to sell my half stake cos it needed more money. Cost me £1500. It was mostly from thieving. All I got was a free ticket. I was gutted, well sick. That's life I suppose. I couldn't be bothered to try again.

> Molly: How will you go raving without money now?
> Stan: Depends on the mood I'm in. If I feel like it, I'll go
>   and nick a car and sell the parts for money. I've done
>   that two or three times since I been here. *(smiles
>   wickedly)* I'm happy. I'm in a happy, thieving
>   mood. Not happy, a thieving mood. I nicked a car
>   last night, so now I got money in my pocket, no
>   worries for the week.
> Molly: What's the money for?
> Stan: I want to spend it on records. Been behind on a
>   record selector for a few months, used to spend
>   £50 a week on it.*
> Molly: But is it worth the risk of getting caught – in your
>   current situation?
> Stan: *(unbothered but pleased at the efficacy of his
>   system)* There is zero per cent chance of getting
>   caught, cos last night's car doesn't exist any more.
>   Everything that needs to be done to it is done. It
>   doesn't exist. The worst they can do me for is a
>   simple offence – Driving Whilst Disqualified in me
>   own car.

This was a rare degree of openness from Stan. It was as though he had decided to take up, albeit briefly, the spirit of Sherborne House, and talk openly both about his offending, and to an

---

* A record selection is a service offering tips on the latest dance music likely to become club favourites.

*unusual degree about himself. But his tone remained confident and
proud.*

My only remand was two weeks in Feltham. Same four as in
the car chase, we went back to the caravans in Essex, got caught
again. Me and my mates were juveniles. The social worker came
down and took statements, and let us go – put us on the train and
watched us go. Actually one of the caravans was mine, bought off
me Mum. The bloke who owned the land burned it down after
£900 of non-payment of rent. I couldn't be bothered.

Then I got drinking – I'm not a drinker – and went back to kick
in the windows of a forty year-old Greek who tried to rape my
sister. The Old Bill didn't do nothing when we told them. I went
back and forth to a party – then went back and he came to the
door and I just went mad and started to hit him. Did this three
times in one night. I knocked on the door, he answered, and I
rushed into him. His brother and sister managed to get the door
shut, so I put my foot through the window and caught his face as
well – gave him ten stitches around his eye. He ended up curled
on the floor.

I was wearing a track suit with a luminous stripe so I was easy
to spot. But I told my uncle who I was living with and he said
'Good on you.' Got a lot of praise from the neighbours cos he'd
interfered with lots of young girls. He used to offer them drugs to
lure them into his flat.

They let me out *(of the police station)* after four hours. He
walked past me on the estate the next day, and he couldn't even
see out of his eye, it was all shut up. I said 'You cunt, I'm gonna
kill you.' I'm still planning to do it again.

*Stan's expression left no doubt that this was true. The violence
of his act had taken us all by surprise, but its motivation was clear
enough, especially if the account of police inaction was accurate.
The approval of Stan's family and neighbours stamped the action
as correct in his mind. He said he was acting out of family loyalty,
and was totally unrepentant.*

I gotta stick up for my sister. My sister didn't want me to do it.
She wouldn't tell me cos she knew I'd go round there. My mate
told me, he was there at the time, and pulled the bloke off my
sister. He was in his forties. My sister was fifteen at the time. I
was sixteen.

Given his persistent offending and the violence of the assault,

Stan had been dealt with leniently by the courts. He had been given a series of non-custodial punishments which had so far failed to impress him. Apart from this attack, none of his offences in themselves would have required custody, but cumulatively they represented a history of the failure of the criminal justice system to influence his behaviour. Sherborne House really was his last chance.

I got sent to Sherborne House once before for theft from a car – got stopped by a copper who took my clothes to the person who called the police and she spotted them. I got ABH for the Greek, Theft, and TDA. They gave me Sherborne House and a year's probation order. Another squeeze. I could have gone away. The magistrate said if he saw me in court again I'm looking at time but he gave me Sherborne House.

I breached it and went on the run. But when I turned myself in, the beak sent me back to Sherborne House again. *(smiles)* My family says I've got the luck of the Irish.

Molly asked Stan how he lived when on the run. He replied:

I used to have a lot of money in my pocket on the run. I financed it with TDAs every day. I paid the rent for a mate's bedsitter, bought cars, flash clothes. I wasted it. I could get up to five grand a week for motors they could ring – BMWs, Rovers, cars they want in Spain, places like that.

Started to save towards the end. I got the idea I'd go down *(go to prison)* and wanted to prepare. I was in a Sierra and went through a brick wall being chased by the police. They did me for reckless *(driving)*, and three TDAs and some burglaries.

The judge called me a 'juvenile delinquent' *(smiles thinly)*. But he gave me bail and put me in the care of social workers. I got a wicked squeeze – a hundred hours' Community Service for one and the same for the other offences – two hundred hours concurrently, but they told me I only had to do fifty.

I only got seven hours left but I can't get up at nine in the morning on a Saturday *(after raving all night on Friday)*. I been warned they're tightening up but *(smiles)* I just can't get up. Anyway, I got a squeeze, man, got a squeeze all the way through. Three times I should have gone away. Just lucky.

I got arrested again just before starting Sherborne House:

charged with driving disqualified, no insurance, TDA, two thefts
from motor vehicle, and breach of Sherborne House and probation
order – all done in '89 except the breach and TDA. My licence
was endorsed three times – I ran into the back of the Old Bill
while having a race in a Rover 2000. I'm on a ban now.

The TDA was when I was off sick, and saw this car with the
keys in the ignition. I just got in, turned the motor over, and the
Old Bill clocked my face.

I don't deny I'm doing things now. But I wouldn't drive in my
manor because of the Old Bill. My face is known. For me driving
is a hobby, like dragster racing. I need £200 a week. *(smiling
grimly at the group leaders).* You give me £200 a week and I'll
stop offending.

*At the end of his time at Sherborne House, in the last group
session, Stan had to guess his best, worst, and most likely future:*

It's obvious ain't it? Best is to be a millionaire. Most likely is
you'll be working. Worst is to be in the nick. In five years I'll be
a millionaire cos I'll get a gun and hold up Sherborne House. *(This
was the sort of remark that gave the impression he was only biding
his time there.)* Don't know where I'll be living.

The best would be security, and a roof over my head. Could be
cardboard city, don't know. One thing's for sure, I ain't staying
in the same job for more than three months when I get out. *(Stan
had a job waiting for him at the People's Dispensary in East
London).* One bloke's been there forty years for £106 per week!
I'm moving out of the area, and making a fresh start.

Want to be an apprentice mechanic. I know how to set it up –
I'm not a complete idiot! How do you think I do my work? I know
people in the trade. I know how to do it already but I want
the degree. *(He said this with no expression, and never raised
his voice, or his eyes. Then, suddenly:)* If anything goes wrong,
I'll get me own fruit stall in the market, take in two, £300 a
week!

*Then he returned to his usual detached ironic self, smiled at the
group, and diverted their attention to someone else's future.*

*The staff view of him at the end was mixed but basically posi-
tive. The group leaders felt he never took responsibility for his
actions, and showed his youth (still seventeen). They felt him to
be sly. Even his punctuality – he travelled from north-east to south
London to reach Sherborne House – was suspected to be based*

on stealing cars to drive there, and ditching them too far away to be caught.

On the water-skiing outing we piled into the staff's own cars. Stan took one look at Molly's battered Capri and offered to buy it:

I'd do it up – alloy wheels, a five-speed RF gear box.

Molly realises Stan is serious – despite his having proclaimed how broke he is repeatedly over the past weeks.

Molly: *(tactfully)* I wouldn't sell it to anyone I know.
Stan: I wouldn't sell it, just to run around in.

En route, Stan was a real back-seat driver. We had to follow the craft instructor in the other car and lost him several times, much to Stan's fury. Sitting in the back, he was as relaxed as a reformed alcoholic in a pub. He told us on the way that he was on a ban but was applying to court to get his licence back, using a letter claiming he needed it for his work. He then coyly asked to drive.

Molly: Why?
Stan: Cos I'd drive right up his arse and stay there till we
     got to the docks!
Molly: But you've got no licence!
Stan: So? We need to get behind an ambulance and cut
     in and out with him. *(undoes his seat belt and is ticked
     off by Molly).* Don't like the feel of seat belts. I wrote
     off a car at 125 *(mph)* and walked away. Why
     don't you drive down the opposite lane, it's empty!
Molly: I don't like to cut people up.
Stan: I drive to cut people up.

After the skiing, which he managed with aplomb, Stan finished dressing before the others. When we all went into the car park to go home, Stan was sitting in the driver's seat of Molly's Capri, smiling, having broken into it. Molly was furious, but Stan said, 'You got no sense of humour.'

The craft instructors all found Stan creative, patient, and resourceful. He made his lamp away from the original design given by the staff and it turned out well. Tom, the avuncular woodwork instructor said, 'If Stan likes what he's doing, he does it well. In the workshop when it's noisy he seems distracted, but he's actually into the work. He doesn't look it but he is.'

When the base of his lamp was completed, Stan obtained some money from Tom and went out to the shop to get some wire. He returned and realised he'd forgotten a lamp holder, which meant more money and another trip. On his return he said, 'I'm not going again.' Then he realised he'd forgotten a bulb. When he got back a third time, Tom asked dryly, 'How are you going to plug it in?' Stan laughed, and went again. The lamp, a small round base made of fourteen different woods, looked wonderful.

I grew to like Stan the more I saw of him, but shared the staff view that he saw life as full of chances, and sailed very close to the wind.

When Dane was thrown out for driving illegally, Jack mentioned to Stan that he 'owed him one' because he'd been spotted as a passenger and could have been nicked for allowing himself to be carried in a stolen car:

Stan: What? I never –
Jack: It's on the file. 15 August. It's a criminal offence –
Stan: *(quickly)* He said it was his cousin's. No way would
      I have ridden in it if I knew it was hot. I got too many
      TDAs. *(then, with professional pride)* I know his
      scam. You nick the petrol cap and get the key
      made. My mate does it with Cosworths.

With a job and a steady girl waiting for him, Stan should, because of his intelligence and wit, be able to make a productive settled life – if he doesn't get his deserts in the courts in the meantime.

Nine months after Stan left Sherborne House, I interviewed his new probation officer:
Stan came out of Sherborne House and lived at different addresses. He kept no appointments for three months. He was caught reoffending with cars in December and spent last Christmas in Feltham. He had a job in the People's Dispensary for Sick Animals, in Stoke Newington, until he went in. When he came out after Christmas, he had the chance to go back there. But he had a fight with someone there and left in February.

He was very erratic – never kept any of his appointments before his last offence, kept some appointments in January and February, and was very pleasant. I tried to get him into the Ilderton Motor

Project in South London cos he was mad about cars, but he went down for a day or so and then didn't carry on. He moved back to his Mum in Romford, and I offered him a chance to report to the Probation Office there, but he refused.

One year after Sherborne House, I interviewed Stan himself in Feltham Young Offenders' Institution. Finding Stan in prison was not a complete surprise in the light of his professed offending even during Sherborne House. His confidence was not dented by being in custody. His strong physical presence clearly protected him there. He smiled a good deal during the interview. The only apparent difference in him was that he now looked well-fed and quite a few years older.

As he talked, sitting in a prison office surrounded by the numerous noises off of others like him, I felt Stan almost physically making sense of himself, coming into focus like a polaroid photograph. He was far more willing to talk about his past than he had been at Sherborne House.

I was eighteen in February. Doesn't mean anything. It just means I can drink, legally. The only difference is you get money when you get out.

When I was young I'd nick a fiver off my Dad or Mum, go out and spend it on chocolate and on the machines. Then I got addicted to fruit machines. When I was seven I started nicking £100 at a time off my Dad and step-Mum, and that's when it got out of hand.

At one time I nicked £550 mortgage money and done it all in two hours in fruit machines. My Dad took me to a psychiatrist. I came off the machines, but then started again after about six months, so he sent me to boarding school.

I was at boarding school from the first year junior, to first year senior, because I was an uncontrollable child. I used to thieve and that. I got cautioned for a forged £20 note when I was eight years old. I nicked it from a car – got caught the first time I broke into a car. Also I nicked three loaves of bread from a doorstep on a paper round.

My Dad sent me there to try to sort me out. It was alright. There were only twenty kids. You'd do a couple of hours' work a day, the rest just mucking about. I caught up on my work. Then I went to another one, but I was on day release. When I was fifteen, I went to a comprehensive but I dropped out at the beginning of the fifth year. I wasn't doing much work, and I couldn't really be bothered.

At fifteen in Romford, I ran away from home to Edmonton and nicked lots of car stereos. Course I'd done it before. I used to nick stereos when I was ten, on my own, on the way to work in the market on Sunday mornings in the East End. I'd sell them in the market and then tell my Dad I'd done well.

My scar was a car accident when I was two years old standing on the kerb. My little scar was a cricket bat. I got hit by a rioter in the Tottenham riots when Broadwater Farm went up. I was looting, I weren't there to beat up the Old Bill. Me and my brother heard the alarms go off and we went down there to see what was happening, and just to raid a couple of shops. I was only about twelve. My brother was what, thirteen or fourteen. We got out a van and was filling it with videos when this geezer runs by being chased by a copper. He hits me and keeps on running, and so does the copper. But another one got me. I got a squeeze *(no conviction)*. They kept the van, and I went to hospital. Got five stitches and a result. Just did it to get a bit of cash. We was only on about fifty pence pocket money in those days.

My Dad knew *(what I was doing)* but he didn't ever hit me. He just told me not to get caught. He did the same things at his age. But he spent most of his youth in custody anyway, so he knows that I'll 'learn by my own mistakes' as he put it. That's what I'd tell my son if I have one: I don't mind, if he don't get caught.

What stopped him was five years in Brixton *(Prison)*. While he was inside he did a brick-laying course, come out and got a job as a labourer. Done that for about ten years, got to be foreman, and now he's got his own business, and doing alright. He still wheels and deals, you know what I mean? But he don't go out thieving. He buys the odd hooky thing now and again.

I wouldn't work for my Dad. I get on with him well, but we'd end up arguing all the time cos my Dad likes all work and no play. My brother and he are always having arguments.

One of the government's ideas is to make parents responsible for the criminal acts of their children. Stan seems to support this view but his mother's tough reactions had little influence on him.

My Dad would have kicked shit out of me if he was getting the fines. That would have affected me a lot, cos one thing, I have got a lot of respect for my Dad in that way, I'm shit scared of him. It probably would have worked for me. He tried to stop me but I was just like any other kid. I wouldn't listen.

When I got out of Sherborne House, I had a job with the People's Dispensary for Sick Animals. That's the job I had open for me when I was at Sherborne House. Moving to Romford it was just too far to travel, so I gave it up. I've just been thieving since then.

For a streetwise young man a job tending sick animals seems surprisingly soft. But Stan also liked working at an old people's home when he was doing Community Service.

It was sweet. You come in any time you wanted, stop when you wanted, wash the windows, make the old dears a cup of tea, whatever needed doing. You was never forced to do anything. Just had to write it down in the book. But you didn't get too involved with them cos we weren't allowed in the old people's rooms. It was nice. It was alright. But my fucking probation officer told the court I wasn't doing it when I was.

Again, the system was against him – without him having any part in his future. Yet Stan had only one day to go to complete his Community Service Order but didn't manage to get out of bed in time one more Saturday morning. For a natural rebel, his views about Sherborne House were a surprise.

I thought Sherborne House was brilliant. Great. If I had the chance to do it again I would.

Stan appeared to be serious. I was astonished.

My probation officer tried to get me back in there, but they wouldn't have it cos I was living out of London. At the time I didn't think it was. It's looking back at it. I think it was great. In all ways really. There are a lot of activities, plus you get to talk about your own offences and hear about everyone else's. I just thought it was brilliant. I joined in sometimes and I got a blinding report.

I was having real trouble believing him. I told Stan he had been the most unresponsive person in the entire place.

I'm a quiet person. I'm just a quiet person, a bit shy on the side. I was paying attention, believe it or not. It's up to you, innit? I was interested in it. If I had the chance to go back I would. I made a lamp in woodwork, and a chest which I never took with me.

Liked the music, and some of the activities, but I weren't really too much into the talking side of it. I told the truth in groups, the whole truth, and nothing but. But looking back, if I had a second chance, I'd do a lot better. Though I did get a right good report at the end of it, and my solicitor always reads it out in court.

I got well involved in the *(counterfeit)* £20 notes, I think everyone was. It was in the paper the next day, the day after we all went out doing them. 'Twenty pound notes flying around South London.' We must have done about twenty grand's worth in the area between the lot of us. Nobody caught that I know of.

It didn't make me want to go straight, but then again, nor does this place. I'd say a good eighty per cent of the people in here are likely to reoffend when they get out.

After Sherborne House, I done a sentence here at Christmas for a month, for two TDAs. Then I got out and got arrested again in February, again for TDAs, and I absconded. I was just caught in October. I was on remand for a month, and I've just been convicted, two weeks now. Ain't really a lot happened. I've moved to Romford, living with my Mum.

One important change since Stan left Sherborne House seems to be that he no longer goes joyriding. Like the reconciliation with his mother, it is an important sign, though he clearly has a good way to go before he gives up offending altogether.

I don't think I'm on that buzz anymore. I was on it for a couple of years but I'm not really into it no more. I do it for the money purely. If I nick a motor now I stay all calm, take it nice and easy.

It's hard to explain the buzz really, you just get behind the wheel and you're there ready. Like you love it, and you just think, 'Yeh, I wanna do it again, I wanna do it again' – just like smoking. It's like drugs, you wanna keeping doing it, but then after a while you keep doing it so often, you ain't getting the buzz no more.

I've said to a couple of people in here, one in my cell, he goes out nicking Astra GTEs all the time just for the fun of it. I said, 'If you're gonna do it, don't go out for high speed rallies and all that. Do it for money, or don't do it at all.'

I drove to Sherborne House a couple of times, but not in stolen ones as it happens. I got two of my own cars. I got a Mark II Escort RS2000, and an Escort Van. It's like a project and I'm still building it. It's all bought legitimately. It's in my brother's name. I can't register it in my name, with me driving it, cos I'm on a ban. I've just been given another three years, from the 21st October.

I've been on a ban since I was fifteen anyway. I was banned when I just bought a little motorbike and I was sending off for a provisional *(licence)*, and I got banned. By the time I was sixteen I had another ban, and another one at seventeen. Hasn't affected my driving.

The government's planning to extend the punishment for joyriding. I've been listening to it on the radio. I don't think I'd like to do a two year stretch. But I can't say it'd stop me joyriding, or if I had a sale for the car or the parts. It's hard to say.

I told Stan that, in Belfast, joyriders were shot at by the military and beaten up by the para-military, which seemed to excite them; in fact one joyrider who'd been knee-capped for joy-riding, stole a car as soon as he came out of hospital – on his crutches!

I wouldn't carry on joyriding in Belfast, I wouldn't risk my life and limb, definitely not; though cars are something I've always liked since an early age.

If I seriously hurt myself, I'd think twice about doing it again. I've been lucky, I've had a couple of crashes, but I've always walked out unharmed. When I see someone else has been killed, I just think that's them, being silly. When you got a car, doing handbrake turns at seventy mph and all that, you deserve it. Now when I nick a motor I don't do it to show off. I might do a little wheel spin if I see one of my mates, but I don't exceed the speed limit by much, I don't go down a thirty mph road at ninety mph, you're just asking to get chased.

The guys *(joyriders who hit a lamppost and died)* who got killed in Newcastle – I don't think that puts people off, it's just part of the excitement. They do it for the buzz, purely for the buzz. Nothing else gives you that kind of buzz except rally driving or something. That's what I'd like to do, as it happens, when I get out. I've done a course, about six months ago. I went away for a week rally driving. I'd like to get into it properly.

I can do that on a ban cos it's all done on private land. But after about a year, if I've kept out of trouble, I'm going to go back to court and ask for my licence back. I know a couple of people who've done it. Just say that I want to start a new life, and that I want to drive legally.

They was going to put me on a motor project but I absconded court. I'm not living in London no more, I can't go on this course. It's the same as Sherborne House, they were going to send me back there, but now I'm not living in London I can't go, so they sent me to prison.

Stan in prison is costing us nearly £400 a week — twice what it would cost to send him to Sherborne House, or to a motor project, if either existed in his area.

I don't think prison's got an effect, cos you're banged up with a load of people most of whom are in for the same thing as me. There's a couple of mates on this wing for joy-riding. Prison's alright as long as you get a job, otherwise you're banged up in a little room for twenty-two hours a day and it just gets on top of you. I'm working as a cleaner so I'm out of my cell all day. Just do half an hour's cleaning, then watch TV and play pool.

I gave up burglary anyway. Burglary's no buzz. I done three burglaries in Malden Court. I got fined £150 for them. I've done a couple with Raga *(Bren, another member of the group)*, as it goes. We used to go off in the afternoon, but I never got into it. Me and Bren did one day, but they come home while we were in the house. We shot out down the back garden and got away, but it's not really the sort of thing I'm into. You get a terrible rush to your head at that sort of moment, you're just para[noid], terrible para.

Bren does love a burglary. He was in here when I first come, and he got shipped off. He said I had to get caught in the end, I was out there every day. He's doing eighteen months in Dover Prison now.

He came round my area once, and everyone raided the off licence — a load of champagne and that, I got nicked for it. Cos I went in with them, and they knew me in the off licence, and Raga was there, grabbing the champagne, but they thought all that was nicked was four cans of lager. I got a caution. There were loads of bottles of champagne, they were filling up a sports bag with it.

Sunny* said Raga came into his flat but didn't realise whose it was. Obviously Raga drew the line there cos he was a mate. Though people do thieve off other thieves. There's a couple of people in here who every time they go to the canteen they get robbed — cos they won't stick up for themselves.

There's a geezer where we are cleaners, there's four to a cell, and everyone just harassed him for his canteen *(money)* today.

* Another group member — see Chapter Six.

He's got nothing. £3.55 canteen, and he ain't got no tobacco, nothing. They robbed him of everything. I went round trying to get some of it back, I got him a couple of bits back. I couldn't get everything cos some people weren't letting off. They said 'he deserves it if he ain't going to fight back,' which is right really, if he ain't gonna stick up for himself. But I feel sorry for him, and he's my cell mate – I gotta put up with him. And when he ain't got no tobacco he's going to start asking me for some.

I suppose I got two sides to me. I got a good heart, and I'm also a thief. But if he was in a different cell, I wouldn't have done it. It's only cos I have to put up with his moaning. I haven't fought that much. I just stick up for myself. If someone comes up to me and wants a fight, I'll fight him, but I don't really go out looking for fights. Did you hear all the screws rushing down when I was coming in here *(to the interview room)*? They thought something was going off. It was a false call. The screws're alright. As long as you treat them with a bit of respect, they treat us with a bit.

I'm not into mugging, it's not my sort of thing. I've never even tried it. I might try it one day, and like it and do it again, but I'm not the sort of person who can front someone and rob them. I couldn't go up to someone and grab something. I'd probably feel sorry for them afterwards and go back and give it back. *(He said this convincingly enough, but at Sherborne House he admitted doing it once.)*

I never thought about the people I took from. I know what it's like cos I had my house burgled, and I've had one of my cars stolen – but it's part of life innit? If I didn't do it, some other cunt would!

When it happened to me I was sick, but I just went out and nicked more stuff to replace it. If I'd caught the person who did it to me, I'd have a row, but then again, everyone would.

If people leave cars unlocked, they deserve it. I've nicked cars and found spare keys in them. I've even found keys in the ignition and nicked motors at four in the morning.

Even if they deadlock cars like the new Astra, I can get round that. I don't nick Astras anyway, they're too dodgy. There's no such thing as a thief-proof car, not that I've come across. But if I see a motor and it's got a deadlock and alarm on it, I'll still nick it if I want it bad enough, if I know someone who wants bits off it, or if I do myself. Get a small crowbar behind the deadlock and just force it off, and with the alarm, get underneath the car and pull the earth wire off of the gear box and that stops everything working. Pop the bonnet, rip the alarm out, and connect the wire back up, scoffold *(sic)* the car or whatever, and just drive off.

Don't take long, it depends on the car, anything from thirty seconds to about two minutes. Five minutes at the most if it's got a crook lock. Often people forget to put their alarm on. You just rewire it and put it in your own car, and send off for a new key. What I'd do to protect my own car is lock it up in a garage. Garage alarm, car alarm, it's too much to bother with. I wouldn't bother with it.

Although he seems prepared to carry on offending, at least as a source of income, Stan's domestic life is taking shape at last. He has a steady girlfriend and is reconciled with his mother.

I went to live with my aunt for a year, which is where I was living when I was at Sherborne House. Then I patched things up with my Mum and I was living there, though most of the time I was round at my girlfriend's flat. My Dad and I, we keep in touch. I've got a couple of letters off of [my Dad] since I've been in here. When I was fifteen I went on holiday with him to Greece. I used to pop round there when I felt like it, just to keep in contact.

My father don't have no contact with my sister, I can't explain that one, I don't know why. My Dad has never spoke about it. But when he took me, he never took my sister. I was the son he wanted. He wasn't really interested in my sister. When I was at home, I used to get taken everywhere, and she used to be left at home with my Mum.

My sister travels round all the DIYs selling garden things. She's got a company car, she's doing well. She's seventeen. She's got a pager, doing alright for herself. I'm pleased for her. I'm not jealous, she's looking after me while I've been in here. She's sent me a radio in, sending me stamps, envelopes and all that. Me and my sister are really close.

My Mum was in the court. I've written to her, but I've got a feeling they're not sending my VOs *(visiting orders)* out. I sent her one first week I came in. I sent two letters out on the same day, and I got a reply on the other one. I've sorted it out though. I kicked up a fuss on the wing.

My girlfriend is well into her career – she works at a bank. I'm not ready for a kid or that sort of thing. I'd like to be stable with a nice job before I got involved. I want reasonable money, something that would see me, her and the child alright. About two hundred a week.

When I wasn't working, I'd spend my days sitting around with my mates, having a puff *(cannabis)*, listening to records, that's about it – working on the motor. I don't think I'd like to do it for money. It's just a hobby that I like to do at my own pace. *(A year before, at Sherborne House, Stan was clear he wanted to become a mechanic.)*

Most of the time before I was arrested, I was really getting stuff for my own motors. Like new seats, or if someone asked me for something, I'd go out and get it. I weren't really just going out just for the joy ride any more. I was only doing it if I knew there'd be money in it if I got the motor. No more high speed chases. But I had one when I got away from the old Bill in a Ford Sierra Cosworth. Now I just keep to speed limits, drive normal.

I been thieving for money. Had no work and I ain't been signing on cos I had two warrants out for my arrest, so the police would just be there when I signed on.

Even if I kept the job, I don't think it would have stopped me stealing. It's hard to tell really. The only time I've stopped was when I was at Sherborne House I suppose, that's about it. Felt alright. But it didn't give me a taste for a different kind of life. Didn't make me feel different when I wake up in the morning and walk down the street.

I'm thinking about going straight when I go out, I want to settle down with my girlfriend and that but I might do it occasionally. It depends how the situation is with work. If I need money desperately, I admit I will go out and nick a car, or get it some other way.

People only stop thieving if they want to. It's work, having enough money coming in, that will do that. Some are hooked on drugs and might want six hundred a week, which they ain't going to get, but we're not all like that. I suppose thieving is wrong, but a good eighty per cent of the population does it.

I don't think of myself as intelligent but I can read, I can write, the only thing I've ever been good at is maths. I was working at a greengrocer's at the time, and I had to use the maths in my head as there weren't no till or calculator. Most people can do that. It's not special.

I trust anybody till they turn on you. Parents, a couple of mates, girlfriend, family and that. That's about it. Only people who've let me down are a couple of mates – that's about it. I've never thought about it really.

The reason for me to stop is I'd be worried about getting caught. I don't really think of it when I am thieving, otherwise you're just on a para' all the time – just paranoid. As soon as the police look at you they can tell you're paranoid, so I just don't think about it.

Your book sounds good. Maybe people won't be so hard on us after. When I go on the tube, everyone clutches their bags. I go into a shop and everyone follows me around, right up my arse. *(This was a common complaint among most of the group, including those who shoplifted regularly.)*

There's only one person that can make me go straight and that's me. I'd like to settle down, live with my girlfriend, find a decent job. What's nice about it? Not a lot; *(laughs)* it's just you ain't got to look behind you all the time, see if the Old Bill are there. That's about it really.

Stan's experiences test the various means by which young offenders might be diverted from crime. Despite his broken home, Stan was intelligent and resourceful enough to hold down a straight job in the market and impress his employer. He did the same at the People's Dispensary. He is personable and disciplined enough to do more or less what he wants. It is tempting to conclude from Stan's own account that if his father had been firmer it would have made a difference to his behaviour. Yet his formidable mother was vigorous in her disapproval to no avail. Moreover, his father was himself a convicted offender, which may have spoken more vividly than his punishments and warnings.

Prison might have been a plausible deterrent, but to those who adapt to it as Stan has done, it is simply part of the process. They say on the streets and in prison, 'If you can't do the time, don't do the crime.' Much as he liked Sherborne House, within a year of leaving it, Stan had been reconvicted and sent to prison twice.

Stan was quite open about his criminal activities. Apart from the fun of joyriding, there was a practical basis to it: he was broke, could not get enough to live on from the DSS, and knew how to get it himself through stealing cars and selling the parts. Jack, the

Senior Probation Officer at Sherborne House, said to me early on, 'Crime makes a lot of sense for these young people.'

This raises an important question: how quickly can we expect the programme to effect change when the circumstances that prompted the offending have not changed?

For Stan, the teenage joyrider, his slow movements towards going straight represent the onset of maturity. This squares with the notion that young offenders simply grow out of crime. Perhaps none of the interventions we make hasten that process. Sherborne House in that sense is like prison – it keeps them out of trouble while they are in the building. This is a minimalist doctrine – but one used by judges and magistrates all the time to justify the use of custody. As one distinguished criminologist Professor Leslie Wilkins put it, 'Maybe what we need to do about young offenders is a four letter word – less.'

But to keep out of trouble, they will still need a job, and for that they need training. Perhaps Stan's desire to return to Sherborne House is based on his sense that now he is ready to take full advantage of it.

CHAPTER THREE

MARK

Is it worth it if I get caught?

Mark is a multi-layered personality, although this only emerged slowly over the ten weeks at Sherborne House. He was at first sight perhaps the most amiable of the group. Large framed, solid, clear-eyed, half-caste, he looked Greek or Lebanese but his close haircut with stripes shaved into his temples showed he considered himself black.

At Sherborne House, Mark was easily liked. He fitted into all the activities, co-operated with all the exercises, played all the games no matter how silly the others thought them to be. At first he appeared to be involved in only one offence, and presented himself as a good citizen who had been prosecuted for a quite reasonable act of family loyalty – protecting his brother by wounding a neighbour who was endangering his brother's life.

His family plays a vital role for Mark. His parents split up, and he and his brothers were raised by their mother who died two years ago. Two of his brothers have straight jobs, but his older brother Peter was always in trouble, and it was through him that Mark wound up in court. I met his father, a small middle-aged black man who had just returned from living in Florida and clearly felt himself a guest in his ex-wife's home – or at any rate, lacking in authority there.

The house sits in a North London enclave of solid pastel-coloured stucco fifties houses that offer more security than the long strip of overgrown wasteland they face. The part of urban landscape that is Mark's home ground contains a wide cross-section of ethnic groups, including a strong community of Hasidic Jews, whose uniform of black hats, beards and coats stands out from the jeans, smart baseball jackets and trainers worn by Mark and most of the other young men on the streets nearby.

The house itself was kept clean but sparsely furnished. Mark's own room was distinguished by the presence of two large matt black corner units of shelving, on which sit two gold and black pharaoh's head lamps – both of which he made at Sherborne House. I visited him at home, a year after he finished at Sherborne House. Unlike many of the others who went there, Mark's distinct view of himself was that he was not a criminal. Yet he wanted to be seen as tough and worldly. How he defined and judged his actions was born out of the scene in which he moved.

A lot of people are carrying knives, but I never have done. When we go out, there's so many of us, nothing happens. You don't need a knife. You just feel safe. A couple of my lot carry something. They are hard criminals. But some of us are working. We've known each other for years. Some turned to crime, some got jobs.

At one stage all my mates were going through a crime phase. Most of the ones who stayed with crime were from broken families. The government want to punish parents for crimes committed by their kids but I don't think that's right at all. I know a guy who's adopted, they've got their own kids who are fine. And this guy doesn't need to steal. He goes out and does robberies, everything. It's not for the money, just, it's the thrill and being part of a crowd.

Crime can never finish because no matter how much money some people have got they will always want a bit more. Top executives are committing crime all the while, fiddling books all that sort of stuff, bent police, screws in jail bringing in rum, crime is everywhere.

White people with money seem to get off things a lot easier. I wouldn't say all police are racist, I would say a large percentage of them are. I've had so much abuse from them, they want you to retaliate so they can kick shit out of you. I've got so much hatred for the police, the way they go about their business.

One time me and my mates were coming back through Dalston at about one in the morning and a police van was driving past and one of the policemen wound down the window and said 'you wankers.' So we shouted it back. The next thing we knew they'd come round the corner again with another car and they nicked us for aggressive behaviour or something like that.

I did okay at school, did alright in my exams. I enjoyed school, I had a lot of friends, and I got on well with most of the teachers.

I left at seventeen. I wanted to do a carpentry apprenticeship; I got an interview with Camden Council and when I went down there they said, 'Sorry, all the carpentry jobs have gone, but we can give you a painting and decorating job.' I thought, 'Nah, not painting and decorating.' I wasn't really interested in that then, and it was thought of as a low job with bad money. So I didn't bother.

I've got two brothers who live here, and one in prison, and two younger half-brothers. Martin is in Florida on holiday, a caretaker with his own phone business, Luke is doing computer studies. My Dad divorced from my Mum when I was seven and I lived here with her. Two years ago she died and then Dad moved in here. He's staying here for the moment.

With him here again, we're trying to be a bit more tidy. Before we'd always have our friends around, for a drink or a smoke, but now it's different.

There was nothing she wouldn't do for us. She used to work really hard, she had two jobs. She brought us up as best she could. It was hard, there were four of us. When my Dad was here it was quite strict, but we used to muck around and rebel against our parents and try to enjoy ourselves as much as we could. My Mum was soft on us, she wouldn't hit us or nothing. With Dad not there, things were different as we knew the consequences were not so serious. But as we grew up we started to slow down a bit and everyone started to try their best, except Peter.

Peter's my half-brother – he don't live with us. He's always been in and out of prison, normally for fighting. He's a bit violent. If Mum and Dad had stayed together there probably wouldn't have been so much getting into trouble, and Peter might not have been in and out of prison all the time.

Peter had a different Dad to us, and sometimes he'd say we were getting better treatment than him from our parents. It did seem as though if there was any trouble between us it would be me and my brothers against Peter. He got in with a bad crowd really, he used to drink heavily. Him and his mates would go to football and have a good fight, that sort of thing. He's always been like that. He's twenty-eight now. He was about twenty-three when he was doing all that stuff.

When Mum and Dad split up it seemed like it was everyone for themselves, everyone was going out and doing their own thing.

Peter was a lot older than us, and there was no way we could stop him.

I got into trouble with him when I was coming home early one morning from a party and I saw Peter in a car with a few people. He said they were going to a club. But first we went back to Peter's flat and had a few drinks and a smoke. Then as we were leaving, it was dark on the landing, so my brother couldn't see the keyhole to lock his door from the outside. He knocked on the next door to get a torch or a candle. Its dog started to run out. I thought it must be another friend of his because it was about four in the morning. The guy opened the door and he and my brother started arguing. The guy said he didn't know Peter and shut the door and came back with a carving knife cos he had a baby and thought we was going to attack his family. He took a swing at my brother who had quite a few to drink. Peter went really mad and the guy slammed the door. My brother's mate kicked it open and the guy came running out again with a knife in one hand and a cleaver in the other. My brother wrestled with the guy to keep him away, but as Peter went inside the doorway he fell, cos he'd been drinking heavily, and the guy started swinging and threatening him with a knife.

So then the next bloke from upstairs came down with a machete and said, 'What's going on?' He thought someone was breaking in. He knew my brother, so I said 'Peter's inside, help me get him out.' So the guy gave me the knife and helped me push open the door. I said to the neighbour holding Peter, 'Let him go, he's drunk,' and the guy swung at me and cut my arm. So I swung back at him, more in shock than in trying to attack him, and the guy ran into his bathroom and we managed to get my brother out.

It was then we got nicked. We was a bit shocked by the blood but just left him *(the neighbour)*. Got downstairs and start jogging across the road and a police car pulled up alongside us. We hadn't done it so we had nothing to hide. They shouted 'stop' and just started questioning us. They didn't know nothing about what had happened, so we could have just gone.

But one of them started being cheeky and said, 'where you black bastards going?' and things like that. A WPC spat in my face, cos I was swearing at her, cos she was calling us 'black bastards' and stuff. So I spat in her face and slapped her. So it turned into a little row with them, and they nicked us for assaulting a police officer. It was only later they found out about the other thing.

I knew that I'd cut the guy – on the neck, in the chest, on the legs – but he'd cut me first. It was in self-defence because he had my brother in a doorway. Then they referred it to the Old Bailey and that's when it clicked with me what I'd done, cos the only time I'd seen the Old Bailey was on the news for murderers and stuff.

We were going for Self-Defence in court. But the next-door neighbour was saying we'd come there to burgle him. If you go into someone's house and you hit them, even if you don't take nothing it's classed as Aggravated Burglary.

Our barrister said he was going to make a deal with them, that if we go Guilty on the assault, I would probably get about eighteen months and Peter will get two years because of his previous.

All this was dragging on while we were inside. I'd already done six months on remand, so I thought, 'yeh eighteen months, I'll probably have to only do a year and I done half of that.' It wasn't too hard in there, so I said, 'Yeh, we'll go Guilty on the Assault.' He said if we went Not Guilty and they'd found us Guilty for Aggravated Burglary we'd might well both end up with six years each. So we went Guilty on the assault, but they did us for Attempted Aggravated Burglary too. The Judge said he would give us extra cos we didn't plead Guilty from the start. 'Aggravated Burglary's a sickening crime and it's on the increase.' And he gave Peter five years. I didn't hear what the Judge said to me.

I was really worried. They put me back for *(Social Inquiry)* reports cos I never had no previous *(convictions)*. I was in Rochester Prison one day and the screws came in and said I had bail. I was out for about three months and I came back to court. I was two hours late cos if you think you're going inside you have a little smoking, drinking session the night before. I'd been to see Sherborne House and they accepted me but they said they couldn't see me getting anything but prison. Instead I got two years' probation and Sherborne House. It was the happiest day of my life.

I still really can't believe it. My brother is still inside. The geezer attacked us with a knife, he cut me first, he admitted that. I don't think it's fair really.

At Sherborne House, Mark described these events in the daily group which discussed their offending behaviour, and what could be done to change it. *He showed the same sense of outrage at the unfairness of being punished for defending his brother. Mark claimed to have tried to calm things down, which won the group's sympathy. They were already impressed by the extent of the violence, and his having been at the Old Bailey.*

In an effort to make Mark see how he could have avoided offending, the group probation officers explored the situation further, looking at it step by step. They pointed out that the whole event took place in the dark at four in the morning, when a neighbour with a small child opened the door to three large figures at least one of whom was angry and drunk. Mark was unmoved by this explanation.

At our age it's nothing at all to be up at that hour, or call on someone at 4am, specially when you're drunk. Anyway, he was twenty-two. He must've been up.

Mark's view of family loyalty transcended any mitigating details, including his brother's record: 'Violence, fraud, stabbing someone, things like that.' It was also pointed out that Mark had risked a very long prison sentence. But he would not accept the suggestion that he had a choice.

Walk away from my brother in danger? Never. I wouldn't sink so low. And I couldn't have stopped him. He's my big brother, he would never listen to me. Anyway, the other geezer was mad and swinging a knife and a cleaver. I maybe saved my brother's life. I'd go to prison to save my brother's life. If I walked away and he got killed, that'd be a life sentence too.

The next day Mark returned to the group a bit more sombre, having clearly thought about it a bit further.

I'm not saying it's all the other geezer's fault. We were all a bit drunk, and I probably steamed into him a bit too hard. I got a bad temper.

This was an important concession. Mark was one of several group members who had attacked people in defence of their family, as Stan had done on behalf of his sister. Despite the severity of their violence, it seemed to them clearly justified. This blurred the efforts to make them reconsider their other criminal acts.

In the first five weeks, Mark was one of the leaders of his group. On the outings he went rock climbing and abseiling, dry slope and water-skiing and riding, and met all the challenges with physical courage and a minimum of bravado and complaint. In the craft

*sessions and workshop, his work on the pharaoh's head lamps
and shelf units also progressed well. He managed to be popular
with both the staff and the other young men, black and white.*

*Discussing the merits and demerits of crime, Mark showed his
diplomacy:*

You make more money in one night than in a week, but when
you work for it, you're careful how you spend it.

*But, as the course at Sherborne House progressed, Mark's virtue
began to slip. The influence on him of the more cynical group
members grew stronger. (This, of course, is a danger in such
groups, but it is almost inevitable in prison, unmediated by positive
external influences.) It showed in the way he presented himself as
a burglar.*

I only did it once on my own. I needed the money and I hate
the police. I saw the chance and I took it. I lost my head, but it
seemed right at the time, and I couldn't back out. If I saw an open
window and a TV inside, I'd still grab it.

*This account suggested he had acted impulsively, on a rare
occasion. Yet when the group was asked if they'd stopped offending, he put himself on the sheet as quite active: forty per cent of
his original rate of offending was still going on – an odd admission
from someone who had previously implied he did little in the way
of crime, and had no previous convictions. When his group
leaders, Lenore and Deb confronted him about this discrepancy,
Mark somewhat defiantly produced a different story:*

It's not on my record but I've been burgling with my mates
every two weeks since I could walk. Not since I could walk, since
I left school at sixteen, seventeen. Never got caught cos I was
lucky. My mates got caught cos they had a criminal record – I
didn't. I was never fingerprinted. I just happen to do it if I happen
to be with them. Same with street robberies. But if I have money
in my pocket I wouldn't.

But I don't see myself as a burglar or a robber. I wouldn't sink
that low. I do giros, family allowance books, things like that. You
get someone else to fill out your giro and cash it, then you go and
say it's lost. If you haven't signed it, the loss isn't down to you. I
got a friend who gets a personal issue dole cheque delivered to his
door and he does it every week. *(Personal issue cheques involve
turning up in person with the cheque to collect the money.)* The
worst they do is ask for your ID. They don't come out and grab

you. Or you can change the numbers on a cheque. It's a risk, but then every criminal activity's a risk.

After the session, both Lenore and Deb agreed they simply did not believe him. They suspected this account was Mark showing off rather than coming clean, and that he was not a habitual criminal like the others. But their view of him altered as the group work continued. In the exercises involving moral dilemmas Mark revealed himself as quite ruthless and unprincipled. When talking about what he would do in a pub if drunks at the next table insulted him or his girlfriend, Mark was clear:

Mark: Don't wait. Move quickly. Just hit them! Take
    them by surprise. Don't give them the chance.
Lenore: *(appalled)* Would your girl expect that?
Mark: Yes.
Lenore: But it would ruin your evening!
Mark: It was the people who'd started it that ruined the
    evening.

The rest of the group agreed with Mark that such violence was both inevitable and proper. Asked whether he would lie in court under oath to help a friend, Mark was equally certain it was acceptable behaviour:

Everyone does it. I gave a false alibi in court for a mate and he got away. It was worse than affray – someone burnt someone's house down. But the geezer deserved it.

Mark smiled while reporting this, sitting comfortably in his chair, legs crossed. It was not at all clear whether he was pleased because it raised his standing in the group, or because he was simply unconcerned with the morality of his actions. When thieving too, it was the need for money that justified it. Another exercise listed people in your life – parents, brothers and sisters, friends, acquaintances, and teachers – and asked if there were circumstances in which you would steal from them. Mark told the group he would steal from acquaintances, such as a teacher who had given him a lift home:

Mark: I have stolen from a teacher – the tea and coffee
    money, and even something simple like a video
    tape. Can't say I saw them as losing out, really. I
    wouldn't steal from every teacher. Just ninety-five

per cent *(smiles)*. The other five per cent I wouldn't
steal from if I liked them.

Lenore: What if one had given you a lift to her home?

Mark: I'd steal from a teacher even if she gave me a lift,
and I was in her house and saw a £20 note and I
knew she wouldn't know it was me. I know they did
me a favour but I was just taking advantage – just
being friendly. I'd pretend to like someone, then take
advantage. But if I genuinely liked someone, I'm not
sure. I'd probably do it if I was desperate. I do feel
guilty when I steal but I do it. Loads of people do. I'd
do it if I was desperate and there was no brother
about to help me out.

*This was a turning point for the two group leaders. They seemed
genuinely shocked at Mark's attitude towards people who'd been
kind to him. They were especially troubled by his admission that
he pretended to like people just to take advantage of them. But
Mark was now well into describing people from whom he'd stolen
in the past – but no one knew about it because he'd never been
caught.*

I started nicking things when I was about ten. This older kid
came in with about £100 that he'd nicked, and five of us nicked
it and shared it out. We had around £20 each, and at that age, it's
a lot of money. Police came round to my house and my Dad had
to pay it back.

I nicked things from the DSS. They're just a bunch of crooks. If
I was desperate, I'd even steal from the girl who gave me my giro
if I was certain of not getting caught, if she wouldn't recognise me
– I'd do it if my bros *(brothers)* or my parents weren't about.

I wouldn't steal from friends or relations. I wouldn't sink that
low. My parents brought me up, they changed my nappy. They
give me money if I need it. I suppose I can't say I never would
steal from friends, but not as I am now. They help me. I always
pay them back, even if I have to steal the money. I suppose it's
not very moralistic. I never thought about it before. But it wouldn't
change me. It might slow me down. It would hurt me not to do it
– if I owed someone £10 and had no money to repay it. I could
choose not to steal it but I'd feel bad not paying my debt.

*In another group on moral dilemmas, Mark was asked what he
would do if a friend stole £20 from him.*

Mark: I wouldn't mention it. It would only upset him.
But I also wouldn't trust him.
Lenore: Do you think it's right that friends should steal
from each other?
Mark: No. But you can't always tell if they're real friends.
Lots of people hang around together, and pretend to
like each other just to take advantage. I don't trust
my friends anyway.

*Talking in the staff room afterwards, Lenore and Deb were dis-
mayed by the deviousness and fragility of Mark's relationships. It
seemed completely at odds with the way he had presented himself
in the groups from the beginning. This is a familiar predicament:
how much do probation officers hear that is true, and how much
is simply what their clients say to amuse themselves and their
mates, or just want their particular audience to believe?*

*Near the end of the ten weeks, Mark disappeared for a while.
When he came back he was harder, less agreeable, often cynical.
He complained often of being bored, and that the staff had
changed and were much less pleasant. Many of the group agreed
with Mark. It was observably true. Both Lenore and Deb seemed
disappointed and angry with the way he'd apparently taken the
whole group for a ride, including them.*

Lenore: I think you've been misrepresenting yourself in
this group. You want everyone to think you're a
nice guy who was forced into doing what you had
to do through family loyalty. But I think you're far
more devious and unscrupulous than you wanted
others to think. You've already said you'd steal
from your teachers, even if they gave you a lift, or
brought you to their home. You pretend to like people
to take advantage of them. And you don't trust your
friends.
Mark: I'm just like everybody else. Everyone hides things
in here. Nobody tells you what's really going on
with them.
Lenore: I don't accept that. You just can't imagine that
other people behave with more integrity, and loyalty
to their friends.
Mark: You just don't know what's really going on. I'd

never ever betray my family. And I've got friends.
I'm just realistic about them.

*Lenore and Deb attributed Mark's absence and the change in
him to his having been swept along by the others into unfamiliar
criminal activities until he was out of his depth. He hadn't gone
on the sailing trip after originally planning to do so because, they
believed, there were no other blacks going. This was further proof
of his insecurity. They felt that Mark's 'boredom' meant his facade
had fallen, and that he was being made uncomfortable by the
exposure of his true self. This was a theme they developed over a
number of sessions towards the end of the course which did change
the atmosphere in the group.*

*Discussing Mark in the staff meeting to prepare his final assess-
ment, Lenore and Deb also worried that he'd deceived his probation officer into feeling sorry for him. They felt she didn't really
know him, and that Mark realised it and took advantage of that.
Because his record was so short, it would seem she only knew
about his one serious offence, and did not see how much work
needed to be done with him. They were frustrated by the way he'd
played them along. Lenore said mournfully: 'He looks you in the
eyes like he knows he's lying.'*

*They saw Mark as having many good qualities – he was bright,
well-mannered, fitted in well with the others, and could work well
and hard when he wanted to. But 'his weaknesses make him prey
to the bad.' They saw this as a deep and enduring character problem. And what he called his 'bad temper' they believed were serious
mood swings. They put all this to Mark at the final assessment. It
was an intense and difficult encounter, but he refused to open up,
or move from his original position:*

I was nice until you stopped being nice. I treat people the way
they treat me. That's life. I don't think there's anything wrong
with me myself. It works for me. *(He smiled.)*

*One year later, when I spoke to Mark at his home, he claimed not
to be impressed by Sherborne House, or the people who worked
there, despite his many and varied experiences.*

I had no feelings for any of the people in charge at Sherborne
House, and I'd have stolen from them. I reckon everyone who was
at Sherborne House would have stolen from the probation officers.

Talking in the groups in front of them was different. Everyone was different in front of them. But outside at dinner time when everyone was having a smoke we were talking the truth, what they would do. Inside there it was hard because people thought the POs *(probation officers)* were prying into what they were doing and that then they'd write a report and tell the police what we'd got up to.

I don't think they could create a situation in which people told the truth. Even if you had ex-cons doing it *(leading the groups)*, people would still think 'they're working for the probation service, and that's connected with the police, who've put them there to deal with you.' I knew nothing could really come out of it, that it was just talking, and I told the truth. But a lot of people didn't think like that. They thought everything they'd said was being written down, that police would follow them.

I was surprised at some of the things people got up to – burglaries every night. You're bound to get caught. Stu was big time. He was making a lot of money. We were meeting at Sherborne House at eight o'clock at night to do business with the *(counterfeit)* £20 notes. What it did, the same as prison, was get you contacts with criminals. You're learning things all the time.

Lunchtime, we used to buy lager, have a puff, nothing serious. Most people were getting the duff £20 notes to get them changed for real money. I was buying them and making the shopkeepers get change. Everyone made a few hundred pounds at Sherborne House. Stu made a few thousand, selling them for £6 each. Dane was coming to the place in stolen cars every day. Everyone I've spoken to has said it was too easy.

Getting people to talk about what they've been up to is not going to change them. They speak about it every night anyway. It seems all they were doing was putting questions to us and waiting for answers, not trying to really change us. If people have been going out doing burglaries and stuff since they were twelve you can't change them. I mean, people were getting nicked while they were at Sherborne House.

I think they were trying to play a game to make everyone come out and talk about these things to try to get them to mend their ways. But it was easy to talk about it just like it was an everyday thing. It was a lot easier than being banged up in a cell for twenty-three hours. Sherborne House didn't really change my view on anything. It seemed more like a laugh, a get together, meet new friends. As long as you could stick it out you were safe. It was too

easy compared to prison, locked in a cell. When you're in prison
you can't lie to yourself.

The only thing is prison. I wouldn't wish it on no one. But if you're
in a single cell it makes you think. Feltham Young Offenders' Institution is okay, because you're let out of your cell. In Feltham there
are so many bent screws it was easy. We were getting so much smoke
in there, and bottles of rum. My *(younger)* brother would give me
£20 on a visit, and the next day I'd give it to this bent screw and he'd
bring in an orange bottle filled up with rum.

Feltham's really clean. And most of the time if you have a prison
job, you're out of your cell. A lot of the time we were just watching
TV. But Brixton shook me up. Brixton is bad, you're not even
human no more. It was so dirty. So many people on one wing,
banged up twenty-three hours a day. You're let out to eat and
walk around the yard and that's it. One little window in each cell,
bed sheets all ripped up, you got to slop out with a bucket. It's
really degrading – if you're in a cell with someone you have to go
to the toilet in front of them. You're treated like an animal. It was
a shock to me, especially the first day. But then you see people
you know so it gets easier. But it makes you think about your life
and what you've been through.

At Sherborne House, when you're there you know in a few
hours' time you're going to be free to go out and do what you
want to do. But in prison you're just lying on a bed, thinking. It
has made me think: the police can fit you up with what they want
to – and it's probably stopped me doing about fifty per cent of the
things I would have done. *(On the other hand, if he was telling
the truth, by his own account at Sherborne House, he had stopped
doing sixty per cent of his normal offending while he was there.)*

I wouldn't have done nothing serious, but it stopped me going
out fighting with mates, acting like louts or taking car radios, that
sort of thing. I've never been into burglaries cos I wouldn't want
to get burgled myself. I wouldn't want to see my house turned
upside down and all my personal things gone. Somebody's house
is their life. *Despite his earlier claim to have told the truth in the
groups, this squares with the group leaders' private impression
that Mark was not a habitual burglar, whatever else he was up to.*

On the other hand, I didn't really want to leave Feltham, I was
having such a laugh. You're living for free. Some people can't
handle too much pressure. But when I look back I think it's not

worth it. I thought 'if I'm going to get nicked again it must be for something that has made me some money. It is not worth going out on the street and getting nicked for a car stereo you're going to sell for £15. It would have to be a lot of money. Over £500.'

I wouldn't do nothing now while I'm still on probation. It ain't worth it. Once that's finished I won't be charged with what happened with my brother, so I won't be so worried about going out to do something *(criminal)* – though it doesn't mean I will.

Mark casually explained his philosophy on crime and violence which placed his actions to save his brother in a different light.

They charged us both with Attempted Burglary, but who would burgle their next-door neighbour with people he knows? I wouldn't go out and do something that stupid.

Like I can't understand people who go joy riding. They're not making a profit. If you kill someone you can go to prison for manslaughter. But if you can make a lot of money you have to weigh it up and think, 'Is it worth it if I get caught?'

It don't need to be £500, it could be a tenner. It depends what the thing is. If someone says 'Go and beat someone up for a £20,' I'll think 'Yeh, £20 for five minutes' work, not bad.' But if someone says 'Go and steal me that car and I'll give you £100,' it ain't worth it if you get caught. If you beat someone up for £20 and you get caught, you could say, 'We had a fight'. You got a case. But you can't say 'Someone told me to steal a car.'

I did once *(beat someone up)* for £100. My mate's Dad was owed money, about £2000 by someone. So he said 'Go and get the money, if you can't, beat him up.' He didn't have it, and we didn't want to come back, so we just gave him a little bit of a good hiding. There was nothing he could do. He'd never seen us before in his life. It was a good deal. If someone had said 'I don't like this guy. Go and beat him up,' that would be different. But he owed him money.

The funny thing is, about three months ago some guy come round to me and my mate. He said him and some other mates were going round to get a guy who'd been messing around with his bird, and they needed help. He'd said he'd give us some money. But when the guy came back; him, his mate, and a girl in a car, at the last minute we changed our minds. It just looked funny; I thought, 'What's a girl doing in the back of the car if we're going to beat someone up?' I had an uneasy feeling about it. Two weeks later the guy was in the paper for kidnapping a couple. He beat them up bad and tortured them. And he came for us to help him. He was a good footballer, and a lot of big clubs were coming in for him, and now he's messed it all up.

I'm getting £62 a fortnight to live on. That ain't money. So I'm desperate a lot of the time. I go shoplifting, but not from people I know. I don't say it's always right – it depends on how they come across to me – but everyone would steal if they thought no one would know. That's life. You get a run of bad luck and you keep on stealing till you get caught.

But Sherborne House didn't really keep me out of trouble cos I never really got into trouble in the first place (*meaning he was never caught for most of the offences he committed*). I try to make my money as legally as possible. I'll only steal if I'm desperate. When I say legally, I mean without me having to go out and do it. If someone comes to me with something stolen I'll buy it and sell it on at a higher price.

It's when the weekend comes and you haven't got any money and your mates who work are going out that you turn to crime. It's so hard living off £62 for two weeks.

During the week, I'll be trying to get money. I know some shoplifters, they come to me with stuff, clothes and that. I buy them and sell them on for a profit. I sell suits, bikes things like that, mostly to shops round here. People will buy anything, for themselves, not for the shop. I don't go into pubs cos you never know if there's a policeman in there – though half the time it will be a policeman buying the stuff! It's more fun buying very cheap, forcing the price down, and then selling more expensive. (*smiling*) I'm a good liar. I do it for greed. I feel proud I can do it. I do some shoplifting myself from time to time – but I never do it to a Jew. Round Stamford Hill they all stick together and they'd come down on you really heavy.

The more the better. No one's got enough except for billionaires. I don't just spend it. I use it to make more. Buy more and sell it on for my cut. No one gets hurt, but it ain't legal. I'm a pretty safe person. I don't do cars, or drum (*burgle*) people's houses. If I bring you a ring and say it's gold and you believe me, it's down to you. (*smiling*) I like to work alone. More money's involved.

At weekends I rave till I drop. I move around with a group of about twenty people. There's always something to do. We don't cause trouble. Sometimes I'll bring my girlfriend, but not when there's so many of them around! We go to my friend's house, we'll have a few drinks, have a smoke. About one or two we'll head to a party, then maybe head on to another one. Get home around 10am.

A good party's got good music, plenty of girls, plenty to drink. Sometimes they're in houses, but usually halls. Just have a good laugh, see who can pull the nicest bird. At 10am, you feel horrible. Sometimes you've smoked so much you forget about things. I'm not into Es (*Ecstasy*). Most of my friends are. I don't cos you wouldn't put stones in the petrol tank of a car – it'll damage it. A lot of people don't know anything about what they're taking. It's more of a trend than anything else. I used to deal hash, but it's too much hassle, people coming round all hours of the day. If you get nicked, caught with bags, you're classed as a dealer. But I know someone who's never had a job in his life, and he's earning so much money from it.

I ain't as bad as I used to be. I've just turned twenty. I feel older. I was glad to be finished with being a teenager. People look at you in a different light if they know you're twenty rather than nineteen. It feels like I should be taking on more responsibilities, finding work, things like that.

I've been with my girl for about three months. It's helped to quiet me down. I get bored of a girl easy, I don't know why that is. Three months is a long time for me. Course I don't use a condom. It's down to her what happens.

I want to learn a trade – plumbing. So I won't have to go out 'earning'. (*In other words, he sees his buying and selling as only involving hot goods, not a business he could engage in legitimately. The plumbing trade is seen as work, the other is 'earning'.*) I've done some private work, painting and decorating, and that always went well, but the work has dried up lately. I've always wanted to do a course, an apprenticeship, but I never got round to doing it. There's always something that puts me off. I thought they wouldn't want anyone who'd been inside. Like now I think, 'oh no, turning twenty, they won't want me.'

If I had a job, I wouldn't get up to no crime. I'm not saying I wouldn't get into fights or have a smoke now and again, but nothing else. At twenty it's not good not to be working, and it's a real disappointment.

*

Mark is a kaleidoscopic character, whose moral centre is hard to find. The only consistent theme was family loyalty throughout the changes in the way he presented himself – honest man among thieves, street-smart but with integrity, a dealer but not a burglar, violent only for a good family cause, but for sale as a heavy if the price was right.

He was equally inconsistent in his performance and judgements at Sherborne House and in prison. He spoke seriously of prison as being a direct deterrent for fifty per cent of his offending, while the probation programme was just an enjoyable talking shop, an excuse to meet other criminals. Yet he found being in prison was actually fun at Feltham – where so many youths have committed suicide. For all his lonely reflections, and fear of harder prisons like Brixton, the almost certain prospect of going back inside if he were caught still left him offending half the time. (At Sherborne House, he suggested his offending had dropped to forty per cent.) He now avoid fights but that means he's raised his price for beating someone up on demand.

Like everything else he has said, it would be unwise to take his disparaging comments about Sherborne House at face value. Assuming that at least some of his accounts of his criminal activity before Sherborne House were accurate, and bearing in mind the milieu in which he lives and operates, Mark could yet be an interesting example of what Sherborne House staff regard as a delayed reaction. This emerges in the gradual reduction of the seriousness and frequency of crimes, and an equally gradual assimilation of more positive choices and values. Moreover, research on the Hereford and Worcester probation programme suggests young adult offenders who've been to prison before doing the course are the least likely to reoffend afterwards.

Although Mark's violent streak seems almost pathological rather than just a 'bad temper', he wants other people to like and approve of him. This vulnerability is coupled with shrewdness and ingenuity, all qualities that could be put to positive use. His is like many black families in which the parents have split but the children hold onto some kind of family spirit. Most of his brothers are straight and have regular jobs, about which Mark is proud. It may take years, but Mark seems to me impressionable enough to become a law-abiding citizen like them if he can find a job that also brings with it friends who support this direction.

CHAPTER FOUR

JOEL

Stuck in a little world and it's hard to get out

Joel is short, red-headed and wiry. He slopes around with an amiable detachment not unconnected with the fact that he's been smoking marijuana every day since the age of eleven. Despite the damage he has done to his body and brain from the consumption of a variety of illegal substances, Joel is bright and witty. His freckled face wears a permanent smile that becomes a smirk when deployed as part of his street persona. He is a likeable young man, whose unrealised potential is painfully obvious – even, on occasion, to him.

At Sherborne House, to which he was sent for drugs offences, Joel was often, literally, very laid back. Despite his appearance of being near or in sleep, he was a keen observer, rising from the horizontal occasionally to inject a sharp remark into the conversation.

Joel also had moments of surprising energy. In view of his oft-expressed loathing for sport, he took to water-skiing and riding with humour and unexpected aptitude. In the drama workshop run by a young pair of actors, Joel entered into the games with gusto and imagination, and without the preoccupation of keeping his dignity which hindered most of the others. But he was a natural maverick, whose erratic performance at Sherborne House gave an idea of what he must have been like at school. On the journey to the Family Planning Clinic, the group travelled by tube. Joel was girl-watching when they changed trains, and never caught up with the rest of them. On another outing – a long walk by the beach – Joel led a breakaway contingent that was discovered by the probation officers playing snooker in the pub, next to where the van was to collect them. It was presumed, though never admitted, that they had hitched a lift.

Joel lurched in character between a cynical streetwise Jack-the-Lad and a witty, thoughtful, rather sensitive person who glimpsed how differently he could live his life. He reflected on that when I visited him a year after Sherborne House, in his mother's roomy and comfortable council flat. She lived there with her two daughters, and, depending on the state of their relationship, occasionally with Joel. His father had left long ago, though he was still much missed by Joel, while his elderly step-father, a tall, conservative Trinidadian, had recently died. In the preceding years, his step-father's old-fashioned, strict ideas about how children should behave drove first Joel and then each of his younger sisters to leave home. After their step-father's death, one by one the children returned to the flat. It has a splendid view of the trees on their estate in Kentish Town, the mixed urban area in North London that was Joel's home ground.

I reckon there's three categories: drug takers, drinkers and straight people. But eighty per cent of the kids I know of around this area all take drugs. The other fifteen per cent just drink and say drugs are bad, though they have tried them, and the other five per cent don't do anything. That's just the way it goes. I've been used to taking drugs all my life so I don't know any other way. I'm not really qualified to say if I'd like to be one of the five per cent or not. There is a part of me that thinks that I would, but I just couldn't live one of those lives, cos I'm not straight basically.

I suppose I think of myself as a criminal. In the eyes of everyone else I'm a criminal. I don't think about it. It's alright, know what I mean, it's just usual innit, normal? I steal for money, for clothes, for booze, for drugs – for life!

I was born in Ladbroke Grove and moved to Kentish Town when I was about a year *(sic)*. We were squatting and then got a council house which turned into a squat cos we let everyone come and live in it. There was about five different families – a big hippy house and then my Mum got pissed off so we moved into a council flat. But my Dad was just lazy really, never really worked; he was an alcoholic and a smackhead – totally fucked up on drugs.

He's still like an ageing hippy. Man, I love him, know what I mean? He's an alcoholic though, he'll never change. My Mum was the most responsible for me. They were both on the dole, but she would go out to work, a cleaning job, nothing special, but it brought more money into the house. But now that we're growing up she's training to be a librarian. Two more years and then she'll be qualified. She dropped out in the sixties and came to live in London.

We used to go to Stonehenge Free Festival every year. I've been about eight times, Glastonbury, Deeply Vale up in Yorkshire, a big hippy gathering. I was brought up listening to Jimi Hendrix, Pink Floyd, Hippy Music; and I was brought up around puff, so it's second nature. I started puffing regularly when I was eleven, had my first when I was ten.

They were the ones that turned me on, my Dad did. My Dad puffs and he's an ex-addict. But he don't thieve or anything. I was brought up around hippies and puffing. I know quite a few kids that were brought up like that. Even if their parents are dead straight they let them puff, cos they know it isn't that bad. They know that drink would probably fuck them up a lot more than having a puff now and then.

I learnt to roll *(tobacco)* when I was about thirteen. I used to smoke it pure in a pipe. Then I progressed on to a joint and that made me start smoking cigarettes. There haven't been many days when I haven't been under the influence of something in the past seven or eight years. The longest gap was when I was in prison for two weeks *(on remand)*. I'm nineteen, nearly twenty. I wish I was younger.

Everyone's got a criminal record round here, so it doesn't really matter. If you haven't got one, it's more strange. All the people in my age group round the area, they're all into crime: car thefts, things from cars, thieving to buy drugs and clothes. It's just the way I was brought up.

When I first started, hardly anyone puffed and then a lot of the kids were into gas and tippex thinner. No glue, cos the government warnings put me off. That progressed to going into a shed for a puff at lunch, where everyone used to just sit and skin up. You could see the teachers walking towards you so you could put your joint out. They'd see Rizlas *(roll-up cigarette papers)* on the floor but couldn't do anything about it. I think our year was the last nutty year in that school. In the last year me and my mates were dealing and supplying younger kids.

We used to go out shoplifting from the age of eleven, but the first time I nicked a car stereo I was probably about fifteen, and that's quite late now, cos a lot of kids start at fourteen or thirteen.

Sold the gear, and just had a laugh with the money. Bought some puff, speed or drink, that's what we were into at that age.

At Sherborne House, in the session on drugs Joel became dynamic, was far more well-informed than the probation officers. In an almost comic encounter, their attempts to point out the disadvantages of the drugs were constantly interrupted by Joel's first hand accounts of their merits. In what ended up as a lecture by him to the rest of us, Joel showed that he had the capacity both to make articulate and intelligent judgements, and be aware of the damage he was doing to his brain. A year later, he was still struggling with drugs. In our interview, he expanded the lecture at my request to explain the intricacies of the drug scene, and his continuing part in it:

You just go through phases of different drugs, know what I mean? When I was a little nipper, I used tippex thinner and gas lighter fuel. We'd take a lot of trips when we were about fifteen or sixteen. Then I progressed from grass and hash to speed, I hated speed, it's just a cheap and nasty thing that keeps you awake all night and you can't eat and that. But *(acid)* trips are a brilliant experience. I think you can learn quite a lot about life and yourself by taking trips cos they help you to search the corners of your mind what you haven't searched before, know what I mean? I've never had a bad trip and I've taken hundreds of them. I've never had a flashback either.

Ecstasy, that's the best drug cos it's plainly for having a good time, it won't fuck you up or anything. You take them when you go out raving, they give you energy and a rush, it makes the music sound good and dancing is brilliant. When it first came out it was called 'the love drug' as everyone in there would be your best friend and you would have never met them before. You could pull up at a rave and not worry. My mate left his keys in his motorbike all night and when he came out in the morning they were still there. At anywhere else someone would have nicked it.

The Americans used it on Vietnam soldiers cos it gives you so much energy – brings you up. It lasts between four and eight hours for £15. Some people take ten in a night. They get really out of it – they lose a lot of weight dancing all night. Apparently great quantities gives you Parkinson's Disease in later life. It was called the Love drug cos it turns girls on. It's brilliant making love to them – wicked, man. It's the best drug ever made.

It was the bad press – that was when they started busting them. 'Illegal drug barons getting kids addicted to drugs that turned them into raving animals.' Because, when you're under the influence of an E it makes your jaw come out and you look really out of it. You've got so much energy dancing, and to them, cos they were on a totally different normal buzz, you just looked like you were going mad. They must have thought we were nutters.

All of a sudden things changed. The police started nicking people holding the events and giving them big sentences and fines. It just pissed you off – why did they want to spoil what was a good thing? It made you depressed and pissed off more than paranoid. And with E, you lose all your inhibitions – you're totally open with everyone. We'll be singing 'All we wanna do is dance,' and saying 'why do you go messing with us when we're trying to have a good time? We're not hurting anyone or affecting anyone.' It just pissed us off that everything young people get into – hippies in the Sixties, the Punk Scene, then House, police just hate it and try to stop it. It's just the way it goes.

The government said they were having this War on Drugs but really they made it much worse. In 1989 when the *(acid)* House scene started to die out because of bad press, coke began to hit the streets. They brought in stronger sentences for Ecstasy so there was less of it about and cocaine became the thing. That's when I started taking Charlie myself and then crack.

Cocaine is a nice drug in moderation, take it now and then, have a little chat and a drink with your mates and a little line of Charlie. It makes you chatty and electrified and the centre of conversation. It's like you're a battery and someone recharges you. It gives you confidence but if you take it a lot that confidence can turn to paranoia. It starts with you using it to be sociable, then if you start licking it – washing it up into crack and taking it like that, it starts fucking you up. You've got to have it every day – go out and thieve to get some more.

One lick will last between thirty seconds and two minutes. Then you've got to have another one. £30 of crack will last twenty minutes to half an hour. Straight away after you've taken crack, you'll cluck for more – clucking is craving. It keeps you awake for hours. You feel rough. But you have a couple of hits one day, the next day it's all in the mind, you want a lick – even though you don't really like the buzz – just the first little thirty seconds.

The first little hit is really intense rush. After that it's just terrible, it's just a craving for more. But it's the best buzz going. That's why people get hooked on it. You try it once, you like it so much that though you may not think you're hooked, you're thinking 'when can I get some more?' It just progresses like that – it plays with your mind – it's not a physical thing.

When you're clucking for crack, you're going through hell. You get a bad paranoid depressed feeling for an hour and three hours after taking it. It's just not normal, and you're craving for something to take you down off that feeling – either drink, puff or smack *(heroin)*.

I was addicted to crack for about a year and a half. That's a lot of the reason I was getting into trouble. Since I've been into crack I've been nicked four times – for two car systems, and two intense supplies of puff. But I don't take crack any more, I do now and then, but not every day like I used to. I used to spend grands a week on it. Like one night, between four of us we done a thousand pounds' worth of cocaine, but it was only a thousand pounds' worth cos it was in one lump. If you broke it up, it would have been about two grand's worth.

By the end of the next morning we had taken so much we were feeling ill. We didn't want any more. I ended up going home. And not wanting another lick after you've had some, it's impossible really. But we had just taken so much.

My friend's uncle was a Charlie dealer so my friend used to get ounces on tic. He had an ounce and we all went up his house and we washed out a gram of it and had a bit, and then that progressed into washing out a quarter ounce of it, and then that progressed into washing out the whole lot and just caning *(taking)* it all.

We literally promised our lives and our mother's lives that we would pay him back but we never. *(laughs)* He's a mate. He was a mate. Younger than us, taught him never to trust again. That's a good lesson.

That's what it's like, you'd knock anyone to get your crack but it's not YOU doing it, know what I mean? I've made myself a bad name, people who trusted me before don't no more cos I've knocked them for money. But I ain't worried. They won't cut *(stab)* us. Cos if they cut you and don't kill you, they'll be hunted until you get them. I ain't that bad.

I weren't ever actually on smack *(heroin)*, I've got more sense. I just take it now and again. It takes a while, every day for a month, till your body starts wanting it. Crack is so expensive – my mates have been through so much money, they're getting into smack.

Smack is a totally opposite effect to crack. If you've been taking crack you're used to being paranoid and hearing noises and that and not speaking to your mates. When you take smack it knocks you out, makes you feel mellow. It's a nice buzz. You can chat and that, which you can't do on crack.

To me smack is like glue. When I was at school, I seen all the publicity about glue sniffing so I didn't do it. Glue sniffers was like some kids see smackheads now, it was seen as the lowest drug. I said I'd never do smack. But I did cos I was addicted to crack, and that was an easy way of *(getting high and)* not spending all that money.

I'm favourable of smack in moderation, I'm favourable of everything in moderation. It's just when you start to take it every day, it fucks you up.

If you know people it's easy to get any drugs you want. Anyone can go down King's Cross and get drugs any time of the day or night, just walk up to someone in the street and ask them for it. The police got surveillance, but they're not doing it right.

I know a lawyer who does lines of coke with a judge between sessions. Rich people put out bowls of Charlie instead of peanuts. Most rich people take Charlie. That's not a myth. That's a fact.

There's quite a few crack houses opening up – that's somewhere they sell crack with guns and dogs so they don't get ripped off, cos like some people when they're clucking for crack they'll do anything from robbing their best friend to mugging somebody – just crazy things.

The drug takes over. When you're normal you wouldn't do these things, but when you're under the influence of the drug you just don't care. And you'll do almost anything to get some more.

Crack mixed with Marvetol *(baby laxative)* is an evil drug. It makes you think of things you wouldn't normally do. Some guys nick from their own Dad and Mum. *(Joel says this with touching outrage.)* I been clucking like that but not any more. The main reason I stopped is cos if I carry on thieving I'll go down and I don't want to do that. If I still had loads of money coming in I'd probably still be taking it. You stop by just telling yourself you don't need it. But even though you've stopped, if you go to the pub and have a drink and everyone goes to get some rocks *(drugs)* and you've some money, you're going to end up doing it. You want something to bring you up, like a line of Charlie or Es.

It's totally different now. All the raves are legal and haven't got the same atmosphere. A lot of Ragas *(tough black youths)* started going. Before, everyone was friendly. The Ragas tried to mug people and gave it a bad atmosphere. People got stabbed at the Michael Sobell Sports Centre in Islington recently. They had a rave and there were ten thousand trying to get in, with only room for three thousand. Loads of Ragas came nicking peoples' money and stuff.

I've never mugged anyone, cos I ain't into that. It's a liberty. I've never done any pick-pocketing, but I'll try anything once, I suppose; *(laughs)* it just ain't my scene. Rent Boys? I've never been that bad. I wouldn't know where to begin. I'd never stoop down that low. When you say, 'You'll do anything,' it's only like immediate things that are around you. You're not going to plan something cos by the time you've done it, you're probably going to be off the effect of the drug anyway.

But another thing we used to do for money was go out to night-clubs and sell moody Es, Vitamin C tablets pretending to be ecstasy tablets. *(chuckles)* You could earn between £100 and £500 for an hour's work in a club. I felt bad, but it was my cocaine money. It was just to support a habit, cos you'd spend about £300 on Charlie some nights. But I wouldn't do it now cos I'd feel a cunt about doing it. I was doing it when the House scene had died out and there was only a load of mugs. The only person who'd buy an E off you must be a mug. So it don't really matter.

My mate sold these black kids these moody Ecstasy tablets, and since then my mates have been having fights with them. Whenever we see each other in the street, we just lay into each other, and someone gets stabbed or something like that. I'm not really a violent person myself, it's just come to me through my mates.

It's been going on for two years, but got worse recently. Two years ago these kids jumped my mate after we sold them the tablets, and my mates gassed them with CS gas and stabbed one of them. Then these kids knocked on my friend's door and spat in his father's face. So whenever we see each other in the street it just goes off, basically.

About six months ago I was carrying a knife around all the time – there was more of a possibility of running into them cos I used to hang out more. It's just a pen knife with a three-inch blade. But some of my mates carry around big cleavers. One of them's got a cosh. It's always best to carry around a tool, cos if you haven't and you bump into them you're fucked basically. But me personally I'm not out looking for trouble, but if the trouble comes I've got to protect myself. I wouldn't go out looking for one just to stab him, know what I mean? Well, I would one of them, cos he done that *(scar)* to me.

I don't see how it's gonna stop cos they take the right piss. Like I was walking down the street and four of them jumped me. They always hang around in large groups, you'd never see them by themselves. Four of them battered two of my mates a couple of weeks ago. I can't see it stopping in the near future. One of my mates said he ain't going to rest until he slices up some kid. Even if he has to carry a knife for the rest of his life, he ain't going to rest until that kid is sliced up.

Nothing to do with the police, cos no one grasses on each other. Like if you get stabbed you ain't going to go to the police and say 'Excuse me, so and so stabbed me.' That's just the worst. You don't go to the police, you go and stab him yourself. I haven't personally started anything. It's them, and I've carried it on. I don't think it ever will stop.

To Joel and so many others like him, life on the streets was a chaotic and unpredictable mix of boredom, excitement and danger. Sherborne House, with its strict routine and emphasis on self-awareness and positive activity, was a drastic and not always comfortable change. During Joel's time at Sherborne House, two particular events stand out. He and Sunny were in a photography session on Monday afternoon in the middle of the ten-week programme. They asked if they could go out to take pictures – using the expensive cameras that belonged to Sherborne House. This is normal practice. Ellie, the crafts instructor, was nevertheless wary of their request. Neither Joel nor Sunny had been a regular in photography but since the ethos of the place is to encourage people to grow and take responsibility, Ellie had no grounds to refuse.

When Joel and Sunny were late returning, she wandered the corridors of the old building cursing herself for having trusted them. Each passing minute seemed to confirm her worst suspicions.

Eventually they returned, agitated, and without the cameras. Joel described how on their way back from taking pictures they were set on by a group of black youths carrying baseball bats. In each telling, the threats and actions varied – at first they were actually beaten up, but by the third time round it seemed they were threatened with a beating only if they did not hand over the cameras, which they did. Their delay in returning was, they said, because they went to the police station to report the incident.

In the staff meeting that followed, most were inclined to believe them, despite Ellie's fury at what she saw as an obvious charade. But the staff were all understandably discomfited by an event that suggested the programme had been mocked. The place had been burgled of equipment before, but by strangers, or people who Sherborne House had refused to accept. This time, as Ellie saw it, two young men in the middle of a course designed to change their lives, may have stolen these cameras and proposed to carry on as if nothing had happened. Most of the others preferred to believe Joel and Sunny were telling the truth, and were now victims of the kind of crime which previously they might have committed themselves.

After much debate, Jack, the Senior Probation Officer, made a plan to see Sunny and Joel in the morning, and to test their account of going to the police by making them call the station for the crime number. Their reactions would be the only evidence the staff had to go on.

The next day, Joel did not show up, but Sunny did. When asked to call the police, he did so with calm and confidence, and obtained the crime number. Jack was pleased to recount this later to the staff, who, except for Ellie, seemed content that their original account was true.

But Joel's continued absence seemed a worrying sign. He returned one week later, just at the point of being thrown off the programme. When a detective arrived to see him, Joel was electrified with anxiety – it looked as if he thought the game was up. But it emerged that Joel thought he was being arrested for another outstanding warrant. Instead, he was interviewed as a witness to

*and victim of the theft of the cameras. Still tense but amiable, Joel
told the DC the same story with variations: the group of black
youths stopped them on the street:*

DC: Which street?

Joel: *(quickly)* Don't know which street, I'm not from the
    area. Then this geezer says 'What you got?' and took
    the cameras. He had his hand in his back pocket like
    he had a blade. That's where they keep them. Then
    he said, 'Let's see what you got in your pockets,' so
    I ran off. *(In this version, he was beaten up later
    in the day.)* But I don't know if it was the same guys
    that took the cameras. They jumped me from behind.
    *(The detective said he knew Sunny of old, and
    invited Joel to say that Sunny sold them.)*

DC: I don't give a shit about you. I won't bother
    prosecuting you.

Joel: *(after a beat)* I told you what happened. That's it:
    that's the way it goes.

*Joel returned smiling to the rest of the group who'd been waiting
anxiously to get on with that afternoon's water-skiing trip, and to
find out what would happen to him. Driving to the docks with
Molly, Joel showed he had obviously enjoyed the role of victim.
He was still wired:*

They want me to go to Brixton and look at photos. But I don't
want to. Can't make me. Don't bother me. Not my camera.
Would've been different if it was. Past caring. *(then with half-
serious rage, as he watched the other group's car disappear in
front of them)* Look at that cunt go ahead! I hate women drivers.
They got no guts. You should get into all the spaces – like behind
an ambulance and cut in all the way. Women are like cars. They're
only good to ride in. *(He turned on the radio, found some House
music, and sang along with it loudly, until they were stuck in
traffic again.)* I'd go down the other *(oncoming traffic)* lane. It's
empty. *(quietly, to Molly)* Do you think I'm mad?

*Months after they left Sherborne House Joel told me what really
happened:*

Sunny asked me to nick the cameras with him days before, but
I said no. Apart from any other reason, it was too fucking obvious.
But when we was out and about on photography he said we should

stop in at his place which was on the way back and have a quick smoke. That was sweet. So we go there and light up when these big black geezers arrive with baseball bats and take the cameras. I didn't like it, but I wasn't gonna get beaten up for cameras that weren't even mine.*

It was a characteristic episode: it also highlighted the difficulty of being precise about the truth of any information provided by the young people regarding their experiences. Any variation of their account of events could have been the true one: local youths know and mistrust Sherborne House, and could easily have spotted the cameras on previous excursions before Sunny and Joel took them outside. Sunny, who is small, thin, and vulnerable, as well as criminally minded, could have been blackmailed into getting the cameras. Or he might have proposed the idea himself. Joel swears he had no part in it. As Joel is a habitual drug taker who thieves, whereas Sunny is a habitual thief who takes drugs, I'm inclined to believe Joel.

The second important event for Joel happened during Project Week: the sailing trip across the Channel. He had only a modest amount of money – earmarked for drugs – and a hankering for French-made US-style jeans that were said to be half the price they were in Britain. Although Joel said he had been a Sea Cadet, he complained as much as the others about mucking in with the routine of the boat, and slept relentlessly between watches. But he was cheerful, and good company throughout.

Onshore in Ostend the first night on the Continent, Joel swaggered down the road leading the other lads. 'Too bad there aren't more of us. We could terrorise this fucking place,' he said, kicking the coke machine in the railway station.

It was a beautiful, warm, moonlit evening, as we moved down the high street from one side to the other admiring shop windows full of attractive goods. Joel, an experienced shoplifter, was in heaven, despite his regular outbursts of 'Belgium is shit, man. Fucking Belgium is fucking shit.'

The others followed close behind Joel like a shoal of fish.

'Fucking Belgium' was more an expression of frustration than of disapproval. That bicycles were parked unlocked outside discos seemed to Joel and Johnnie both stupid and too good to be true.

---

* See Chapter Six for Sunny's version.

Joel wanted to take them all back to the boat — indeed he suggested we steal a different boat and escape — but the presence of police with machine guns and dogs calmed him down.

The next day in Dunquerque, while Johnnie actually bought a jacket, Joel eyed a particular pair of jeans with the dispassionate interest of a barracuda sizing up its prey. He exercised great restraint — which he later regretted — and left them behind, but could not resist stealing a T-shirt. He dealt with Jack's ruling (that any stolen goods brought on board would be seized and either thrown overboard or returned) by putting the shirt on as soon as he had returned to the boat. Jack said nothing, and neither did anyone else. Joel felt he had honoured the spirit of Jack's diktat by not stealing the jeans, and a great deal else besides.

On our return voyage, Joel was excited:

I've just been told *(jokingly by one of the probation officers)* I'm good-looking and wear nice clothes. I feel really full of life from that. I want a job so I can get a bank account and roll up loads and loads of debts. If I get half a million, I'll retire. With money you can go into buying and selling.

Looking at the boat, Joel had a 'brilliant idea — sweet'. He offered the captain half a million to go into 'a little smuggling business'.

Captain: I've got what I want.
Joel: But we'd have made a fortune running drugs this trip.
Captain: You'd have been caught. Everyone always is. I was. I spent six months inside — care of HM Prison in Winchester. For fraud.
Joel: *(astonished that someone 'straight' should have a record)* For how much?
Captain: More than you'll ever see.
Joel: *(gamely persisting)* I'd risk it if enough money was involved. If you think paranoid you get caught. If you think positive, you'll get away with it.

The captain just shook his head sadly, as if to say Joel was a fool who didn't know what he was talking about. Joel kept his smile but fell silent.

*

Despite his enjoyment of the trip, Joel returned to the same situation — he was broke and homeless, while estranged from his mother. Near the end of the course, Joel's attendance was so erratic, he ran out of points and breached his court order, but the staff liked him and sympathised with his situation — enough to let him continue the programme. They knew he was sleeping on a succession of friends' floors — not ideal circumstances to construct a viable new life. In the final sessions, they tried to encourage him to put his life in order, and more immediately, to finish his work in the workshops. Ellie had found Joel a constant pain in the art workshop: he kept making sexist remarks, and insisting on doing his silk screen T-shirt his own way. That it turned out well made him still more smug in his dealings with her. Joel had maintained a teasing relationship with all the group leaders that parried their efforts to make him think more deeply about himself, his past actions, and his future. As he had done on so many previous occasions, Joel hinted that he knew what was expected of him — and that he could, if he chose, go in a different direction. But he preferred, for the moment, to stay floating on whatever cloud he had stopped on. Joel's puckish tone was not generally offensive, but it allowed him to keep his distance.

One year after Sherborne House, when I interviewed him in his mother's flat in Kentish Town, Joel seemed to have changed few of the attitudes he had held before the course. He still showed little remorse about his criminal activities.

I'd say about two per cent is how much I've been caught, and ninety-eight per cent I haven't. I've done about twenty burglaries, and that was just one summer. The number of cars I've nicked from is endless, I couldn't possibly begin to imagine, know what I mean? Probably going into the thousands. About a thousand, I guess.

Got started with friends, just walking round, looking in cars, nicking things. It's fun. When you're out thieving you get a good buzz, especially when you get a nice touch, know what I mean? The buzz of being alert and paranoid and getting chased, it's a laugh, especially when you're young. Ain't so much fun now.

I started burgling Spring and Summer '89. Going out burgling in the day and raving at night. Cos it was during the summer people leave their windows open. Everyone I hang about with has done a burglary at some time in their life. It's brilliant man, going through other people's stuff and finding brilliant treasures, it's a wicked buzz. Almost as good as any drug, finding loads of money and that. But it's harder now cos they've got these special crime squads. They know me as having done two burglaries but they don't know me as a big burglar cos I was only doing them one summer. If I was still doing them I'd probably get two years straight away and I don't want that.

I ain't had a hard time from the police, not really, but they've come up and harassed me just because they know my face. They searched me cos I looked out of it. But they've never beaten me up or anything like that. I been caught by being actually seen on the job, or by fingerprints, or by police knowing my face and pulling me up in the street and searching me.

For thieving, I got two cautions when I was under sixteen, but I haven't got any juvenile offences. I started getting proper sentences when I was about seventeen. Getting cautioned is nice cos they give you another chance but it doesn't deter you cos they just say 'Don't do it again, see you later' sort of thing. But it's better than actually getting into trouble at that young age.

My first burglary I got two years' probation. Some people only get a caution. But then again, some get a year in prison. I think if you get used to prison at an early age it'll make it worse, cos it's harder to break out of that sort of pattern or cycle of life. I've been there four times, but only on remand. Four weeks is the longest time I've ever been inside. I hated it.

It's definitely deterred me. I could still be out there making loads of money but the thought of going into prison is stopping me. I'd rather be a bit skint than have all that trouble.

I hate it: being locked up and thinking about all your mates having a good time while you're in your cell; self-pity, thinking about your life and all that. And everyone in there's moody. A lot of people in there are all out to prove something. Like who's got control over everyone, who's the hardest, and all that, know what I mean? I just hate it, and it has deterred me I think.

I suppose it's different for everyone. I've met people, one of them was at Sherborne House, he got breached and he went back to prison. He's been in and out of prison since he was fifteen and he didn't care if he got a sentence; he'd spent more time in than out since he was fifteen, and he wasn't bothered.

The only reason I have done well in the legal system – got no prison sentences – is cos of the way I was brought up. I tell people about my background and how my Mum and Dad split up and that, and how I've been moving between the two.

Community Service's alright, but if you're doing something like that you should be getting something out of it, and they should give you a qualification. I don't see the point otherwise. It's not going to help change your life.

It's supposed to be punishment, but they should look at alternatives to punishment. I wouldn't mind making it up with someone I burgled, doing something for them to square things. Might make a good friend out of it.

In a nutshell, Joel has grasped the case for victim-offender mediation, the kind of alternative to traditional punitive justice that leads to positive outcomes: reparation and explanations for the victim, and some kind of positive resolution for the offender in coming to grips with the consequences of his actions.

I pressed Joel on what kind of sentence he thought might have made him stop thieving, and what he made of Sherborne House now. His answer was more realistic than the expectations of those judges and magistrates who think it can work miracles overnight. Ten weeks is less than one term at the schools and universities to which those who sentence these young people would have gone at their age, and to which they send their own children.

I think Sherborne House was a good sentence. It got me into a routine for a while, and it kept me out of prison, and I had a laugh I suppose. It never stopped me from thieving. I bought some duff £20 notes and we used to go for a puff at break time. It was like a youth club cum school, where you could meet fellow thieves and associates, know what I mean? It weren't really this great new beginning. *(laughing but serious)* It never transformed me into a new person. It was a change, but it wasn't this amazing bridge to a new and better life, free of crime and drugs and destitution. It's meant to show you a new way, to change you. But it's only you that can change yourself.

Ten weeks is too short. I think an alternative to Sherborne House would be a sort of training scheme where you come out with a qualification at the end, and if you don't turn up you go to prison. Then at least you have something under your belt when you've finished. I mean what did you come out of Sherborne House with? Something saying 'This person done well' or something like that.

Because I was there all the time I never had any opportunities of earning money in any other ways apart from going out getting a little earner at night-time, so that's what I done. I thieved whenever I was skint, cos I was going out at the weekends.

Anything from shoplifting to mountain bikes to car systems. You can get a lot of good things out of cars. My mate found £5000 out of a car. It was in the glove compartment. It's like robbing a bank, ain't it? Especially around this area of North London, man, there's so many nice cars with nice systems in, that if you're really clued up you can go out and get five systems, and you can get £300 easy.

Ninety-five per cent of them, even though they may be distressed and in trauma cos you've gone through their personal property, they all get it back on insurance. I've never done any council flats or anything like that. I've only done houses in Primrose Hill, Belsize Park, Hampstead, places like that, all sort of rich and posh areas. And most of them get it back, so it doesn't really bother me. I mean I do feel a cunt about it, but I'd never rob off someone who weren't well to do, and I'd never steal off a friend. Like even though you're a thief, you've got your morals, know what I mean?

To tell you the truth I don't really feel bad *(about thieving)*. I have thought in the past, it's hard to explain. One time we got into a house, and it was an old grannie's. We never knew until we'd got outside and we'd nicked a couple of boxes and found all these old war medals. So we went back and put the stuff on the doorstep. I know what it's like cos I've had things that have gone missing of mine.

And another thing, ninety per cent of the houses I've burgled are done because the owner has made a silly mistake and left their window open. I've never forced entry into a house, so it's their own fault in a way, know what I mean? Like one of the houses we went into we knocked on the door and there was no one in and there was these big sliding glass doors that were open, so we just walked in and picked up whatever we wanted and walked out.

A thief's job is to nick things and if people are stupid enough to leave their things about then the thief does alright. Even for people that aren't thieves, if they saw a big bundle of money they'd think 'go on take it', know what I mean?

If I had money in my pocket I most probably wouldn't thieve, cos I'm a bit more sensible now. I'd think of the implications of what could happen to me first. I've never thieved off anyone I've worked with or anyone I know or anything like that. It's obvious if you're working somewhere you don't want to mess your job up just for the sake of a little bit of money.

I only thieve off people I never knew, who were rich – with big BMs *(BMWs)* or a big house. They don't deserve it cos they might have worked hard for it, but it might affect them like 'Oh no, I got burgled. What a pity' but that's about it. Sometimes they're probably happy in a way that we done it cos they stake big massive insurance claims. Like some burglary I done we got a video and a clock and a little camera and they was trying to say it was worth two grand. That was just waffle! Good luck to anyone who wants to earn their money. They're just the same as common little thieves but on a higher level I suppose. Everyone has got their price to become a thief. Politicians, Presidents and all that. Even armed robbers, as long as they don't blow away innocent people, they're sweet, I don't mind them. As long as they're only using those guns to get the money. And they're robbing banks, not ordinary people, so in a way your common burglar is worse.

I think the legal system is bollocks cos in the end it's just up to the judge and his views and attitudes on life. And all them judges, they're brought up in upper-class backgrounds, and they can't look on life from our point of view, know what I mean? Rapists and child molesters are the scum of the earth, and what really makes me sick about the legal system is that child molesters and rapists get away with two to three years, while someone who robs a few grand can get five years. The law puts more of a sentence on money than they do on people's lives. I think that's disgusting.

I trust my family, a couple of friends, that's about it. I trust you, cos you're not really them sort of people. There's a couple of friends that if I lent them money I might not get it back sort of thing. But there's different degrees of trust aren't there? I've never known a teacher I could trust with my secrets, cos they're always trying to help you so they'll probably tell someone.

I've had birds but don't at the moment. I don't use condoms, man. For a start I wouldn't go with a bird, like some rough old slapper with Aids, I'd only go with a bird who's had a few partners. I've never used a condom and I doubt I ever will unless a bird makes me use one. People say I'm just as much at risk as anyone else but I don't think so, and if you're meant to get Aids you probably will. No one I know uses a condom. I think it's mainly among the older generation, cos younger people, they're not born with Aids, so if you stick with them you're sweet.

There's nothing else to do in this life apart from have a good time, innit, while you're here. Nothing would have made me go straight cos all the people out there having a fun-loving time, a good time, all take drugs. All the other people they're just what you could call proles; they're either normal yobbos that go to the pub and have a drink every night, or they're just normal people who work hard and all that.

I should be getting on better than I am now for my age. I should be stable with a job and a car like a lot of people I know my age. I'm just floating about in limbo waiting for something to crop up; like, things aren't going too well. I'm just skint all the time cos I don't thieve no more. A lot of my friends, their parents have bought them cars, even though they're still drugged up junkies. If they never had their parents they'd probably be living in squats but they've got a stable background and get their jobs found for them.

Like one mate of mine was given a job with his brother on a stall and fucked that one off, and he's been given two cars. Then they got him a job doing a milk round with his own float and he fucked that one off. Then they got him a job at the same place as a supervisor of the floats and he fucked that one off too; he's just a right junkie, but he's alright. But if it weren't for his parents he'd be on the floor, worse than me. They're not really from poor families. They're just well-to-do working class.

My Mum, cos she ain't got much money, like if my mates are on the dole, their parents won't expect any money, but if my Mum had her way she'd have every penny off me. But I just give her £30 or £40 out of my £60 (dole for a fortnight) and keep the other few pennies for myself.

Even if I had a good job and that, I'd still take drugs. The only reason I'd give up is to clear my head a bit cos non-stop for all that time is bad. Non-stop anything for all that time is bad, know what I mean?

I was going to start going jogging and weight lifting and give up drugs over this autumn, winter and spring but I haven't managed it. I haven't really tried hard. Tell you what I'd love to do if I had the money and that's make my own music, but I need loads of equipment. But I don't care what I do basically, I haven't got any one thing I want to do. My head's mixed up and that. I would take almost any job at the moment.

In his last week at Sherborne House, Joel had seen Derek, from New Bridge, the voluntary agency that helps ex-offenders find training and work. He told Derek about his work experience:

I've worked doing painting and decorating for three weeks and I worked in a factory for about two months after I came out of school, but that's it. I've just been living on the other side of the law all the time. The first job was rubbish, man, cos we were getting paid about £80 a week, but my second job was alright. I was getting about £180 a week, but that only lasted for three weeks on one contract. They probably didn't like my work. The advertisement in a shop window said 'painters and decorators wanted, start straight away.' It must have been cos they had to get their contract finished – they was hiring extra hands, know what I mean? That was before Sherborne House.

Derek was impressed by Joel's school record which included two distinctions in Maths. In their discussion, Joel said 'I'd like a job that used my head, but guess I can't without qualifications.' But like Johnnie, Joel would not accept Derek's proposal that he go into training, and earn very little in order to go to the head of the job queue and earn more later.

Joel made an appointment with Derek for the following week. But in the event, he neither kept it, nor rang to explain why or make a fresh appointment. As Joel explained to me one year later, he hasn't worked since.

I've been to the job centre, and I've had a couple of interviews but I didn't get anywhere with them. I don't really know where to start, I've never worked. I think the best way to get a job is to know someone who knows someone.

After Sherborne House, Joel carried on sleeping on friends' floors. His probation officer managed to find him council accommodation, but Joel never turned up to see her so he lost it. Since then, his mother has allowed him to stay with her and his sisters in their flat but they quarrel regularly. His mother wants him to get a job, or a place on a course, and certainly give up drugs, while Joel tests his manhood against a houseful of women.

I moved back *(here)* after my step-father died. He was a nice bloke really, but very strict, very old-fashioned. Had no idea about teenagers. We didn't get on at all. It was impossible. He made me leave home, then me sisters went. We each thought something was wrong with us but it was him really, he just didn't understand and wanted us to do everything his way. Now we're back but I'm still fighting with me Mum and me sisters. They don't really know about the harder drugs. They would be angry. My Mum found a burnt spoon and she freaked and kicked me out. But I promised I wouldn't take drugs in here and she let me off. I haven't kept my promise, no.

My sisters want me to get up off my arse, but I mean they've been brought into the drug scene just as I have, and all their friends. I never used to live with my little sister. I never knew what she used to get up to and I couldn't believe she was taking acid tabs with all her friends and that, at fifteen, I didn't think she was into that. I found out she was a trip head, an acid junkie.

I don't mind. I've told her I don't want her taking trips, but I went to get her some, so I contradicted myself *(laughs)*. Every kid goes through it and if I didn't get them for her it's only going to be someone else, know what I mean?

One sister's got a job, works for the government, but that don't mean she's straight. She's taking just about everything, puff, and smack, Charlie. It's just the norm, like having a drink. Grass to smack is like lager to whisky, just a totally different spectrum.

I don't know what would have stopped me. If they had the answer to that I reckon they'd be using it wouldn't they? *(laughs)* If I had the answer to that I'd probably be a rich man. A different circle of friends would have deterred me, if I'd started hanging around with all posh people, know what I mean? Then I might have done well at school. I was quite bright but I never got into school work. All we used to do was mess about, smash things up and make the teachers cry and stuff. It was mad, school.

Recently I tried again. I did Maths and English GCSE, but I got fed up cos I had to pay for the course. Only £20 a term, but I need money for everyday things, getting there, and eating and stuff. I was getting pissed off with the homework. I left after about two weeks. I thought 'Fuck this, I'll look for a job instead.'

Like everyone tells you when you're young, 'Get your exams, you'll be glad, you're going to need them in the end,' know what I mean? But you just think it's a load of rubbish, because you know people who've got exams and they ain't working, and that's your excuse. So you just mess about all the time.

I know I could do really well at college if I tried my hardest, but I haven't got enough self-control. I've got partial control. I'm not positive thinking enough, basically. I can't stick something out for four years with no money. If I had the money to do it I would, basically.

I talked to my probation officer about grants and things like that but she's well useless. All she does is tell you what you should do but doesn't help you, know what I mean? I was meant to go up to the guy from New Bridge again, but I never got round to it, I forget about it or something like that. I'll call him and see what goes on, what's happening.

This vagueness was characteristic of how Joel lived his life: good intentions drifting into drug-induced haze. Two months after Sherborne House, I saw Joel running along the street while I was driving through Kentish Town. In a friendly but brief exchange, he told me he was off to visit his Mum – progress from the state of hostility they'd been in before – but he wasn't living anywhere. He promised to call me, but didn't. A few months later, trying to keep track of his whereabouts and how he was managing, I called Joel's probation officer, Mary, a friendly Irishwoman in her late thirties. Six months after he had left Sherborne House, Mary didn't know where he was either:

I first met Joel fifteen months ago. I haven't seen much of him. It's been more like holding onto him than doing anything for him. He was rearrested, and he hasn't kept many appointments. When he did come, it would be at the wrong time. I tried to engage him but he's really stumped about what he wants. It's been six months since I saw him last. I'm at the end of my tether with him. He doesn't communicate when I do see him. It's the age. He thinks I'm his mother. I'm sure he dismisses me the way he dismisses her.

I know he has a difficult time with his family. His early childhood was awful – his father was an alcoholic who used to abuse his mother. Mother's now married a black man much older than she is. Maybe I'm being racist but when I met them all I was struck by how dominant he was. There's no interaction at all. The step-father just said how things were done in his country, and what Joel was going to do – that was that. Joel never said anything – and the step-father got really annoyed. There's obviously a generation gap. He thought I was siding with his step-father but I wasn't. *(Mary had not seen Joel for so long she was unaware that his step-father had died.)*

I really don't know what to do. He had a chance to be rehoused by the council but he's blown it. He tried to blame everybody else, but finally admitted he couldn't get his act together to fill out the forms. He's not just lazy, that's not it. He's lethargic. I think psychotherapy might be helpful. It's an awful thing to say but I suppose his lethargy at least keeps him out of more trouble.

Mary was present at his final assessment at Sherborne House. His group probation officer, Molly, told Joel she regretted he'd missed so much at Sherborne House because he'd have had more benefit from it.

Joel: I didn't miss so much time on purpose. I'd have come here, and finished the work in craft but they thought I didn't have enough time. I'm pissed off I missed the time here – I wanted to make some tapes.

Molly: You also seemed to miss a certain amount while you were here, by being so sleepy. You slept most of the time on the boat. It's the effect of the drugs. It's a matter of control.

Joel: I'm always sleepy. Quite a lot of the time. It's not the drugs. I don't use drugs, you should know that! It's up to me ain't it?

Molly: There are consequences for everyone.

Joel: I only use drugs for pleasure, experience, to pass the time. It's not that I got no control – I got partial control.

Molly: I'm sorry you missed so much here. I'd have liked to get to know you better.

Joel: Nobody knows me really well. Even outside of Sherborne House. Could be wrong. Maybe because I'm shy.

Molly: How well do you know yourself?

Joel: Too well.

Molly: What we do know is good: you're sharp, have a
good sense of humour.

Joel: I don't have a good sense of humour. Ain't used to
daytime. Used to night-time. None of me mates get
up at 9am ever.

*Molly said he had energy when he wanted it. She reminded Joel of
his passionate row with Johnnie about politics, when he discovered
Johnnie was a Tory.*

Joel: I like to put my views across.

Molly: *(with suppressed frustration – it's the most
important question)* Why can't you be like that more
often?

Joel: *(genuinely puzzled)* Like what?

*Discussing his future, Joel was still more doubtful. His best hope
for the short term:*

Joel: To be free of all my outstanding court cases, in a
job of some kind that pays £150 a week, and either
in a new flat, or on the way to having one.

Molly: More likely?

Joel: I'll still be muddled up with my cases and living I
don't know where – in a cardboard box, or most
likely on a friend's floor.

Molly: In five years?

Joel: I want a flat, a job with prospects, and a steady
relationship. But not without a flat to put my things
in. More likely I might get the flat, but without the
job or relationship, I'd still be in a horrible mess
with money, struggling with debts, trying to
decorate the flat. It would just be an empty shell.

Molly: What's the worst outcome?

Joel: To be sentenced to Feltham or Brixton for eighteen
months, or more. Or, at the age of twenty I'll be six
feet under if I carry on the way I am now.

*One year later, the first time I visited Joel in his mother's flat, he
was watching the State Opening of Parliament on television.
'What d'you think of the single European currency?' he asked. On
another occasion, he was watching BSkyB's sub-standard version
of* Blind Date *with equal interest, while his sisters and their friends*

came and went, making dinner for him as well. He is open to whatever influences are at hand.

I watch the news on the telly all day long, like what's going on around the world and that? Everyone is interested in that really. It's just been born and bred into you, knowing what's going on around you, away from your own little room.

I need someone to put me in line to tell me what to do and tell me off and that, do you know what I mean? I need some authority even though I don't like it. Mum, she tries, but she doesn't do very well. She's really pissed off because I went to college and I never stuck it out, and I'm not working, and she's really skint at the moment.

Watching him prowl the comfortable confines of his mother's flat, politely offering us tea and coffee at regular intervals, Joel seemed to be itching for stimulation – for contact, for surprises, for a challenge, or just for distraction – from television, from his friends and family, from anywhere.

I'm too rebellious man, I dunno, I'm weird, my mind swings, maybe I should give up taking drugs for a year and that would help me to clear my mind and sort my life out and that. Cos I could be interested in one thing, and think, 'Yeh, this is what I want to do,' and then one little thing goes wrong and I'm pissed off with it, and I'm saying 'Ah, fuck that.' Stuck in a little world where it's hard to get out.

But even if I didn't take drugs I probably would go out and thieve cos I haven't got an income. The people I hang about with are worse than me. We go to a rough pub where the geezer who runs it is sweet with us so he lets us do the business. People know about it so they go for business. Anyone who's not accepted gets seen off by four or five geezers with baseball bats and cleavers.

They do a lot more drugs than I do at the moment. That's why I've stopped hanging around with them so much. I don't go out to look for earners like I used to, I go out to look for jobs instead, and on the way to the job centre if I see an earner I'll probably do it, a car with a handbag which has got a cash card and pin number and a cheque book and card and which has got loads of money in it. I've found two, but I've known people that have found quite a lot. But I'm not out there specifically looking.

I puff most of the time, go out with my mates for a drink sometimes, watch telly, and sometimes I'll go out and look for a job with no success. That just makes me even more pissed off so I'll go up to my room and cry. Nah, I don't, but I feel like crying, know what I mean?

The police keep after you. Where I used to live in a flat in Finchley, a letter got put through the door that they wanted to speak to me about a serious incident. They think I possibly committed a murder cos the description fits mine and apparently the blood of the same group as mine was found at the scene. So the police want to question me about it basically. I've got to go to see them next Thursday with an alibi, but I don't know what I was doing, in which case they might hound me, and bang me up for ten years. But my solicitor said there's about 150 possible suspects, so I'm not really that worried about it.

I didn't do it, and it's most probably cos I got a criminal record that they picked me out in the first place. If I never had one I might not even be in the inquiry.*

I haven't got any court cases coming. I'm totally clear. I've just got to get off my arse one day innit? I think whatever is meant to happen in your life will happen. I'm just waiting for that opportunity to come along, and I'll jump on it.

I wouldn't move anywhere else in England. It's just the same in other parts. But I wouldn't mind moving to Australia or Canada or something like that. But I like London, it's alright, sweet. I've been painting a bad picture of bad drugs scene, bad violence, destitute life, but it ain't like that, know what I mean? Even though I was strung out on drugs it doesn't mean it was really bad, know what I mean? I just went the wrong way and got fucked up on it. It's sweet. I have a good time.

I don't know, I'm just not mo . . . I can't think of the word, man, motivated enough. I haven't got much self-confidence either, and when you're used to living in one little world it's really hard to break out of it and join the big world. It's hard, but I know I've got to do it one day.

Some Sherborne House staff thought that rather than being a compulsive criminal, Joel was a sensitive person who was profoundly depressed. His mix of lethargy and self-awareness could just be a result of drugs. But his latent desire to live differently

---

* There's been no further contact from the police at the time of publication.

and his inability to act on that desire in even the smallest ways inclined me to share that view.

His intelligence and laid-back charm grew on me as it did on most of the staff over the ten weeks. In the subsequent interviews this impression was confirmed – he is a substantial person, trapped in the conventions of his situation on the street. Even though he went to a good comprehensive with a mixture of children of all abilities and backgrounds, Joel's drift into criminality echoes Johnnie's who also went to a good school. They both had broken and difficult home lives, and needed more support to make use of the opportunities and the obvious intelligence they had at their disposal.

Joel actually had strict parental guidance from his step-father, but in a form that forced him out rather than encouraging him to toe the line – a frequent occurrence among young offenders. Yet again the conventional assumption made by politicians that family life equals good and effective discipline is inadequate. Despite his family difficulties, Joel loves his shiftless and destitute alcoholic father, and spoke warmly about his late step-father.

I believed Joel's real need was simply for something to do. As it happened, through Book Aid, our campaign to send one million books to Russia, there was a place in the warehouse in King's Cross for able-bodied helpers. Having urged Joel to get a job, I decided to back my own instinct and offered him the chance to work there as a volunteer. I warned him that if there was any trouble, or he didn't come up to scratch, he'd be out. Joel accepted with surprising eagerness. He came nearly seven days a week, and worked diligently alongside men, women and children of all ages and social classes who travelled from all over the country to sort books. Joel fitted in gradually as his wit and commitment came to be appreciated. He was as surprised as they were to be among such a motley crew, with such altruistic motives. As the weeks passed, Joel lost the sleepy, hooded look that made him appear rather sinister at first. He came to be genuinely liked by everyone who worked there. The probation officer in charge of his Community Service arranged for this work to qualify instead of his original sentence.

But near the end, Joel began to slip – he was late, vague and ineffective, all worrying signs that he was back on drugs. I asked him point blank, and after denying it at first, Joel rang me back and admitted he was using crack again. He had fallen out with his mother over his attempts to be the boss in the house. After a particularly nasty exchange, Joel kicked in the front door panel and was thrown out to fend for himself again. Installed in a series of grimy hostels for the homeless, Joel ended up sharing a room with a heroin addict. It could have been his nemesis. But after a further desperate week, he had the strength of character to seek help – and then to choose to kick the habit on his own before it overtook him.

Joel moved in with his alcoholic father – himself an ex-addict who told me when I visited his squalid flat in West Hampstead that he'd kicked heroin fifteen times. A small hunched man who looked far older than his years, he was still pursuing the life of an ageing hippie, drinking and sharing his dole with vagrants and attending free festivals. Unaided by his father's passive cynicism, Joel came off drugs over a long weekend. He returned to the warehouse looking more like the clear-eyed and alert person his co-workers had come to care for and respect. Joel kept clear of drugs for the month until Book Aid ended. He was taken on by the producer of a modern dance spectacular which used the warehouse for a fortnight: he declared Joel to be 'one of the brightest and hardest working young men he'd ever encountered', and vowed to hire him for his next production. Joel himself found the dance fascinating. Another local studio gave him a brief stint of painting and scene-shifting – nothing steady, but enough to keep his self-confidence intact.

Joel is at another crossroads: he plans to help his father give up drink and clear up his flat. But his father doubts Joel's success at kicking drugs, blames the mess on Joel, and claims to have been threatened by him in fights over his living habits. He himself threatens to kick Joel out onto the street.

One week after his probation order ended, Joel was arrested for intervening on behalf of a friend being roughly handled by the police. He is on probation for another year. Joel is now struggling to persuade his father – and his next employer – that he has changed for good.

CHAPTER FIVE

SAM

Let them stand in my fucking shoes

Sam is white, small, and wiry. At seventeen, he was the youngest in the group at Sherborne House but looked younger still – he seems about fourteen when he's tired. He has jet-black hair and small eyes set in a clear sea of a face that lights up when he smiles – which is seldom – or breaks up into contortions when he's angry, which is often. Energetic and restless, at Sherborne House Sam wore an almost permanent scowl which hid his essential good nature. In fact, he's likeable, wayward, and impulsive – given to bouts of mock fury as well as real anger.

Sam thought of himself as street-smart, and had considerable experience of crime – largely burglary. But his youth and almost innocent directness belied his criminal career in the making. Sam's intelligence was also masked by his serious reading problem. Despite presenting himself as illiterate and awkward, he was capable of mucking in satisfactorily in most situations, and paying attention.

But at Sherborne House, Sam's posture of being Puck's bad boy – making provocative remarks, staging tantrums, and providing a regular display of general waywardness – stopped him from fulfilling much of his potential. But he was also vulnerable and appealing – his rages seemed a form of acting out which was hard to take seriously – except for the fact that Sam, who is a slim five foot six, was sent to Sherborne House for committing Grievous Bodily Harm on his much taller neighbour:

It started over a banger (*firework*). I dropped it on the floor (*in the street*) – it went off, and he came running out and smacked me in the face. We started fighting between cars. I ran across the road and grabbed a pool cue from one of my mates, who was standing there watching, came back, and cracked him round the head. He used a dustbin lid as a shield. Anyway, it turned out he got a broken collar bone. He was bigger than me, about thirty years old. I got a probation order and Sherborne House.

He *(the Judge)* didn't really let me off did he? Cos if you fuck up Sherborne House you go down automatically. So for eighteen months or however long your probation order is, you have to behave.

At Sherborne House, Sam was a source of constant amusement and frustration. Despite having less money than any of the others, being apparently homeless, and persistently objecting to being there, Sam was the second most frequent and punctual group member. His language was filthy, but he was fastidiously clean about his person. His behaviour was consistently disruptive, yet with Peter, a member of his group bordering on mental illness made worse by drugs, Sam showed concern and surprising resourcefulness in helping him to behave properly. Moreover, Sam achieved this after other group members had failed. (Some were unwilling even to try, and retreated into supine daydreams when either Peter or Sam was causing trouble.)

Sam misbehaved at least as often as Peter, and never ceased complaining about what he was asked to do. Sam was wired much of the time, full of unexpressed frustration, springing out of his chair when unable to get attention, or his own way, no matter how trivial the matter. He was restless and combative, regularly interrupting the group to test the rules and regulations. On one occasion Sam threw a cup of tea (which he wasn't supposed to have) out of the first floor window and hit a woman passing by, who became decidedly irate. Sam was sufficiently ashamed to go down to apologise, but found her anger so offensive that he went back upstairs intending to squirt her with a fire extinguisher.

Sam's reading problems were a favourite excuse for his refusing to co-operate with most of the exercises. During the group on self-assessment, each member had to fill out a questionnaire listing their positive and negative qualities. Sam refused even to try.

Sam: *(defiant)* Left it blank. *(Molly threatens a warning so he starts, haltingly)* It'll take time cos it's hard for me.

Peter: 'Attitude Problem' would be a good one for him, I must say. *(This group brought them to talk about each other for the first time.)*

Sam: I'm pissed off easily – 'Bad tempered' –

Molly: What makes you angry?

Sam: *(mock ferocious)* The way you keep carrying on!

Molly: *(patiently)* Am I not being reasonable?

Sam: Four days a week, all we talk about is offending! I
    hate this worse than prison.

Peter: What's this place going to do for you?

Sam: *(shouting)* Fuck all!

Peter: *(surprising us all)* You got your freedom, Sam. You
    learned how to build a bed *(in the tech shop)*.

Sam: *(almost unable to argue with Peter of all people –
    good group dynamics)* But this group is shit!

Molly: Since you won't do the list I'll tell you what I
    think – you're kind/sensitive/friendly/moody/
    bad-tempered *(Sam interrupts, and won't let her go
    on.)*

Sam: I'm bored. That's what I am.

Peter: You're just bored cos you won't listen.

*This stopped Sam in his tracks, and left the rest of us astonished.
This was a remarkable and moving exchange – to see Peter, himself
barely able to keep his focus in the group, championing its value
to Sam.*

*Despite his insistence that he could not read, Sam showed flashes
of literacy at convenient moments. When he was given special
language tutoring on the computer, Sam seemed able to read the
instructions of the games that were part of his tuition. He played
well and quickly, swearing at the screen throughout the lesson and
virtually ignoring the tutor. She was late for one lesson and failed
to turn up altogether for another, thus feeding Sam's general sense
of grievance. On the second occasion, I stayed with him to play
pool while we waited for the tutor. When I showed myself much
less adept than he was, Sam took great care to help me improve
my game.*

*The session on race which separated blacks and whites showed
Sam at his most awkward, including his intermittent illiteracy. On
this occasion he was not the only troublemaker:*

Lenore: *(reading from a list of popular prejudices she had
    drawn up with the group)* Let's deal with 'They
    smell.'

Sam: Everyone smells. Only they go over the top. I know about two hundred in my road. The Pakistanis – *(Having been stopped previously for calling them Pakis, Sam has said the whole name, but Lenore stops him anyway, and says he's 'lumping them all together'.)*

Sam: I'm only calling them what everyone else calls them, which is what they are – Pakis, Pakistanis, what's the big deal? *(Lenore tries vainly to get through to him but he isn't close to listening. The others are on Sam's side but grow bored quickly and move in on the exchange to insist 'they all smell.')*

Joel: When you pass a Pakistani you smell curry. I lived in a block of flats where you had the smell of bad curry morning to night. Nobody else smells like that.

Sam: Pakis smell! *(Deb stops him again)* I wouldn't have come out with any of this stuff *(if you hadn't pushed us)*.

Joel: *(to Lenore and Deb)* You can't say that all Asians have greasy hair and smell of curry but most of them do. Admit it. Even if ten per cent of white people smell – they don't smell of spaghetti Bolognese.

   (The staff are frustrated. Deb announces there is no tea break, not a popular move.)

Joel: *(realising they are stuck, and smart enough to know they've gone as far as they can in one direction)* I know black people get a hard deal but they make too much of a thing out of it. They can go somewhere else and just accept that that's the way it goes here.

Deb: *(emphatically, without her usual cool)* Where can they go?

Sam stomps out to the lavatory, as does Joel, without answering. Deb tells them not to leave.

Sam: *(furious)* I don't give a fuck! It's fucking quarter to three and time for a break. You didn't tell us there wouldn't be one.

Deb: I'm telling you now.

Sam throws his chair across the room, goes to the table in the midst of the group and grabs the papers, heading for the window. Lenore asks for them back.

Sam: Stick them up your hole.
Lenore: That's going to cost you a warning. I find that very offensive.
Sam: I don't care. Give me a fucking warning. Put it in writing, I don't give a shit!

Lenore has a list of twenty facts about blacks, including surprising numbers of successful inventors and supreme court justices, war heroes, and the like. She tries to read while subjected to constant interruptions.

Sam comes back to sit down, almost quiescent, then leaps up again. He patrols the room with rolled up sheets of paper, while Stu starts singing.

When Lenore attributes the invention of the light bulb to a black person, Sam interrupts:

Sam: They changed that. It's all lies. We were taught James Watt did that.
Lenore: *(reads out)* He assisted Thomas Edison.
Joel: *(leaps up in his excitement – the first time in three weeks he's done that except to leave for break)* You shouldn't have written that – he was just an assistant! You're doing my head in.
       (Lenore reads out that Edison's black assistant really invented the light bulb, and finishes the list of black achievements.)
Sam: So what? What's that got to do with us? *(picks up the list)* They're all black! *(He reads some names surprisingly well, considering he's illiterate.)* 'First black Mayor of Battersea in 1914.' Wowee! 'First Asian MP in 1982.' They should have shot him on the spot!
Joel: You see, all these people – it proves we're not racialist.
Stu: All of you vote Labour, don't you. *(Stu does a slow handclap, and Sam joins in. Stu yawns. Johnnie and Luke stay quiet.)*

Joel: That's just the way it goes, throughout history. We
     can't change it.
Sam: We can't do anything. We're all racialist.

*They're all exhausted now. As the group ends, Joel manages a
decent exchange with Deb about the fact that school-books lack
that sort of information about black achievements. 'My mother
told me that at school,' he tells her.*

    *But as the final seconds approach Stu can't resist turning to
Molly: 'Did I annoy you, Molly? You looked annoyed.'*

*Sam's financial state preoccupied the staff almost as much as he
did himself. He came each day in the same pink T-shirt and black
jeans – somehow managing to wash them overnight. Having fallen
out with his parents, but refusing to talk about it, Sam was apparently surviving somehow, somewhere on £8 per week, most of
which went on 'fags and boxer shorts'.*

    *Notwithstanding his precarious financial and domestic con-
dition, Sam was alert and energetic if not attentive. He took full
part in the workshops and sporting activities, except those few he
thought 'too childish'. That meant he also refused to do one of
the key exercises – the cartooning of the crime that sent each
of them to Sherborne House. This was intended to show offenders
the stages leading up to the criminal act which involved choices
that could have been made differently.*

Sam: I'm not writing two-year-old's pictures. It's a
     downright fucking lib *(liberty)*.
Molly: We'll have to find some other way to talk about
     your offending.
Sam: I'm not drawing and I'm not talking about it. You
     can't make me. It's a lib.

*One afternoon at the dry ski slope known as the Becton Alps in
the deepest East End, Sam learned to ski quite well. Both he and
Peter tried to move on from the beginners' class at the bottom of
the slope to take the rope tow to the top, or at least to climb up
from the modest height at which the class had been conducted.
Despite his evident excitement, Sam was continually abusive to
the instructor and about the experience. He delivered his verdict
at the counter where he returned his ski boots:*

It was fucking boring, man, fucking shit, boring. An hour felt like seven seconds – I've had more fun when I'm asleep.

Sam resented his shortage of money intensely. When he left a girlfriend's jacket in the Sherborne House van while playing football, it was stolen. His own carelessness was evident from the fact that he had left his money belt as well. This was not stolen – an oversight that prompted Sam's contempt for the thief's stupidity! But Sam demanded darkly that Sherborne House give him £90 to replace the jacket. As the van was left unlocked, and in view of Sam's situation, the staff accepted responsibility. It took many weeks to obtain the money, during which Sam grew increasingly threatening about what he would do to the staff and, like Stan with his dole money, that he would burn down Sherborne House if it didn't arrive. Sam's need was genuine, but he told me with quiet amusement that the jacket had cost only £30, and he regretted not asking for even more. On another occasion Sam told me about playing cards with a fellow lodger who lost £300 to him.

All day and all night, he never won a fucking game. I gave it back to him ninety-nine per cent but I let him squirm.

This reflected both Sam's hidden competitiveness and still further hidden compassion, in the light of his poverty. Despite staff efforts to extract more from the DSS, they had to resort to 'the poor box' and a small special grant from a private foundation to get Sam £100 to buy another set of clothes, which by condition of the grant had to be second-hand.

During Project Week, Sam came on the sailing trip with very little money and only the clothes he stood up in. But he would not accept the loan of my jersey. At the last moment, he was given another special grant of £23 in pocket money by the probation service.

Most of it went on the first night in the fruit machines of Ramsgate. He stood as if hypnotised, pouring coins into the machine, while row after row of video games and one-armed bandits let loose a cacophony of gunshots, bells, and explosions against a background of pulsing rock music. In this atmosphere of aural violence, Sam looked like a lost soul in an outer circle of Dante's Inferno. When I told Sam I didn't understand the variables of fruit machines, he said ruefully:

I wish I didn't. Johnnie *(who was nearby, expertly playing two machines at once)* thinks he's not addicted but I really am. After every burglary it's straight to the arcade. I stop when I run out of money. Simple as.

On the voyage itself, Sam was a comic nightmare, refusing to leave his bunk at the appointed times of his duties. As we set out across the Channel, Sam decided he'd been unfairly singled out for early turns. He cursed anyone who asked him to do anything with his ferocious but somehow charming scowl. He threatened to leave the boat as soon as we reached the other side.

Onshore in Ostend and Dunquerque, everything we saw was 'fucking shit. Belgium's shit. France is shit.' But Sam was fascinated as well by the comfort, the cleanliness, the quality of the food and drink. He tagged along cheerfully with the others, who were a year older and had more money. Sam was not as expert as they were on the nuances of house music or trainers, but they did not tease or reject him as they might easily have done. Joel aptly and affectionately called him 'Grumpy' from Snow White and the Seven Dwarfs.

In the marathon hunt for Johnnie's perfect jacket and jeans, Sam handled his own poverty gracefully – stealing only a cheap pair of sunglasses:

I had plenty of chances to nick things in fucking Belgium. I didn't do it. I think it's OK to steal at home, but not in someone else's country. Simple as. Anyway I don't fancy doing time in foreign jails.

His complaints were like Eeyore's, a form of expression that had little to do with reality. Sometimes they meant the exact opposite, as though his vocabulary could not stretch beyond his lexicon of abuse. As we strode down Dunquerque's main street, he said, 'God, this place is fucking rubbish. I really slept well!' He loved steering, though he refused to do it when sulking. At one point when we were heading into a sunset, he said, 'Go on and fuck off in, sun!'

By the end of the voyage, it became a standing joke that Sam's consistent fury meant he had enjoyed himself hugely. On the last night, Sam, Johnnie and I stayed on board, while the others went ashore at Sheppey for a drink. Johnnie complained he wanted one too. Sam responded angrily:

You don't need a fucking drink! I didn't have no fucking drink last night and was happy as hell!

It was the only such admission I heard in his ten weeks at Sherborne House.

In the final week, Sam was presented with the staff assessment of his performance. It felt to me like the first time anyone in authority had taken the trouble to communicate with him successfully.

His probation officer wasn't there – more grounds for complaint. He saw Molly, one of his group leaders, alone. Shown the staff meeting notes about him written on the pages of a flip chart, Sam laughed at the handwriting. He refused to read, claiming he couldn't. Molly was not so sure about that but chose not to make an issue of it. She read it to him:

Molly: 1. Can be childish.

Sam: Who wrote that? *(chuckled, then yawned, then suddenly objected to 'childish')* Just cos I don't like going to groups and talk about the same things.

Molly: You work hard in groups.

Sam: *(surprised by the compliment, but still wanting to complain)* You ain't got no choice. Just groups and more groups.

Molly: *(reading)* 2. Setting self up for failure. 3. Can listen, learn. 4. Can do good work. 5. Lacks confidence. 6. Sees value of education.

Sam: *(having listened in silence)* Ain't pleased with none of it.

Molly: *(trapping him, with a smile)* You say unpleasant things about the groups but yet you choose to work, and you've got the most *(attendance)* points.

Sam: *(wouldn't have it)* I'm just storing up points so I can bugger off at the end! Simple as.

Molly: You've got more at stake here than you want to say.

Sam: *(wriggling now – it was fascinating to watch him try to resist her proof of his achievement)* I just want to say something rude like I said to the other lady.

Molly: Will it happen again? Can you control it?

Sam: *(truthfully)* Not really. Just like with the Old Bill. *(They were now dealing with the stuff he needed to hear.)*

Molly: That's the main way you let yourself down, not being in control.

Molly went on to stress Sam's positive points: that he worked well in art, and in the tech workshop, listening and learning – but sometimes he didn't want to know. Sam agreed.

Molly: *(gaining on him)* You've got the ability and the choice whether you use it.
Sam: *(still holding out)* I just come in because I can't go get work in these clothes.
Molly: *(gently)* But six others in this group can't get it together to do that. Too difficult for them.
Sam: Too difficult? It's been difficult for me for the past year and a half!
Molly: *(serving for the match)* Exactly – can you give yourself credit?
Sam: *(purposely misunderstanding)* No, cos I'll just end up in debt.
Molly: What about the future?
Sam: It takes care of itself.

This view is nearly universal among young offenders, even those with small children. It is one of the defining differences between them and much of the rest of society.

Molly: Do you believe that – that you have no choice?
Sam: I can't just walk into a shop and say 'gissa job!' To get work you need money to travel, for clothes.
Molly: But you got here, which shows you can value it.
Sam: *(still not having it)* What if I didn't? I'd just go inside. I don't want to go in for eighteen months!
Molly: *(reading from the notes)* Does 'lack of confidence' sound like you?
Sam: *(sourly)* I ain't got confidence in nothing.
Molly: Have you any confidence in yourself? *(Sam sighs)* How about education?
Sam: What's education nowadays? *(with contempt)* Just so I can read a newspaper.
Molly: *(smiling)* I suspect you read a newspaper already.

> Look at the exercise we did called Five Facts About
> Me – you read that!
Sam: *(insisting now)* Only with help.
Molly: But you did it.
Sam: Only with her help!

Molly handed Sam his typewritten report – and he actually read it, in silence. Molly offered to read it to him, but Sam declined and put it in his pocket. He agreed to give his probation officer her copy in the evening. Molly then read the results of an exercise in which cards describing positive and negative qualities were awarded by group members to the person they thought most deserved them. Sam had received many complimentary cards.

> Molly: 'Flexible/Shown ability to learn/Goes for it'. They
>   think you've got a lot going for you.
> Sam: *(suddenly almost weeping)* Let them stand in my
>   fucking shoes and see how little I got going for me! I
>   got fuck all going for me!
> Molly: I think you've got a lot more qualities than you
>   allow yourself to recognise by your childish
>   manner. Any goals?
> Sam: Just the way I dress.
> Molly: Anything else?
> Sam: Yeah. Can I go?

The encounter exposed Sam's feelings and worries, without his having formally engaged in any dialogue about his obvious vulnerability, and his genuine inability to find a way to show it comfortably. He knew he was safe with Molly, but needed to give in to his pleasure at being at Sherborne House in order to allow himself to admit that to himself.

When I asked him, one year later, Sam's verdict was characteristically curt and dismissive:

Sherborne House was alright. I made a bed. Somebody cracked it, and one of the woodwork men glued it together.

In his workshop project during the ten weeks, Sam had made a simple but well-crafted large pine double bed. It was mysteriously broken the night before the last day when all the work is put on exhibition for the final visits of the probation officers. No one

could discover who had damaged it or why, though many suspected Sam might have done it himself in one of his rages – perhaps
this time against having to leave. Astonishingly, Sam took the
damage almost in his stride. Not so his other crafts project: he
had been making a set of moulded clay chess pieces and a board
– an unusual project for someone who described himself as stupid.
By the end of the programme, none of the group members quite
finished their pottery, and so were not allowed to take them home.
Sam's reaction was special: he destroyed his chess men with a
hammer, and stabbed the board he had made with a knife.

Such a final gesture might seem to give the lie to the staff conclusion that Sam had matured while at Sherborne House. But
in spite of his antic performance, there were signs of a growing
commitment: his punctuality, and helpfulness to Peter, and his
behaviour on the day out in the country near the end of the programme. This last was meant to be a walk by the sea, replacing a
sailing lesson that could not be arranged. The group – including
Sam – protested about the change, and strongly objected to the
walk – 'What's the fucking point of a fucking walk in the
country?'- but when they arrived, Sam set off alone along the cliffs
at a pace which left the probation officers behind, while the rest
of the group hitched a ride to the pub.

Sam left Sherborne House with a long way to go. But in our
conversation one year later, Sam confirmed the impression that he
was becoming his own man in a positive way. His ability to resist
being drawn into the orbit of the others engaged in crime and
drugs showed remarkable strength of character.

I steered clear of the illegal stuff going on (at Sherborne House).
I heard all about it, but didn't get involved. I liked most the holiday. That was alright. I hated that ginger haired guy,* he was an
idiot, he came out with enough stories about drugs. He ain't got
no will-power to stop taking all that stuff. Cocaine is harder to
stop than thieving. But I tried it and let it drop. People also say
'Once a thief, always a thief,' but that's not true.

When I was working, I didn't burgle. I kept out of the way of
my mates. As long as I have clothes on my back and money in my
pocket, I don't thieve. Simple as.

Our interview was taking place in a coffee bar around the corner

* Joel. See Chapter Four.

from Bow Street Magistrates' Court. Sam was being tried for peddling hot dogs without a licence – for the fourth time at least. On the latest occasion, he was so fed up with being hassled by the police, he shoved the hot dog trolley onto the foot of one of the plain clothes detectives trying to arrest him. He was taken back to the station, and the knife which he used to cut the hot dogs was found in his back pocket. So he was also charged with carrying an offensive weapon – the most serious of the charges.

In court, the magistrate was so impatient with the police for bringing this charge, he threw out the whole case against Sam. But he warned Sam that if he failed to pay his outstanding fines soon, he was looking at custody.

Sam realised he had escaped lightly, but resented the fines as much as ever. The prospects of finding the money to pay something towards them looked bleak. He could not carry on selling hot dogs – the police would keep the stand for weeks, and the owner insisted on it being used in Trafalgar Square. Without his hot dog job, all Sam had was his modest dole. Like so many youngsters on the edge of poverty, for Sam crime does pay. It is the only available source of sufficient income, especially for those under eighteen.

I was nineteen in September. First I was pissed off at getting older! But it's not that bad. Going down the pub's easier and so is getting money. Before I turned eighteen, I weren't getting no money from the dole cos I couldn't go out to work – because I was at Sherborne House! So they wouldn't give me no money.

This was not a mistake: it was policy. In 1987, the government – more specifically, the Department of Social Security under John Major – stopped the dole for sixteen and seventeen year-olds not living at home or registered with an employment training scheme. The theory was that this would keep youngsters at home longer, under their parents' watchful eye and presumed good influence. Unfortunately for those like Sam who fall out with their parents and leave home, this virtually forces them into crime, once they assess the options open to them. But when the Home Office, a different government department, sent them to Sherborne House to stop offending, they were deemed 'unavailable for employment' and were 'punished' accordingly by the Department of Employment, and the Department of Social Security. Despite its serious training in wood and metalwork – and the shortage of such training places nationally – the Sherborne House programme was not

*considered official training by the Department of Employment, so
all the participants lost the small extra payment.* Until he was
eighteen, Sam received the princely sum of £8 a week while living
on his own.*

I had to pay £5 a week rent and that left me with £3. My
washing comes to £20 every two weeks. A wash is £2.70 now,
and there's the spin drying as well. My probation officer got me
some money from a trust fund, about a hundred pounds. Out of
that I had to get clothes, trainers, a toothbrush, things like that.
The money was soon gone.

So I was nicking videos, tellys, hi-fis, car stereos. Got my money
that way. The probation office weren't going to give me any
money, only for fares, so I went out thieving again. I got caught,
so I stopped. Then I turned eighteen, and started getting dole
money *(£28 per week, paid fortnightly).* When I left Sherborne
House it took me six weeks before I got any money again, so I
just carried on doing it *(thieving).* Simple as.

But I wanted to get out of that life so I went up to Manchester
for a while.

*This itself seemed a sign of maturity. Although homeless,
estranged from his family, and living on a pittance, Sam had managed to establish a place for himself in a house in Manchester, while
still at Sherborne House. He told me he had a job waiting for him
on a building site. A few weeks later I found the probation officer in
Manchester who had taken over his case, and rang her to see how
Sam was doing. She was at a loss to tell me. He'd been into her office,
as required by his probation order, but was accompanied by 'strange
people' – a middle-aged overweight woman pushing a trolley full of
bags, who looked as though she slept rough, and several other older
people who also looked to the probation officer like vagrants. Sam
told her he was 'alright', but could not find work. She liked him on
first impression but did not know what to make of his entourage.
Six months later, having caught up with Sam at court, I asked him
about his time in Manchester:*

I was sharing a squat. Anyone who wanted to could sleep there.

---

* In 1992, after an extended battle that went all the way to Downing Street
with no success, Sherborne House made an agreement to become a sub-contracted
training centre to render the group members eligible for the slightly higher dole
given to young people on certified training schemes.

There was no work, not even on a building site. I looked everywhere. Came back South cos they were all doing crack, so I got out of it. I didn't want to get involved. In London, I started doing the hot-dogs *(selling them from a stand in Trafalgar Square until 3am)*. As I was working, I stopped thieving. I was alright. On a Monday I was taking home £60, Thursday, Friday and Saturday I was taking home between £150 and £200. But you're paying out in fines with your other hand, and hot-dogs are not doing so well now. Some of the blokes have given up cos they're not making enough money.

I enjoy working, it's much better than being on the dole, I ain't stuck indoors. But it's like the Old Bill don't want me to do nothing straight. If they stopped nicking the hot dogs, they'd have to do some real coppering – nicking the big-time drug dealers, things like that.

Thieving started with my mates taking money out of phone boxes when I was eight – with two other kids, one younger, one older. I first got caught when I was ten. The old style telephone boxes; then car stereos, with match sticks down each side to push a spring or just a screwdriver. We used spark plugs to break the window. We used to sell them to minicab offices. They'd always pay £25 for one, even a cheap model. Can get eighty or even a one-er *(£100)* if you're lucky.

I used to spend it all in one day on the fruit machines. One thing led to another, I started doing houses: smash the window, get in, take what you want. Wear an old pair of trainers, put socks over them. Put something over the glass, smash it round the back, and crawl through. Got caught by the Old Bill. I was under surveillance. Me and my mates were doing three a night. One night the Old Bill followed us. They know me round my way.

For all his energy and occasional violence, Sam is normally quite soft-spoken. But on the subject of the police, he was suddenly enraged. Unlike the others in the group, Sam's feelings are not just about the unpleasant things that have happened to him at the hands of the police.

If it was down to me I'd set them all on fire. I'd put them in so much pain they'd never forget it. I just can't stand them cos they think they're it. While they're in uniform they think they can do anything they want – go into shops, get what they want. They don't have to pay for it sometimes and they get away with it.

Like what happened to those three black guys down Holloway

Road *(In 1984 a van load of officers stopped in the Holloway Road in North London, beat up five teenagers and drove off. The subsequent cover-up took two years to undo. It was extraordinary that it had made such an impression on Sam, as it had all happened six years previously to other youngsters. Sam would have been twelve at the time.)* A couple of coppers got thrown in jail; all that happened to the others was that they were thrown out of the force. Any ordinary person does that they're banged up inside for two or three years. That's what pisses me off about the Old Bill, they get away with too much.

I been beaten up in front of my Mum. I got nicked for smoking – just a cigarette. These two coppers wanted to be smart. They were having a go at my mates for playing football. I was indoors. My Mum said to smoke indoors, I said 'No, I'm nearly sixteen' so I went out. One of the coppers was black, and when he saw me walking past he said, 'Put that fag out you white cunt.' I said, 'You put it out you black shit.' He said 'You put it out, you cunt.' Anyway, this carried on and then four of them put me in the back of the van. There were punches and kicks and my Mum could see the van shaking. She went down to the station to make a complaint but in the end they said they'd drop the charges for smoking, so I said 'fair enough', and walked out.

Don't carry a knife, and I've never done a mugging in my life or aggravated burglary. People who put another person's life in jeopardy are idiots. When you do a burglary you make sure there's no one in the house. You ring the bell, and if there's no one in, you do it. If they come down the stairs you just ask for someone, and try another house that looks empty. Simple as.

I'm not jealous. I wouldn't want my family to have had more money cos then you're a snob. People with more money think they're better than everyone else.

In the anonymity of the coffee bar, Sam talked about his childhood and his home in a way he had not at any point in the ten weeks at Sherborne House.

Didn't get much schooling, not hardly at all, I was expelled at thirteen. The school sent me to see a psychiatrist to see what was wrong with me, cos I kept bunking off, kept thieving, kept throwing chairs, kept throwing tables.

I started fighting when I was at primary school. I'd go up and smack someone just for looking at me. Not cos I'm short. I'm glad

I was small, got through more holes didn't I? *(If you're)* Taller you can't do nothing.

My parents couldn't do anything. They gave me money but I kept thieving. Nothing would've made a difference to the way I am. Nothing. My Mum and Dad caught me smoking, kicked shit out of me. Every time the police came round my uncle used to boff me too. It didn't make no difference, I just carried on.

My Dad's on the dole now. My brothers and sisters, they're all alright. My little brother's doing A-levels. I don't know why they're different from me. I don't know. I never had any patience at school. I had private tuition, but I didn't turn up for that either. I don't need school. *(contemptuously)* All it gives you is A-levels.

A few months after seeing Sam in the coffee bar, I went to find out how the court cases had gone. First I traced him to a squat in Finsbury Park. The house was slowly being ripped to pieces, but at least it was still dry. A boozy middle-aged man told me Sam was at work selling hot dogs in Trafalgar Square again. When it became clear I was not the police, his girl came to the door, a pretty blonde who looked about fifteen, and was very, very thin. She told me Sam was alright but she worried about him doing this work. Also, they had to leave the squat in a couple of days and had no idea where they would live.

A few weeks later, I went to Sam's parents' house. I was a bit apprehensive because Sam had been so fierce about refusing to discuss them, or why he had left home so suddenly. They lived in an old terrace house facing a railway wall in the anonymous urban sprawl of North East London – a nondescript mix of corner shops, factories and workshops, pubs and rows of terraced houses and council housing estates in various states of repair. Sam's father appeared at the door looking grizzled, restraining a fierce black mongrel keen to attack me. In an old sweatshirt and unshaven, he looked down and out but explained he works as a welder (Sam had said he was on the dole). When he spoke, his delicate round glasses and gentle manner gave him an almost scholarly air that belied the toughness of his appearance. He was a far cry from the belligerent image conjured up by Sam's hints.

The gentleness of Sam's father was not the only surprise. He currently supported no less than six teenagers in his narrow three-storey house. That number now included both Sam and his girl. The previous week, Sam had returned home – a matter his father took in his stride. He observed with benign resignation that the house was always full of children:

I raised my own five plus three others abandoned by cousins or friends. They're all over fifteen now. Funny thing is only Sam has been in trouble with the law. Don't know why. We never could explain it.

He don't think he's clever but Sam's ingenious about money. When there was a bus strike, he went to the local minicab office, persuaded them to give him a remote receiver, and hailed people outside the tube station to provide them with cabs. He got 50p for each customer. Another time he worked in the supermarket – got to know where everything was, then stood by the door and offered to do the shopping for old ladies – 'Give me your list,' he'd say, 'and it'll be done in no time.' The headmistress spotted him and was amazed. She told the school the next day, 'You all know Sam as a terror, but I saw him helping old ladies.' But he thought she was 'stupid'. To Sam, it was just a smart way of earning bread.

I never knew he was into crime until he got arrested. If I had, I'd have removed his head from his shoulders. But once he went to court, I didn't punish him. Not fair – double jeopardy. They sent him to an attendance centre for twenty-four hours – it only meant playing ping pong and football for two hours every Saturday. Not far either, just down the road.

It still took him eighteen months to clear that sentence! There was always some reason why he didn't go. I think it's ridiculous – nobody chased him up or threatened to take him back to court.

I think if he'd gone to prison straight away for first offence he'd have stopped cold. As it was, I put him on a curfew, had to be in by 10.30pm and all that. But it seems he just did his crimes earlier in the day.

The latest trouble he's in makes no sense. I went down to Trafalgar Square to see why he was getting nicked all the time. I saw the police just sitting there waiting for drivers to go up the Buses Only lane after the coppers had folded the edges of the sign so no one could read it. Sam's the same – he's an easy prey for the police to catch him just standing there selling hot dogs. He's not doing anything wrong, just trying to earn a crust. There's no legal way for him to go straight – he's got to stay on the dole and he's trying to pick up what else he can. He only gets £28 a week in any case – by the time he pays his fines he got nothing left. What do they expect him to do, to live on? And how's he going to pay his poll tax?

A year ago I didn't know where he was or what he's up to. I knew he went to Sherborne House but nothing more than that. I didn't know he went sailing to France. He can't read. I think that's his problem. He had a hard time at school cos he wouldn't learn.

Sam is in a situation common to many young people: he is broke, has no marketable skills, and can barely read. Yet he is resourceful and intelligent, and actually wants to avoid crime. His experience of Sherborne House seems to have helped him reach that conclusion. In what could be permanent limbo, many people in Sam's situation turn to drugs.

This, of course, leads them back to crime. But in the coffee bar, one year after his time at Sherborne House, Sam was sure he wanted to steer clear of hard drugs. He was less clear about crime because of his predicament, not the excitement.

I'm not into drugs: just puff, trips, that's about it. When I was tripping I got in trouble with three geezers. I had a fight with them. I hit them with a pole with a nail in it.

If I went out thieving now I'd do it on my own, so that I wouldn't have to look out for anyone. Don't trust no one.

But if I was in trouble I'd turn to my Mum. I think about the money, only the money. I got nothing else to think about. Thinking about it like we did at Sherborne House does make you more careful. But if you're in a bad mood, you just want the money straight in your hand – you just go out and do it.

Sam knows if he is caught again, he will certainly go to prison. Yet prison seems less of a deterrent than simply fuel for general grievance about his situation. Two years earlier while still seventeen, Sam went to prison on remand awaiting trial for burglary and assault. He spent time in Feltham Young Offenders' Institution, a modern youth detention centre where many young people have committed suicide, and in Brixton, one of the worst of the Victorian prisons still in use.

Prison is like a terrible fucking holiday camp. All you're doing is sleeping, eating, playing cards, going out in the yard for a couple of hours. You got clothes, hot water, you got everything you need apart from cigarettes, and you can get those in. In Brixton, I didn't shit in front of anyone. I waited till we were let out. First thing I said to the other guy: no shitting in the cell. It's alright if you keep yourself to yourself.

All people talk about is getting out, getting some bloody money. Working, thieving, going on the dole. After you get out, it can take weeks for the dole money to come. There ain't nothing good to say about prison. Prison don't stop people, one of my mates is in and out all the time. He comes out, there's no work so he thinks, 'fuck it,' and starts thieving again.

I've been looking for a job for a year. No one will take me cos I got a record. I even tried warehousing. I was alright with the hot dogs and now that's out.

My girl and I are getting on alright. I'm not worried about getting her pregnant: if she does, she does. I don't like condoms. Might as well put a plastic bag over me. She's on the pill anyway. I've known her for about six months. She doesn't like me going out thieving. She'd rather be skint.

Now I'm stuck home, my reading has caught up a little bit. Watching TV, reading the papers. I was going to go to college, one of my friend's Mum's got it all sorted out for me. And then I thought, 'fuck it, there's no jobs. If you've got no qualifications you can't get a job and if you've got too many you can't.' If it comes down to reading a book I can't be bothered.

It feels better when you're not thieving, a lot better. I can walk down the street, see a woman I know and say hello to her, knowing I haven't just done her house over.

But how am I to pay my fucking poll tax and my fines? If I see that fucking copper again that stopped me doing hot dogs, I'll punch that four-eyed git in the mouth. Simple as.

Sam's problem seems simple enough: he wants work, needs money, can't find either and so is tempted to steal. But at another level, his experience exemplifies the debate about the welfare state, and notions of good and evil in relation to crime and parental responsibility. Can we argue that the state owes Sam a living? He is able-bodied and willing to work but has limitations on what he can do. He has committed crimes against people and property – even when at Sherborne House. Wrong as this was, it would be hard to describe him as evil. He did neither for sadistic or arbitrary reasons: he has tried to live on tiny amounts of dole while failing to find a job. He now wishes to put crime behind him. His own personality is one of his strengths and handicaps: he has an unselfconscious charm that makes people like him, but a temper that may yet land him back in trouble. He has committed destructive acts, but is capable of kindness, compassion and has a clear sense of right and wrong. Sam wants to do what he and his parents think is right but cannot see how to manage his life to achieve it. He is rightly frustrated. With so many unemployed, how can Sam expect to win jobs against better trained competitors without a criminal record?

What could have been done to keep Sam out of crime? He does not fit the pattern of a broken home: his father is clearly a kind and generous man who even raised children from other damaged households. Both his parents and his uncle were strict with him, and by Sam's own admission clearly disapprove of his behaviour. None of his many brothers and sisters have been down the same route.

Perhaps his school might have given him more support to break through his reading difficulties. But such tasks make unequal demands on teachers' time when schools are already overcrowded and overworked to achieve their normal targets. Boys with behaviour and learning problems like Sam are all too easily lost at school because they are so disruptive and demanding. But allocating blame to his teachers or parents, and to Sam himself seems far too simplistic. Having watched him in a variety of situations for ten weeks, I know he is bright, resourceful, and in his own way, both modest and truthful. After so many years of failure in the system, his only achievements have been criminal. Now that he's committed to going straight, Sam needs both personal and professional support to make something of his life. He had both, briefly, at Sherborne House. He may be ready to receive the former from his parents, but the latter is proving very hard to find. Because he cannot read and has no job, Sam's going to waste.

Few of us rely only on formal channels as we strive to get on in the world. More often in our lives we are helped by an informal contact: a friend providing perhaps a holiday job, or a meeting with an influential person that could open doors to other things. For Sam and boys like him, there is no equivalent network, particularly in a time of recession. His only grapevine is one of crime: the only way he knows to get past closed doors is to climb in the window.

But, at last report, Sam and his girlfriend have moved out of his family house into a series of bedsitters, and are keeping out of trouble while he looks for a legal job. How long he can sustain this must depend on his luck at finding something rewarding to do before his temper and frustration overtake him.

CHAPTER SIX

SUNNY

Nobody tells me what to do

Sunny (short for Sunil) is nineteen, slim to the point of seeming undernourished. Brown-skinned, with a thin black moustache and beard, he looks Asian, but acts black in speech, dress, and physical mannerisms. In fact, he's from Mauritius. About five-foot eight, his posture makes him look smaller. He's not hunched but appears to be holding himself back from standing where he is, as if he had a coat hanger in his shirt and had been hung on a hook. He looks as though he expects to be punched in the chest at any moment. This is not surprising, since he lives in fear of being beaten up. After a disastrous home life which ended up with him obliged to live in London instead of Mauritius, Sunny spent his teenage years in care in children's homes.

The last one he lived in was Ebony House in South London, a special unit for young people from eight to eighteen who are in difficulty. While at Sherborne House, Sunny seemed to be under threat – or worse – from people still living there. The day he arrived at Sherborne House, he was in some pain. He claimed to have dropped weights on his chest accidentally, but the staff believed Sunny had been beaten up and was too frightened to report it.

Sunny's furtive air and quick smile did not inspire confidence in me. But they were no barrier to his winning the support and affection of Lenore and Deb, the probation officers who ran his group at Sherborne House. They worried about his unstable domestic situation, and realised much of his mannerisms and awkwardness in the groups stemmed from a desire to be accepted as black. I asked him about it in our interview a year later:

I look Indian, but actually I'm not. I am black.

People whom I move around with, they are black, I don't hang round with white people at all. Sometimes they might call me 'coolie'. People that knows me treat me like a 'brother'. But there are a couple of people in here who see me and say 'nah, stop talking like a black man' and call me names, but then a friend step in and said, 'Allow the youth, I know where he's coming from,' so from there on they just called me 'apache', a little nickname.

Sunny's concern to be black played itself out at Sherborne House in a stylised way: his hair was cut close, his jeans rolled up, and the laces of his shoes were undone with the tongues hanging out as was de rigueur *on the streets. His accent was slurred and his speech pattern abrupt and bouncy with black argot. He affected the slightly hooded look that some black youths wear when moving in public. But Sunny had his own qualities – nervous energy, darting eyes, and a stutter – plus a paranoid streak that made him anything but cool.*

This internal conflict expressed itself constantly in his perform-ance at Sherborne House. Sunny wanted to be liked both by the staff and his black peer group. This led him into different roles, depending on the audience. Alone with the staff and seeking their help, he was vulnerable and demanding. In the groups he was tough, tricky, and unwilling to be drawn – hoping to win approval from the others by his guarded sarcasm and criminal experience. This was evident in the session when Sunny had to discuss his criminal record:

I been doing burglaries since I was seven, didn't get caught. I was first caught at ten. Sometimes on me own, sometimes with mates. I used to go into a shop fucking stoned out of my mind and take what-ever I wanted. I remember I robbed a woman of her handbag, and I fucking got caught and was sent to a Detention Centre in West London – the youngest person ever to go in there. Course everyone in there was stealing things, everyone. They'd search the whole place, and sometimes we'd get caught, sometimes not. Sometimes the workers there spoke up for me in court. But I got beaten too, and then your feelings start. The guy that hit me was going to get shot.

I don't remember how many burglaries I did – I was caning, doing it every day. I went to court at the age of ten. *(laughs)* There are a lot more offences I was done for than are listed on my record. Not just theft, forging too.

Burglary – when I first moved to Ebony House in Streatham, everyone else was doing it, and they just pulled me into it. That was the way of making money. Going into someone's house and coming out with four or five hundred pound. So I just got used to it. From there I started doing it by myself. Sometimes every night. Just walk around the area, and the first window you see that's open, just fly into it. I'm skinny, I can fit into anything.

Sometimes the people was upstairs sleeping. But I don't go in for nastiness, like shitting in people's bed, or messing up their house. I wouldn't do that. As far as I'm concerned people like that just leave more evidence for the police. I just used to take the telly and video or whatever was there and then I'm out, that's it. Don't bother going for anything else. If you take your time things start going wrong.

You just pick the TV and video and run. I can run – I just pretended there was a pit bull behind me, so then you have to run. More times than not I was stoned out of my head, so I was more hyper, you know? It was only once I dropped the TV. Take it round the corner, leave it there maybe with my dog, get a cab, and take it back home. The driver knew what was going on but never got a cut cos I paid him, but on occasion I'd sell something to him.

Like several other black youths in the group, Sunny enjoyed a certain amusement at the white people who bought his stolen goods. Videos and stereos exchange hands at pubs – or are just a form of 'shopping' as one group member called his burglaries. Watches, antiques and jewellery were often bought by seemingly respectable people, including professionals. They, of course, sustain the market for burglary.

There's enough people out there looking for a little bargain. Any time they see me, I say 'Yeh, just give me a phone call' then they come down and pick it up. Everyone was doing the same thing. There were enough crooks around. I used to take it round to this man's house, leave the telly, get someone to pick it up, tell them to leave the money, and then go and get the cash. You won't believe it but he was a nice little businessman as well, a little yuppie. He knew me from ages, and the people I was hanging around with, so he couldn't do nothing. Even if he did try a skank *(a rip-off)* or anything funny he knew what would happen. So he was wise, he knew what was good for him *(laughing slyly)*. Sometimes I'd give him a couple of spliffs to smoke.

You might say I'm racist, but since I got put into care I didn't seem too fond of white people, I guess the way they was treating me, telling me to 'do this, do that', I just went off them completely.

His general recalcitrance reached its nadir during the rock climbing trip in the second week. Among the sports in the programme, it brought out the best and worst in the group. Some leapt up the crevices like gazelles, helping others – like me – who were frightened. Sunny proclaimed himself 'terrified of heights' long before we went, and when forced to come, resolved to resist every step of the journey. His ability to project hostility was on display in a host of small ways.

The trip began with Sunny insisting on riding at the back of the van with the rear doors open – which was both illegal and dangerous. He shut them under threat of a warning, and then reopened them from time to time as we drove. When we arrived after an hour's journey into Surrey, Sunny gave Lenore, who was driving, instructions about parking that led her to bump the van – much to his and the others' amusement. When we disembarked, Sunny was the only one of the group to throw his tin of Coca-Cola into a hedgerow.

The first ledge we climbed was not very high, but to those of us with a fear of heights it seemed quite a challenge. Sunny refused even to try it despite entreaties, cajoling, and finally the threat of a warning. 'You can't make me' was his final verdict. Then, as we all moved on, we looked back to see Sunny scamper up the ledge. I asked him why he had made such a fuss. 'When I want to do something I do it. When I don't I don't.' He was furtive even about his achievements.

During the third week of the programme at Sherborne House, Sunny was arrested on his way one morning for allegedly stealing a whole box of tinned tomatoes, an accusation he emphatically denied. At the end of the day, the staff meeting was interrupted by Sunny bursting into the staff room, normally off limits to group members. He was bustled out into the canteen sympathetically by Lenore and Deb. He was very upset; his flat had been burgled again, and the door smashed in. He had put an iron bar on the door to protect it, and taken his pit bull to his uncle's. He was shaking and angry:

I know who's done it. I don't think it's racial because there are other Asians in the house and they weren't done. It's dead easy to get into the house. (*emphatically*) I don't want to report it to the police. The council's fed up. They said it was the last door they'd fix. It's not my fault. I need a different flat but my probation officer won't apply to the council.

Lenore and Deb sympathised, and tried to clarify his movements the next day. This involved yet another problem – going to court to renegotiate his outstanding fines, a process that needs repeating if cases are transferred from one court to another. Lenore and Deb were keen Sunny should devise his day to include being at Sherborne House to work in the group, but this made Sunny feel more paranoid rather than helped.

I can't just sit around in that room and have everyone know my business. Like when you said in the group that my flat was robbed. (He was too edgy to stay.) I gotta make a move.

After Sunny left, the two women discussed their concern for him: 'He's trying really hard. He's done what we asked. We said come and talk to us and he came.' I agreed that his arrest for stealing a large box of food on the way to Sherborne House seemed pretty absurd. The police had only the description of 'a brown-skinned youth in jeans and trainers', hardly enough to nail Sunny, who would have had to dispose of the carton of tinned tomatoes before he reached the building. On the other hand, he did not live that far away. According to Lenore and Deb, local police hassled young people around the area, and were particularly unsympathetic to what they saw as the soft treatment given to their most frequent customers by Sherborne House. The staff had made an effort to draw local police into the work but the police officers who came supported the young offenders' views on the need to avenge insults and return violence with violence, so they were asked to leave.

Yet Sunny's manner inspired suspicions in me which neither Deb nor Lenore seem to share. They explained his paranoia: 'If other people know he's been burgled it again makes him different from them, and he wants to be one of them. But it's good he's starting to trust us.'

Sunny's performance in the workshop was characteristically complicated. He decided to make himself some iron gates to protect his flat. But for the first few weeks he was restless and unfocused, frequently moving around the workshop to turn up the radio or change the tape, and asking the instructors to do much of his work. When they refused, he complained. Then as the course neared its end, Sunny suddenly panicked that the gates might not be finished. He asked for extra workshop sessions during lunch or instead of other groups. When these were refused, he again felt hard done by.

Sunny was in daily trouble with the staff for refusing to co-operate with the rules of Sherborne House. But he also sought their help for

*a stream of outside problems ranging from charges of theft
and non-payment of fines to his fears of burglary and violence.*

*Torn between wanting to win sympathy and approval and keep-
ing his personal life hidden, Sunny bore a continuing sense that
others were conspiring against him. Lenore and Deb accepted his
view that the DSS, the electricity board, the housing authority, and
his aggressive neighbours all gave him an unnecessarily hard time,
and that his own probation officer should be doing more about it.*

*Both Lenore and Deb thought Sunny was simply not receiving
the service he deserved. When they rang his field probation officer,
she rejected their pressure and took a different view of Sunny as
lazy, manipulative, and determined to make himself into a victim.
This only reinforced the Sherborne House POs' determination to
help him. They were now so persuaded of his probation officer's
'negligence' they even contemplated complaining to her superior.
They might even ask that she be taken off his case – a request
rarely and not lightly made.*

*But, near the end of the course, Sunny stretched their loyalty to
the limit when he went off with Joel during a photography session,
taking the two expensive Sherborne House cameras with them.
They returned late without the cameras, and claimed to have been
mugged by a group of young blacks. The next day, when Sunny
smoothly called the police from the office – without his usual
stutter – most of the staff accepted his version as honest. One year
later, I pressed him for the truth:*

That never had anything to do with me. *(still laughing)* I don't
know what happened. A couple of my friends came down, and
they saw Joel and set on him. I couldn't do nothing about it.

I confronted him with Joel's version * – that it happened in his
flat, not the street, and with the obvious suspicion that Sunny had
set the whole thing up for a cut. In the safety of prison, he didn't
bother to deny it further:*

Yeh. That's how it worked out, near enough to that. *(smiling)*
I got a cut.

*At Sherborne House, as the weeks passed, Sunny skated as close
to dismissal as anyone in the two groups. Caught smoking cannabis
by one of the staff, he not only denied it, but loudly objected to Jack,
the Senior Probation Officer, following him out of the building to*

---

* See Chapter Four for Joel's version.

prove he was doing it. Like most offenders, Sunny had a highly developed sense of morality in regard to how he was treated by others, but rather less precise values about his own behaviour. It even extended to stealing from one of his fellow group members. Stu, who happened to be white, was selling forged £20 notes for £10 each to others on the programme. Sunny promised him drugs instead of cash, which led to the rumour he was dealing. Talking to me later, Sunny maintained a characteristically amoral position:

(laughing) At Sherborne House I wasn't dealing, I was just sitting down smoking (grass). As for the £20 notes, it finally came to me, I just took it off him. Everyone else was making money off it. One of the guys arranged a meeting to come out on Saturday and bring out a gramme worth (of drugs in exchange for the counterfeit bills). I took the whole lot off him. (laughs) I asked him to let me have a look at one, and he didn't trust me so I taught him not to trust me again, and took the whole lot off him. That way he won't trust me for definite.

For Project Week, Sunny was booked for the cross-channel voyage. But on the Friday of the eighth week, the last day before the sailing trip, Sunny announced he had no passport, and wanted to change his project – expressly against the Sherborne House rules.

This time his credit ran out. The staff felt their credibility was at stake with other group members who also wanted to change but had been refused the right to do so. Moreover, Peter, the mentally disturbed member of the other group, had also failed to obtain his passport. In a gruelling meeting on a hot Friday afternoon, the staff discussed whether to declare Sunny in breach of his probation order and send him back to court. It was a painful debate, deciding the future of two young men who were on the edge of much deeper trouble. Sherborne House was their lifeline. The staff felt that Sunny had understood the rules and simply ignored them, expecting to be given yet another reprieve or exemption. He had to be breached. They were split evenly about Peter, who was less capable of managing his own affairs. In the end they decided by one vote to breach Peter as well. They expected Sunny to make a huge – and legitimate – fuss if they did not. It was a very sad occasion, watching these two young men being cast adrift.

But Sunny's skills had not yet failed him. In court, he managed to win another probation order, rather than being sent to prison as Peter was. (Fifty per cent of all those breached by Sherborne

House and returned to court are given custodial sentences.)

Two months later, walking with Deb, one of Sunny's group leaders, we ran into him near Sherborne House. Sunny was walking his dog, of whom he'd spoken warmly in the groups. He told us with a mixture of pride and distaste that he'd taken a job in a cafe at London Bridge. He seized the chance to hector Deb about letting him have his unfinished gates, despite the firm Sherborne House rule that any project left unfinished by the end of the course is destroyed.

Several weeks later, after further pestering, Sunny reported he was burgled again. The staff took pity on him. On the condition that he come and finish the gates himself, he was allowed to take them home. Sunny had beaten the system yet again.

Several months later, I interviewed Sunny's probation officer on the telephone. I asked her how he was doing, and why she seemed to have done so little to help him:

Sunny didn't start off with me – he was transferred to me because he got a flat in the area, but he was already on probation and had a load of outstanding cases. Our contact has been pretty intense – and wearying. He is always ducking and diving. You never know where he is or what he's up to. He's in terrible debt now. He had a Community Grant of £500 to do up his flat but he blew that. He's been living from hand to mouth – no job, no money, and he utters veiled threats of more crime.

While he was at Sherborne House I didn't write to the council asking for a transfer for his flat because I couldn't see the point. It's not a solution. He'll just become a victim all over again. That's his style.

I suggest he goes back to square one – let the flat go, and go into hostel accommodation just to be free of responsibilities. He certainly can't cope now. He can't prioritise, can't manage. He's closed off all the options. I just don't know what to do next.

He's a very sad case actually. He has a terrible background history so it's hardly surprising he is such a damaged person, and very isolated, and not able to cope with living alone and yet not in a position to live with anybody else.

I tell him, 'I can only help you to help yourself, but you don't take my advice. Money isn't the solution.' He's always after me for bits of money. In desperation, I relented and gave him £3 to visit a cousin in Essex – it's the only one in his family he has contact with. I know I should refuse to see him until he does something about his situation. He projects everything onto me. It's actually effective – I find it very depressing. But I also have to say he's in the most dreadful situation.

I don't know what I can do. Sherborne House didn't impinge on him. The idea is good and so is the practical side but I don't think young people like to spend every morning talking. He found it very trying. He doesn't like to be restricted. The whole situation is totally chaotic.

There's no simple answer. Unemployment and homelessness is part of the problem. They all have this sort of fancy view of their ideal thing – a little house and a little wife and two kids and then everything is going to be okay. One of the frustrations of the job is that we can't offer them that, we can't offer them a house or a job. We can only give advice and write letters. That's why they become frustrated with us as well. But if it came to it, most of them can't cope with accommodation or maintaining a relationship.

How much of Sunny's problems are real and how much imagined I just don't know. He's in terror of being victimised by one person or persons but he won't divulge the names. I'm at my wits' end.

One year after he left Sherborne House, the system caught up with Sunny. He was in Feltham Young Offenders' Institution. I talked to him on his wing in the officers' tea room. Although he had been very guarded with me at Sherborne House – perhaps because he could sense I didn't trust him – at Feltham he looked pleased to see me and spoke freely. He was much more fit and relaxed than he had been at Sherborne House, but still had the conflicting styles of being cool and street-smart, and that of a victim wanting sympathy. The effect on me was curiously disarming. I liked him more, which made some of his actions rather more alarming because they were described in the same engaging tone as his problems. He was still hunched over as he talked, but at least now he looked me in the eye:

In a way, Sherborne House kind of helped me. Talking about certain things, and that. I hate talking to people direct, I don't like people knowing my business, but since being in Sherborne House I find I can talk to people more. There aren't many black people in the probation service. A few. I think there should be more. They can come on a different vibe and talk to people like me and it will get through, and we'll listen to them more.

It didn't matter to me that I didn't finish Sherborne House. Both Liz and Deb tried to help me even after I got kicked off the course. I went to see them a couple of times to ask them for a little bit of advice. They helped me a bit with the council so I appreciate that from them.

The reason they kicked me off was cos I didn't go on that trip. That weren't my fault – I couldn't go off and leave the dog by itself in the flat. My friend couldn't look after it cos he's got a pit bull and every time they want to see each other they want to fight, so I had to look after it. They must be able to understand I can't just leave my dog. I took my dog over to my friend's but as soon as his dog saw mine they just went for each other. I had to pull them apart. My other friends are afraid of the dog and don't want to go near him.

Sunny's dog loomed large in his emotional geography, as an object of affection and reassurance. But Sunny's treatment of him showed how much he saw it as an extension of himself. Sunny described how he didn't always feed the dog regularly, or just gave him bits of rice if he felt like it. Being on the receiving end of so many burglaries and physical attacks, it was hardly surprising Sunny wanted protection, and in the latest streetwise form of a pit bull. But I asked him how he managed such a dangerous dog as a pet.

I'm not afraid of my own dog. He knows what would happen if he attacked me, I'd beat him to death. He wouldn't win with me. You have to show a pit bull who's boss. If you show him you're afraid of him, he's just going to take liberties with you. I controlled him since it was a little pup. Tell him if he don't do what I say, he's going to get a little beating.

Someone gave it to me, a good friend, who was just like a brother to me. He don't come and visit me, but well and truly that's my fault, cos I ain't been writing to him. I ain't been writing to no one. I just want to get my head down and do the time. If they keep coming and see me, I'm going to start getting depressed, thinking, 'They're going back on the out, and I'm going back to four walls,' so I keep it that way.

Since I was mature, in the *(children's)* home, I never really had anyone. So everything I was doing I did by myself. The staff didn't talk to me. I didn't talk to them, so I had everything inside me and

I got used to it. Then when people wanted to come and help me, I said 'No. From the time I wanted you to help me, you wouldn't help me, so what you coming to help me now for?' I just checked *(blocked)* it.

I was in a home from about fifteen. Family trouble, I didn't get on with my parents. I just came over to this country, and I didn't want to stay, and they wouldn't let me go back to Mauritius, saying 'this' and 'that'. They put me in care instead. I started freaking out, doing things that I didn't even know what I was doing.

I started crime, drugs, everything. When I was in the home, half the staff knew that I was taking crack, but they just used to spread it around, simple as that. Other kids knew that 'Sunny, he's a little crackhead,' like they thought it was a good thing. They didn't even bother to try to help me or to talk to me about it. So I just did more and more.

It was good money and a nice life for a while. The money went on things I needed, like champagne. Saw my family who just gave me lectures. Never thought about the victims except once, when I went into a house and I saw the pictures. One was of a big black man and I got afraid, but that's about it.

I didn't really think about it until it happened to me, and from there I just stopped it completely. I thought 'I can't really do that again.' I thought I'd let other people. If they want to do it and sell me the stuff, I'll buy it, but I can't really do it again. I know what it's like well and truly. I've been burgled eight times in twelve months.

But when I was doing the burglaries, I weren't going out and robbing the poor and things like that. I used to go for rich people. I can tell from someone's house, the way it's situated. I don't think about the rich people, they got things easy. I don't feel sorry for them.

They deserved it in a way. Cos the rich people thought Ebony House had a bad reputation cos there were plenty of black people in there. I didn't feel bad for them at all. I just had a grudge against them, as far as I check it. Since I got put into care, I had a grudge against all rich people and that cos as I check it they're the main people that's in control of everything, the poor and that. They seem to be taking the piss.

Mind you from time to time I used to go a bit mad as well, just go on to the street and terrorise a couple of people for the fun of it. Take their money if they had any, jewellery. Just walk up to them. You can tell from somebody's dress, like if they got a chain on or rings, what kind of shoes or what kind of suit. Sometimes you just take a chance and just hold up anybody.

I had a weapon, all the time 24–7, 24–7 *(twenty-four hours a day, seven days a week)*. Plus I had a lot of trouble with other kids in Ebony House, so I didn't leave without it, didn't sleep without it, it was on me all the time, and I wasn't afraid to use it on the people. You're making it sound bad, but if someone pulls a knife on me, I do it back and then it's down to who is the fastest.

I suppose during those days I was young still, and I didn't really know what was going on in my head. I just used to do things cos I thought that was the easiest way of getting my money to go buy drugs. Plus I had a lot of hate inside of me, and I used to go out and just start a fight with someone, and if they're getting the better of me, I'd pull out a knife and deal with them that way, or just beat them up. That's it.

Like now, I'm nineteen, I've seen a few people I knew who've died with a knife, so I wouldn't touch it again unless it was someone who was on my back, on my case, 24–7, looking to do this and that. But apart from that, I wouldn't do it again. But I don't like people telling me to do this and that, cos for a long time I been doing what I wanted. Why start now?

Sunny told the education tutor at Sherborne House that he had done well at school in South London. I wondered how he had accepted the discipline.

School was alright – till I got kicked out. I got put into care, I had a lot of things on my mind, the teacher told me that I was in a home, and I flipped. They expelled me for that. I held the head up and put a knife to her throat. I got moved to a secure place. I was fifteen. But when I was young and I used to get angry it was the first thing I used to go for, go in the kitchen and get a knife, after my grandad died, from about eight. I used to take it out on myself, put my hand through a window. That's why I got all them scars. I also stabbed my Dad in his hand.

Sunny seemed to blame all his recent difficulties on one person, a West Indian boy who was living at Ebony House but actually attending a subsequent course at Sherborne House. Sunny even blamed him for landing him in prison – because of the nervous tension he caused through his attacks on Sunny's flat.

Quite a few new people came over to harass me from Sherborne House from the group after the one I was on. One called Tommy

Tarzan. He's exactly like me, tall and skinny. When I come out I've got a solution, I've got something waiting for him, I got a surprise for him, it's as simple as that. But like, he's just been on my case for too long.

It's a silly little argument. He tried to rob me, so I rob him back. Then he got his friend to beat me up in my flat, broke my nose, so like my friend beat him up, and he didn't like that. So from there he just kept coming on to me, cos like he knows that all the time I'm alone in my flat. He can't come round to where I hang around, cos he knows what would happen over there.

I asked Sunny why he hadn't given Tommy's name amid his many complaints about him. His answer is characteristic of the young offenders' code of ethics. It leads them into further trouble even after they have given up thefts and burglary.

Tommy was at Sherborne House after me but I never said who he was. I told them there was somebody from Ebony House that was troubling me when my house got burgled. I went to Sherborne House to get a couple of tools to fix my door, but I couldn't really say nothing. You can't grass someone like that, cos what they going to do? They *(the probation officers)* can't really do nothing. There's only one language he'll understand.

After Sherborne House course I caught him red-handed in my flat, him and half Sherborne House in there. Raga *(Bren)* was there. *(Bren had been on the same Sherborne House programme but also did not finish and is now in Dover Prison.)* But like Raga told him to back off and that, cos he knew me and he knew my people, and he said 'nah you can't do that to him.' The guy told Raga to hold me while he chased one of my friends, but Raga didn't want nothing to do with it which was wise for him.

After I left Sherborne House, I got a job catering. Then my flat got burgled again, I started getting depressed again, so I lost the job. That's how it started. Tommy coming back to my flat and doing it over again pissed me off, so I tried to get the council to change my flat for me, but they was taking their time, so I just ended up coming back in here.

From time to time I think why I done it. But I'm not too bad in here. It's not too bad in here. Cos like when I was on the out I was getting pissed off with my flat getting broken into too much. I found out the guy that was doing it is coming here looking for me, so like, I'm looking for him as well, the same one.

Sunny at first tried to describe the crime that landed him in Feltham as an accident that had nothing to do with him. Characteristically, he saw it as somehow unfair that he should have been blamed. It took quite a while to get the story straight.

I'm in here for armed robbery. Something just went wrong. I was trying to help out a friend, and was going to stay out of it. But then the robbery never came to plan as he suggested it. I was standing outside the shop and I saw him fighting with the man *(in the shop)*. The man had the better of him, so I rushed into the shop and I started fighting with the man as well. Next thing, I see my friend get up and run. Then I saw four different men get up, come up me, and just hold me down. I couldn't really do nothing.

I just went along with it *(defensive laughter)*. I went there to see if everything went according to plan cos he was using my gun anyway. I said to him,'I ain't going to give it to you and let you walk off with it, I'd rather come with you and see that you do it.'

So, all of a sudden I see him start fighting with the manager and the gun is on the floor, so I rush into the shop and pick up the gun. I put it to his wife's head, that's the worst part of it. And then I started fighting. That's it.

The gun was blank anyway, so it couldn't hurt no one. The barrel was blocked. But that still counts as armed robbery. Any firearm that's involved, even if it's a replica, they think it's real. So I got the top whack – five years for attempted robbery, three years for having a firearm. That's bad. Someone put some bad luck on me – I went to court on Friday 13th!

I went Not Guilty, but they had all the evidence on me, but what I was trying to say was like someone forced me to do it, and while I was doing it I didn't really know what I was doing cos I was on drugs. But they never fell for that.

I had the gun for a long time. It was in my house. I just came across it a month before this happened. I took it off someone. But I hid it cos I wouldn't walk with it. It can't do nothing anyway, so it's not really worth taking it out there. Only if you want to frighten someone, that's the only thing that you use it for.

I got past carrying knives and that. I got previous *(convictions)* for that. But I stopped cos of what happened to one of my friends. One night he got cut up badly so from that day I just stopped carrying knives.

One day I was down Charing Cross Road and all of a sudden

a group of bouncers just rushed us, mistaking us for someone else. All of them just surrounded my friend. Someone took out a knife and put a long mark across his back, cut up his hand, face and like that. They chased me, got hold of me. I dropped, man went to hold my hand. Luckily I reacted fast, took out my knife and cut him across his hand. And I got away.

My friend took them to court and got a little bit of money, that's it. From there I stopped carrying a knife, even though it saved my life.

I don't think the street will ever be safe. Even now, certain people where I used to hang round, older people than me like that's just come back from Jamaica. They ain't got no respect for the police. If they see a policeman in his car, they'll just walk up behind him and let off two gunshots. They can get away with it in Jamaica, but they can't get away with it over here. And like that was just hotting up the area.

It depends what part you go to and what people you're around with, but there's enough people that want to show themself in front of their friend that they're badder than you, that they can do this, they can do that, show that they're mean. I play the same game as them, that's the only way you can top them.

When I was young, I used to do all them things. A bunch of us would board a bus and rob everyone on it – watches, rings, wallets. No one stopped us, cos of the knives. Like since last year I've thought, 'Them things ain't for me.' Like I've grown out of it, you know? If someone came out to me now and put a knife to me I'd react to it fast but I'm like that. It don't matter who he is, what he is.

After Sherborne House, I didn't steal. I found something more constructive to do, a better way of making money, without being caught, without hotting up myself, and just sitting down and just working it neatly: dealing *(in drugs)*. You don't have to go out. They bring it to me. You stay in the house, don't get seen by no one. Sitting down, you get your food there, get your girls there, get your champagne. What more can you ask for, you know? *(laughs)*

Went on for about eight months. I didn't do any more crime. I was getting nice wage at the end of the day – about £300 a day. I used to take half *(the drugs)* myself sometimes instead of taking money, and the rest I used to just spend it out, on anything, records, drink, clothes mostly.

But my flat don't look nice cos of the distress. Tommy *(his attacker from Ebony House)* took my clothes as well. It came to the point where I didn't even bother with my flat, I just used to go there from time to time that's it. I was living at my friend's sister's flat and that was alright over there, and Tommy would never come over there, cos he'd get hit good and proper. The council said they'd move me from my own flat. I was just waiting on that, but nothing happened, they was just messing me around.

I asked him what view his probation officer had taken of his involvement with drugs, yet another complication for his case.

My probation officer knew I was doing drugs, but not how deep I was into it. But then when I came inside she found out. She just took a guess, and I fell for it and told her.

When my probation officer wrote my social inquiry report she told the judge like it wouldn't be worth putting me back inside, it'd be better putting me in a rehabilitation centre. But like the judge didn't want to know nothing about it, just gave me five years. I don't know his name and I don't wish to know it. It was the Old Bailey – cos there was a firearm involved. It weren't too bad, but I thought I'd get a result cos I was told it was the fairest court in England. But it never worked that way for me.

I never got nothing from Sherborne House for the court. I never even thought about them. Sherborne House was alright, it weren't too bad. I don't like people telling me what to do. Don't see why I should start now.

At Sherborne House, Sunny had refused to say anything about his family. He was paranoid about other group members knowing his personal details. But one year later, in the isolation of the prison, he unveiled yet another tale of parental disaster.

I never really spoke to my parents properly. I was brought up by my grandparents since I was nine months old till twelve years old, when my parents were in this country. So I didn't really know them, and when I came over I found it hard to talk to them. I wanted to go back home. I don't know why my parents come here from Mauritius. They must have something wrong with their brains.

I don't want to see my father. He doesn't live too far from my flat, about fifteen minutes away. But still, I don't want to know him, he don't want to know me, I don't want to know him.

Don't make no difference to me. As far as I was concerned my grandmother brought me up. My grandfather died when I was about seven. I had my grandmother and my uncle looking after me. My father didn't bother keeping in touch with me. I ain't got no feelings for him. I'm pissed off with him for making me come over to this country and separating me from my grandmother. I hate him for that. I still want to go back but he's got my passport and I can't really do nothing about that. Social worker tried to get it but he don't want to give it.

He probably doesn't want me to see my grandmother. All I can say is I ain't going to talk to him, and even if I do, it ain't going to be talk, I'd do something to him and wouldn't even regret it. But I got used to it.

I've never even seen my mother in my whole life! That's one of the reasons my parents separated and my father took me home after nine months. They know she's still in this country but they won't tell me where she is. They just sell me their side of the story. Not so much my uncle is against her, but my father. But I'd rather not talk about that.

Maybe I started taking drugs to get all those things out of my mind. Now I realise that however much drugs I did do, it's still going to be in my head, it's not going to go nowhere, whatever drugs I'm taking.

I was on crack since the age of fifteen. When you sell it, it's there in front of you, and I was just taking it more and more. I just got pissed off with everything so I used to take it to try and forget about it. But it still came back the next morning.

The only person I got is my cousin. She's young, she's nice. She works for the BBC. She's the only one who keeps in touch with me. My uncle and my Dad told her not to; all the time they used to slag me in front of her, and she got pissed off with it so she left *(the flat they had been living in)*.

I found that out when I was in prison last year and that nearly killed me. All the time my uncle used to slag me in front of her and she used to defend me. Then it came to a certain extent where she just couldn't take no more of it, so she left and went to a different place. Don't know where she is now. I've lost her address. Nobody visits me here.

I offered to try to find his cousin, through the BBC, and tell her where he was. He declined:

I just want to put my head down and do my time. It would probably just upset me to see her.

I suppose when I was in Sherborne House I wanted to change, and have nothing to do with crime – though I can't say about drugs, but at least crime and that. I wanted to be on a different level, but it never happened that way. Just the way things worked out.

No matter what subject we discussed, Sunny returned to his attacker, Tommy, like a nemesis. From others' experiences, I believed Sunny's account was genuine, but he seemed to haunt Sunny's thoughts and symbolise his difficulties in a way that freed Sunny from taking final responsibility.

The only person who caused me grief is Tommy. If Tommy never came to my flat, never broke into my flat again, I would have still had that job, I would have been making my money selling drugs at night-time, without doing anything wrong. He's the one that's been causing it. If it weren't for him, I wouldn't have been getting depressed.

Well and truly I don't like working for other people, having them telling me what to do. But I made the effort out there to show someone I can do something constructive. Then he *(Tommy)* came on the scene. I stuck to the job, even though I hated it, but when he came I got pissed off. I sat and waited for him to come again. And boy if he did – I had my dog!

Want to settle down, get away from crime, just live my life in peace. But I can't do that until something's done about Tommy, cos if nothing's done about him, he's not gonna leave me alone at all. This has been going on for three years now, over a stupidness, so I can't really do nothing till something been done about him. I can't settle down cos even if I do, no matter how hard I try, I could settle down, have everything there, but he would come along, take everything away from me, and I'm back to square one again, you know? He's just going to keep on and on.

I've tried talking to him, right? Like, took him on the side. 'You can't keep going on like that for the rest of your life,' like, 'I'm in a different vibe, you should try the same thing.' He said 'yeh,' but I never believed him. It just went in one ear and out the other.

So far Sunny has used his time in prison in the tradition of most incarcerated offenders: not to prepare for a positive crime-free future, but to plan revenge.

No way am I gonna be done for what happens to him, not the way I've got it planned. I'm not going to trouble him. It's set up. There's two different ways of doing it. You can do it where you won't get catched or do it and go and brag about it. I'm going to talk to him, on a nice level, give him time and certainty that, boy, if he come and trouble me again, boy I'm going to give it to him, he's gonna get it, I'm not messing around this time. If he don't take that little warning, that's it for him. If something do happen to him I won't be there to see him, I'll be well out.

I know better. Even bragging to you about it. I've only told you as a little sign. That's not exactly what I'm going to do. It might be me doing it or I might be out the country.

If Tommy goes inside, and he's inside for a couple of years, I think I'd be able to go straight. I would. I'd try my hardest, I'd try my hardest. I know I've done it before, I've got myself a job, I've done that, that's one assurance I've got. I can do it again. It's my little hope.

I was learning to be an electrician but it just went out of my mind when I started doing those drugs. But I'd still like to do something like that. Engineering, or work with music and that. I did a little sampling, I was playing for *(the Notting Hill)* Carnival. At least I'd know that I tried. That's the main thing that matters to me, even I don't make it.

I know I'm quite intelligent. I can read and write, and that's more than I can say for some people in here, and I feel sorry for them, but if they don't want to learn I can't help them. If they helped themselves first, I'd help them to read and stuff. That's one of the wickedest things in life if you can't read or write.

I was on top of my class, and I got a couple of certificates saying I'd done good in years one and two. But then everything just went blank. The trouble I had with my family, getting put into care, it freaked me out, I couldn't handle it. I didn't want to live with my parents, I wanted to go back home, but they put me in care instead. When I came over, I had the impression that me and my grandmother were coming over for a holiday, that's what I was told, but things never went to plan. My grandmother came for a year so that she could settle in with me and then when she was packing I thought, great, but then I was told I wasn't going nowhere.

I had lots of girls. They just come and go. There's X amount of girls out there. They're just waiting.

I've been with the same girl quite a while, since I came out last year. But then she told me that I had to stop taking crack. I told her 'Yeh,' but I was doing it undercover. She got pissed off with it, and I told her to fuck off. But she came back again, and tried to talk some sense into me, but I didn't listen to her until I got back in here, and then I thought, 'Boy, if only I'd listened to her. I might not be here.' But that's how life go.

The only people I'd listen to are my *(girl)*friend and my cousin, who I've got respect for, and who I'd do anything for. They thought I was off crack and were really shocked. Don't see my friend in here neither. I'd rather just do the time and then come out see what's happening with them.

For all his anti-social attitudes and behaviour, Sunny shares the 'fancy ideal' of domestic bliss described by his probation officer as the dream of most young offenders. I was surprised and moved by his concern for the fate of the child he hoped for. It seemed a way of mourning his own.

I want to settle down with my girl. Lead my life quietly and peacefully. Want children, but not till I've sorted myself out properly. I don't want to have a youth now, and I in and out of jail. If I've got a youth, I'd rather be out there doing something constructive and doing my part of it, and like it to have things I never had. Treat him more and stay with him more; give him the love that I never had. But I wouldn't have a youth that I can't cater for. At the moment I've got enough of my friends that have got youths where they don't bother to cater for it. That's one thing I can't take. I had a fight with my *(girl)*friend for that. The way that I check it is, if you've got a youth, you must cater for it, even if you don't get on with the girl, the youth is part of you. You must show the youth that you are his father, that no next man that's come in walking in and out the house is.

I'm nineteen now. Twenty in December. So, time is just going by and I'm doing the same thing. I realise it's getting me down, and that I have to stop that, sooner or later. Cos I had my flat, lost that. Blame that on being in here, so that's the only thing that's pissing me off. Plus the dog.

Found out that someone else is trying to make money out of him out there. That's killing me as well. My friend's supposed to be looking after it, but he's using it, so I can't really do nothing. He's making it fight. He's put it back in the ring again. I'd stopped that for about a year. I can't really do nothing about it being back in here, but it makes me realise about doing the next thing *(committing another offence).*

My friend Stephen's family wanted to adopt me, and they're like a second family to me, and have told me what to do and not to do, and I respect them for that, cos no one else really bothered to do that, to take a little interest in me. Apart from my cousin. But I didn't learn from my mistakes, and I just kept on doing on things, but I realise now I can't keep going on like this. I have to stop sooner or later. I'd rather stop when I'm young. I've been to Brixton *(prison)*, and seen people coming in at fifty or sixty *(years old)* and I could never put myself through that. Never. I might as well just change when I'm young – take a little sidewalk, and go and do something constructive, and just settle down neatly.

But I can't do that with Tommy.

Sunny's only visitor is his probation officer, once every three months or so. She believes he is institutionalised already, safe from the responsibilities and dangers he was struggling with unsuccessfully on the outside. He finds the security of the routine comforting, and it allows him just enough room to test his rebellious nature.

You're getting three meals a day and something to do. Food is rubbish. It's cold by the time we come back from the laundry. They don't bother to warm it up for us. I work from eight-thirty to quarter past eleven and then from about half past one till twenty past four five days a week, ironing shirts – it ain't too bad, at least that makes the time pass. But you learn nothing at all, they don't teach me nothing. But you realise crime don't pay, you know? I was stupid to go and do it but I tried to help out someone else.

Feltham Young Offenders' Institution has had twenty suicides and many more unreported attempts in the past year. Because of staff shortages, there is no therapy, and virtually no schooling. The prisoners are merely 'warehoused' in the language of the prison service. Three quarters of imprisoned young offenders are reconvicted within two years of their release. Three quarters of all adult prisoners have been imprisoned when they were young.

Hopefully I should learn my lesson from this one. Five years is a long time; I got three years to go. My first bird *(prison)* as well. It ain't been too bad so far. I've taken it quite alright, it hasn't really clicked in my brain yet that I'm going to be here three years. I suppose soon it will.

And of course you're on your own for long stretches. But I'm used to being on my own. I been on my own since I was fifteen, so a couple more years ain't going to make no difference. I prefer it that way.

CHAPTER SEVEN

WINSTON

To be Winston in Hackney

Winston is black, tall and stylish, usually dressed in a snappy baseball jacket and cap, with rolled up trouser cuffs, and smart trainers to signify he's a 'brother'. Giving off such signals is important to Winston, and a primary reason why he ended up in Sherborne House. But he should never have been there at all.

When I first met him, Winston was nineteen. He looked ominously streetwise, and cut a tall and substantial figure when he moved with the lads. But I quickly discovered Winston was different from the other black boys in his group at Sherborne House. They were aggressive, fast talking and cocky, while Winston was soft-spoken and gentle. Despite his vivid outward appearance, he was quite shy. For the first two weeks of the group, while the battle for the leadership went on between his noisier companions, Winston seemed to be unwilling to contribute at all. But as, one by one, they were rearrested, or dropped out, it became clear that Winston had drawn comfort from their presence and the black domination of the group. When he was the only black person present – as happened more frequently – he fell into a detached, trance-like state from which the group leaders tried, often unsuccessfully, to draw him back.

Nevertheless, Winston's dignified presence was also felt more strongly as the numbers shrank. While both Peter and Sam took advantage of the vacuum left by the departure of the more forceful black boys, Winston made clear his disapproval of their disruptive antics. When engaged in the other activities, Winston showed himself helpful and cooperative in the workshops and on the various outings. Dry skiing he found so exciting, he vowed to return on his own to keep up the lessons. When we arrived back at Sherborne House later that day, one of the streetwise black boys in the other

group asked him what he'd been doing. 'Skiing, man. I been ski-
ing!' said Winston, with joy and disbelief.

Winston was in many ways untypical of the more experienced
young offenders who come to Sherborne House, but he was more
typical of young offenders generally. He did reasonably well at
school, and lived in a relatively settled manner with his mother
and sisters in a pleasant council estate in Hackney. Winston landed
in the criminal justice system very late, during a break from college,
where he was learning to be an electrical engineer. His mother, a
hard-working woman in her thirties, told me later when I visited
their flat that she was deeply disappointed by what had happened
to Winston: there was no obvious cause, nothing wrong at school,
or at home. But his steady girlfriend Tracey was already pregnant
when he began hanging around with a sixteen year-old boy
upstairs, who was into bullying younger children for money. Win-
ston was caught with him and, because he was older, was blamed
as the ringleader. His friend got off, but Winston, instead of being
sent to prison, was sent to Sherborne House for ten weeks. That
ended his college course, and has left Winston in limbo, among
more experienced offenders, waiting for his baby to be born by
the end of the course.

But like many young people, Winston's ambition to establish a
normal life for himself pulled him away from the place and the
people that gave him the most immediate sense of approval: his
peers on the street.

If we have to make good, we have to go to college and you have
to have brains. Then when you do have brains you've changed
completely. You're not down to earth no more on the street, so
you can't win. If you want to get something good, you meet different people at college and you're straining away from the old people
you used to move with. They chief you out *(insult you)*, and say
'Ah, he's not with us,' know what I mean?

You go to college and it just works out you lose your home
friends, and you have to move to the outskirts. And if you ain't
got the brains you don't get nowhere. You just stay with your
family. The people who do move on, we don't know where they
are. They've gone.

I started in the streets just meeting around people, seeing them
at parties. Then you start moving with them, then you learn their
ways.

Sherborne House for Winston was a refuge from the dangerous streets of Hackney, in the East End of London. Normally, he was slouched and diffident, but he was more involved than he appeared to be. Like many of the others, he has developed a kit of masks – of facial expression, speech and body language – to blend into whatever surroundings he finds himself. The challenge for the Sherborne House staff was to reach down to the real Winston, who is moral and responsible, and encourage his growth.

The challenge for Winston himself was and is to resist the blandishments and temptations of his more irresponsible peers while keeping their esteem and, if possible, their company. He is both shy and sociable, an extremely likeable young man.

In the exercise on self-assessment, Winston gave an interesting account of his strengths and weaknesses:

Brave/Friendly/Considerate/Sensible/Shy/Sure of myself/Hard working/Easily led/Caring/Moody/and Bad-tempered. *(He doesn't show those last two qualities at all, unlike all the others.)* I'd like to be ambitious. I was easily led, but I look at myself more. I think of myself before others a bit more.

Winston had changed – it seemed to me – at this point. He denounced offending now, if he was ever really into crime before. His sincerity and dignity distinguished him from the others. He was not playing games.

The group then embarked on the exercise of saying Five Things About Myself from a list of characteristics: what do you like/ dislike/what is unusual/what distinguishing physical feature/one fact about your offending/what ambition: is this ambition realistic?

Winston likes the fact that he stands up for himself. Dane approved of that. Dane did not see Winston as a rival though in fact he was. Winston showed quietly the leadership and moral authority that Dane, despite all his noise, lacked.

Winston's ambition: to go to Canada. He has elaborate plans to follow his family there as soon as he finishes electronics college. The group was surprised and rather impressed, and accepted his ambitions as realistic.

In the group on offending behaviour, Winston had to describe his criminal record. It was very modest compared to those of the others. Despite his street persona, Winston seemed not to be a serious villain. Whatever he had been up to, his criminal record consisted almost entirely of attempted crimes, including three attempted burglaries.

I got caught for the first thing I ever did. Never cautioned because Hackney *(police)* doesn't believe in cautions. *(They are reputed to be among the toughest police in London.)* I did it with other boys – one the same age, the other older. Both are inside now.

Dane interjected that Winston had 'a good criminal record' because he could do more jobs before being sent away. But Winston expected to go to prison for his last offence:

They got no mercy now. About the burglary, I was on the bus with some boys and we passed a house and they said 'that looks fat', so we got off and they did the door. Nearly got away with it — put the video, video camera, and TV all in this quilt. Called a taxi, which was late, so one guy started down the road. I wasn't gonna wait, and as I left some lady saw me, so I smiled like in church but the police came with dogs! Actually it was only one burglary, in a house with three rooms. Maybe that's why they got it down as three burglaries. I didn't run away cos they had dogs and I didn't want to get chewed.

As he spoke, Winston's predicament could be seen in microcosm. He was not much of a criminal, and did not want to be seen as one. Yet he also sought the approval of others his own age: in this group, that approval seemed to hinge on the scale of criminal activity. It seemed to Winston's credit that he resisted the temptation to embellish his modest record.

One other time we was in a bus in Walthamstow, passing by some studio apartments, and one of the boys said 'Let's get some money,' so we come off the bus. They said 'knock' but I said I wasn't involved. Then we set a little girl to knock on the door and ask for Julie. Girl answers and says 'Julie lives down the road.' So we assemble a new description of 'Julie' and ask her to knock next door. No answer. So we go down the sweet shop, give her a pound and send her in the shop and then go back and kick in the door.

My friends, they got nothing to lose, but I wasn't thinking of the consequences. Got away with a camera. It was in my pocket when the police found me. But if I really had got away, they'd have made me do a lot more *(punishment)*. My Mum says I got no luck at all – but that's what happens when you are wrong.

One of them got away – I saw him last week on the bus. To get away from me he'd jumped out the emergency window and kicked out, his legs buckled as he landed.

I got sent to the Central Criminal Court – the Old Bailey. *(The rest of the group was suitably impressed.)* They got people in there for rape and murder! I say 'What am I doing here?' 'Quiet!' says the Judge.

You go in with your parents *(sic)* but then you're on your own. It's dread *(scary)*. There are killer screws saying 'I don't think you're gonna get away with it.' Pat me on the back of the head. A black man too. I said, 'What a black man doing taking this job to heart? You're a coconut.' When I got two years' probation order he was screwin'*(upset)*, man. He says, 'You'll be back!' I said, 'No!'

My solicitor, he's a 'speng' *(stupid)* man. But when they saying things in court about me, I got mad and said 'It ain't true. It ain't true!' and the barrister's wig fell off, so I just burst out laughing. For my sentence, I came in rag *(ragamuffin's clothes – unlaced trainers, baseball jacket and jeans)*. 'Big difference from the way you started the case' says the Judge. I didn't care.

The last case was when I took a day off college and went off with a friend, Tyrone. He saw this Asian boy and asked him for a pound, and then for his bus pass. Then he took him into a garage and I hear screaming so I went to see what happened. Tyrone gave the kid his watch and told him to bring it back later with more money. *(Giving the Asian boy the watch was a way of reminding him of the threat of violence should he not return with both the watch and more cash.)*

But the kid went to the police who caught us both. But cos I was older, they made me out to be the ringleader, which I wasn't at all.

The sheer foolishness of this was clear to everyone, but Winston didn't grass, and accepted his fate with equanimity.

People on the streets carve you up but they also cover up for you. Tyrone gave me an ounce *(of cannabis)* worth £200, so I made something from the whole thing.

At Sherborne House, Winston gave the impression he was the victim of circumstances, ranging from being black and living in Hackney to simple bad luck. But as he talked about the same matters with me a year later, I was unpleasantly surprised to discover he was also quite defiant about his forays into crime, even if inspired by other people. Hanging around with his mates, they would spur each other on to steal handbags from passersby, for which they were never caught.

I had the choice all the time, and my choice was to say yes all the time. No one pushed me to do nothing. It all depends on what it is. If it's streetwise no one can tell me what to do. I decide for myself. No one can say, 'go and do that Win.' I'll say 'shut up.' I didn't give a damn about the victims. I needed the money.

Winston seems capable of being both independent from and dependent on his mates. The same is true of his relationship with his mother, whose approval he values. Part of his problem is that they pull him in opposite directions as became clear when the group leaders pressed him about keeping clear of bad influences.

People I'm with are like a family, they can get jealous. If you kick out *(move away from the gang)* and have a girlfriend it's hard. They don't like it. They probably don't have a girl and when I say 'I'm not raving no more' they don't like it. Normally when they do their stupidness *(crimes)*, I stay away, or I go to a girl's house.

My Mum only really knew *(about his criminal activities)* when the police started coming round our house. I had to decide for myself to give it up. No one could have told me to stop.

For all his style, Winston lacked confidence, like so many apparently streetwise young men. By the middle of the programme, the only other black person in Winston's group was Dane, a smooth-talking car thief from a different part of London, Ladbroke Grove. Dane's more self-consciously dapper clothes and provocative manner isolated him from the rest of the group, including Winston. But this left Winston feeling lonelier than ever. It was a further tribute to his strength of character that he could maintain his authority.

I started late when I got into bad company. I used to move with different boys and go to different areas, but it was too much hassle fight-wise. Like I got cut at the *(Notting Hill)* Carnival by *(Ladbroke)* Grove boys who don't like Hackney boys. They all juveniles, speng boys. They didn't want to hear. They bogus people. So we sold something dud *(phoney drugs)* to them for a tenner and they went away happy and shaking *(dancing)*.

But we sold it for ten. What they sold us was real rubbish, so they stab him *(sic)*. I moved away when a *(Ladbroke Grove)* brave came up to tap me. I took the taps *(blows)* but I kicked out. They couldn't live in the road in Hackney, it's much too dark out there.

Dane and Winston planned a fight at Ladbroke Grove tube between their respective gangs, the Grove and Hackney boys. It was provoked by an apparently mild exchange of insults about their relative stupidity but seemed difficult to stop. I tried to enlist Stan to persuade them to abandon it but he said it was impossible to intervene. He described how East London gangs even on the same estate fight regularly over territory. Too much face was involved. On the appointed night, neither side showed up, and neither Dane nor Winston mentioned it again.

Much as they disliked one another, when they both learned I was writing about the policing of the forthcoming Notting Hill Carnival they were agreed. Winston was transformed by the force of his feeling:

The police make it worse, man. They stop any black youth for the smallest things. There's gonna be trouble, man. You see. The youth is angry, and they want revenge. *(This was alarming coming from as relatively law-abiding a young man as Winston.)*

My friend was in a knife fight outside a pub. He stabbed a white man who admitted it was his fault. But the police arrested only the black youth, and told the white man 'We're on your side!' *(Winston proved to have many such stories which he told with great conviction, as if they had happened to him personally.)*

My friend's brother has locks *(dreadlocks)* and a white girl-friend. The coppers stopped them and say to her 'Why you going with that fucking nigger?' So he hits them and gets arrested. He tells the court but gets fined all the same.

I was shaken by Winston's consuming anger, and by the familiarity of his accounts. There was no telling how true any of them were, whether the 'friends' were people Winston knew personally or just 'brothers' on the street. But the feeling in Winston was real enough. It would make it hard for any policeman, no matter how well intentioned, to make fruitful contact with him now. Yet Winston is a serious and conscientious young man, a potential leader in his own right. I feared Winston's suspicions and resentment would make him overreact to any brusque approach by a policeman and land him in prison instead of Sherborne House and the constructive home life with his new baby that he planned. Being young, black and known to the police from their past record meant

Winston and the others were always close to such simple encoun-
ters that could alter the course of their lives.

In describing his life on the streets to the group leaders, Winston
expressed the same clear sense of morality that incorporated both
the old-fashioned values of a traditional West Indian family, and
the new reality in which he found himself – with professional
criminals from Jamaica and the East End rubbing shoulders in the
clubs frequented by those youths that can afford the prices.

The average criminal world ain't bad. It's the youth, it's we that
hurt people, who do the crime. The big ones here do the crime
but don't hurt anyone.

I think the world is coming to an end. When I was twelve I
didn't know about smoking. I wouldn't even speak about it in
front of my mother, but now they kids do rollups, smoke reefers.
Aged nine, my little nephew is lickin' tits. He doing jobs, he doing
burglaries. He hangs round with eighteen, nineteen year-olds. His
Mum's boyfriend beat him already, but she's still young, still raving. She leaves him with money but he doesn't buy food, he goes
to arcades and buys bigger draws *(cannabis cigarettes)* than me.
He buys things and goes home and there no one there. So it means
she don't care. Nothing I can say to him except 'learn from my
mistakes'.

My Mum is sending me little nephew to her mother – my Gran
in Jamaica but it might make him worse. She is strict, man, strict
to the max. I don't believe it even now but I going to send my kid
there too.

When these youths come up to me I just go 'boom, boom, boom'
(hit them). It's still better to be older. At school, there's a guy,
thirteen, who's the school hit man, dread.

I know someone local who carries an axe – he doesn't do bird
because he's a fruit cake. You just give him a bottle of whisky or
ten pounds and he does someone for you. Only goes to Broadmoor
if they catch him.

It's mean out there on the streets. You got to go live on the
street for a few days. You'll see how it is.

In one of the exercises, the group members distributed cards
assessing each other's character. Winston was astonished to learn
he was regarded as the most mature of the group, that he treated
people equally, and 'gained respect'. He liked these results but was
truly surprised.

Respect is a hot issue among young men. They scan each other alone and in groups for signs it is missing, almost like a chivalric code. If it is missing, they do not hesitate to fight for it. The sad part is they do not respect themselves.

As the weeks passed, Winston evolved from a spectator to an albeit unwilling leader. He felt obliged to intervene when others acted badly or postured to provoke the probation officers. As such antics went on, Winston made clear his disapproval first by sliding into even deeper indifference and then rousing himself to put an end to it. On the other hand, he missed the black company.

Near the end of the course, Winston's girlfriend was due to have their baby, putting extra pressure on him to get his life together. The imminent birth stopped Winston from going on the voyage to the continent – a sad loss for him and us. During the programme, Winston had formed a close friendship with Stan, with whom he shared a passion for music. During Project Week, the two of them worked in the music workshop while the rest of us were sailing. When we returned, it was clear that Winston had enjoyed himself hugely.

On the day of his assessment at the end of the course, Winston's head was cleanly shaved but he felt it already 'needs redoing'. He was dressed for the street, in a smart green suede jacket, and sported the latest facial attire: one earring, a pencil moustache, and a gold cap on one of his front teeth.

Winston's probation officer was Marian, a well-groomed black woman in her early thirties. She had visited midway through the ten-week course, and was told by Molly, Winston's group leader, how well Winston was performing. Marian was clearly surprised, which bore out my suspicion about the remoteness of some ordinary field probation officers from their clients.

Marian: I hadn't expected you to like it here.
Winston: I could handle it
Marian: Didn't you find the questions embarrassing?
Winston: No. Not like I thought I would at the beginning.
Molly: Like talking about personal things?
Winston: I feel safe. *(A major achievement for Sherborne House, this.)*
Molly: You've taken the biggest risks by saying you won't reoffend.

Winston: It's not worth it. I cut out my friends that want
    to do it. I distanced myself. I go to other parts of the
    estate. If I got no money, I stay in.
Molly: *(impressed, like me)* You've made the changes.
Winston: *(smiling)* Yeah.
Molly: And you're sticking to it?
Winston: It's not worth it. I tell me friends it's not worth
    going through what I am going through now.
Molly: How can you speak your mind in front of them?
Winston: *(with admirable clarity)* I know what I want –
    and I got a nipper coming, responsibilities!
Marian: *(out of her depth)* I'm surprised you do that. I
    thought it would be hard.
Winston: *(triumphant)* I told you! It's cos I'm easily
    influenced. I'm easy going on the street, just to get on
    I get in with people – but I don't agree with them.
    I talk to them but I don't listen. The one I really
    talk to is Mark. I talk to Mark cos he's safe. He's
    on my side. He knows what I'm under and I know
    what he's under. It's hard that Mark's in the other
    group – cos you can't relate to white boys! It'd be
    more fun if there were other black boys in our group.

*Molly apologised for the lack of black staff and black boys. It was
a sore point, and Winston's honesty disarmed her. She remarked
again on his leadership role within the group but he ignored her
comment. He was unusually quiet, showing what must be his
normal persona for officialdom but not the way he had been at
Sherborne House.*

Molly: He's designed no less than four pieces in the tech
    workshop!
Winston: Couldn't decide when they ordered the wood,
    and I didn't want to wait so I made a small cassette
    rack. I designed it for a small corner in my small
    room which is a funny shape.

*Molly was really pleased with his progress. She asked if there was
anything he wanted from the programme:*

Winston: I just take it as it comes.
Molly: Any goals?

Winston: *(direct, and angry)* I know what I want to do
and this place is keeping me from doing it. I'm
screwing that I got to do here! My goal is to go out
and get a job to look after my youth *(baby)*! That's
what's so hard for me to keep coming back here cos
this is stopping me! But I just do what I have to do.
I'll finish my course at college and get a job and look
after my youth as best I can.

*Both Marian and Molly were somewhat taken aback by this out-burst. They wanted only a declaration of good intent, but Winston
was against Sherborne House instead of crediting it with his new
position.*

*Marian talked to me afterwards. She was a bit stiff compared
to the other probation officers – less confident, less approachable
– but she put Winston's lack of trust in her down to him:*

It took ever so long to establish a trust between us, which is
why I was doubtful of his success here. But he comes every week
so I get lots of feedback.

She was very pleased, and wreathed in smiles. So was Winston.

*At his final assessment at Sherborne House, Molly asked Winston
how he saw his most likely future:*

Winston: In three months, I hope to be at college, get my
flat, buy things for my flat. The worst I suppose is
there are certain people I just don't get on with, so
I might have to leave and wouldn't have enough
money – so I'd have to look at all kinds of
possibilities to earn money, you know what I
mean? *(brightening)* But that's just the bad luck part.
In three months things could be safe. I want to get
my qualifications and get a job the next day.

In a year's time I hope I won't be in *(this)* country,
that's serious. I probably will be because of my
probation *(order)* but if they allow me to skip I'll be
in Canada. Been getting my green card, and I need
a paper saying I can do some things. I'd be going on
me own cos me Mum and sister are going soon as,
and the baby'll go with them as well. My girlfriend's
not going, that is she ain't made up her mind. She

ain't seen it but when she does she'll like it and
that'll be rough *(good)*.

Molly: Why Canada?

Winston: Canada's good, man. Not violent. Everyone
gets on with their neighbours. Help me to think wiser.

Molly: Sounds like you started.

Winston: Yeah, but the area I live in still gives me grief
– people try to chief me up. I still do walk away from
fights, but you can't avoid it.

Molly: Why?

Winston: To be Winston in Hackney – to be someone –
you got to do things. You could grow up not doing
nothing, but I know what I'm doing on the streets.
I'm not going to just turn soft. You could start out
by just staying in your house if you can handle it
but I'm a person who likes just to be on the street. I
been out on the street since day one. If you saw me
on the street you'd see me as a different person
cause I act that way. I like it.

Molly: You surprise me. I've seen so much of you over
ten weeks.

Winston: On the street I'm not so 'hello, hello.'

All my family's moving *(to Canada)* – my Mum
and my sisters. I wanna go there, make a new life
as far away from Hackney as I can get. But I gonna
wait until I done my thing. I know it's harder to
emigrate with a record.

In five years I should be functioning. I should have
qualifications. I should have me own business. Maybe
do it at home – or have a little shop at first – just
the work I can do at first, but then when I get big
I'll give people a chance who were in the situation I
was in. Give them apprenticeships.

Molly: But what about Canada –?

Winston: It's better here cos lots of little boys come to
me – need to do something for them. Because lots
of ladies *(other boys' mothers)* seen my badness and
seen my changes. They don't know what I'm like in
the streets but they read the papers and we talk
about crime. In those days I didn't listen, I thought

what I was doing was right. Didn't listen to me Mum neither. I'd just go out the house and say 'Yeah, yeah, yeah', and now I listen and I can say to those boys out there to listen. Those boys out there don't know what they're under, or too scared to know what they're under.

I wouldn't bring up my youth in Hackney cos it's too dangerous, too many dark *(dangerous)* people. But I'd take him there to show him what it was like out there – just to put him off living life on the street.

My nephew used to rob people in the streets, he was only ten. His Dad owns a club, so he's always been going around with big boys. He started when he was six, doing sweet shops. The area he was growing up in, the people he was hanging round with didn't help. He didn't know no different. His Mum couldn't control him, trouble with the police, all the blame was on his Mum. His family was on top of him, so he had to go to his gran's for a couple of weeks and he did not like that. It bucked him up and he's alright now.

He used to take knives to school when he was six, seven. All the Hackney kids do it. As a black kid you just go through those things. And white boys do as well. But it's different cos we're always losing.

The way I see it what I went through no way I want my kid to go through. I don't see my Dad. Most black boys don't. But my kid is going to be bona fide.

Molly: But you'll be around.

Winston: Not 24–7. But he knows someone's there for him. My Dad's just a cunt. Lots of black boys just ain't got anyone out there.

The worst would be if I conked out before he was ten. Course I know I might be hurt *(wounded)* too much. Too many of my close friends got hurt. It's too bad. The South London boys put three of my boys in hospital, one friend got slashed in the arm, another got slashed in the head. They're not looking

to hurt him, they're looking to kill him. Where does
that leave me?

We got to go and find out who did it to them. I've
got to help them in the way I can. I keep telling them
to walk away. I say 'You're big if you walk away.'
Cos I see the light but they ain't. So if I can't stop it,
I'll just have to fight. That's all there is to it.

Molly: What's the fighting about?

Winston: It's a way of life. Days was you had a fight and
just lost. These days you don't lose, you go and get
backup, and they go and get backup and you just
keep going.

Not fists. That would be alright. Everybody from
the age of seven carries something, a knife or a gun.
That's why people are in hospital and someone's
going to get killed. The only way you can stop it
is to put some people inside for a while until things
cool down. But after they might come looking for
everyone cos they been inside and try to hurt them.

My friends respect me for not thieving but they
don't want to stop. You need determination and good
friends to tell you if you look like going off the rails.

*One year after he left Sherborne House, I went to see Winston in
his family's pleasant ground-floor council flat, which was bustling
with activity. The large television set was on throughout the interview: Winston's sisters popped in and out of the sitting room until
the door was shut on them; and his one year-old boy walked
precociously between Winston and the sofa. Then friends arrived
and turned on the stereo to compete with the television set, but
Winston switched it off and ushered them out. Despite the constant traffic between the street and his flat, Winston has been
staying home almost continuously. He had the bemused and frustrated air of a newly incarcerated zoo animal.*

I'm twenty now, twenty-one in February 92 – not looking forward to it. Nothing to look forward to. When I arrived at Sherborne House I had a lot of things going for me, but there's no jobs
so you can't start off can you? No money!

Sherborne House made me understand things. They say 'How
would you feel if it was you? – rah, rah, rah' *(and so forth)*, and

everyone's talking and thinking, 'Boy, I'm not as bad as him, check it out. If that was, rah, rah, rah, my friend doing that *(crime)*, rah, rah – no, I wouldn't like that.' It makes you click. Every day you go there and you think, 'I should have been working, I should have turned that way before I turned this way. It would have been different.'

Some of the others thought the same, some of them didn't. Some thought it was just a little holiday to take them off the road, and then they're back out there just the same. But they were given a chance.

Some of them lied just to give themselves a boost. But I was just listening, it didn't really bother me. No one did anything to make me dislike them. Everyone was safe. The ones that didn't really agree with me I just said 'hello' to and kept out of their way. Everyone treated me safe, and I treated me safe. That's it, me.

I made a chair and I'm proud of it. Now people say 'Make me one' and I say, 'I'll have to go back to Sherborne House!' To me that's a joke. I'd like to go back there, not from court, but because I want to go there.

Like Stan, who also wanted to return to Sherborne House, Winston was serious. He tried to go back to college, but two courses in a row collapsed under him because the teachers closed them down. Winston is now stuck at home with literally nothing to do but make the occasional foray for the dole or to the Job Centre. He passes his time peering out the window, almost in pain from the temptation to go back on the streets. His mother cannot bear his being stuck at home, but fears his being on the street more.

There's Mum, two sisters and me. I don't know where my Dad is. I don't want to. He ain't done nothing for me, he don't support me, he never did. It don't make sense me talking to him. He went when I was small, I don't know where he is. We don't talk about it. He's not part of our life no more, we're happy as we are.

Don't see me Mum getting with no one else. She don't need no one, she's alright as she is, I look after her. Everything's safe, she don't need no one else.

She works part-time at a school as a dinner lady. She's a whole lot happier when I'm not doing things. Now if I get into trouble and she goes down the police station she knows if she asks me personally what happened and I tell her 'I never did that' she knows I didn't, she's got much more trust in me now. And if I did it, I'll tell her bluntly.

I didn't do good at school. I wasn't paying attention to the teachers, I was mucking around, looking at the girls. I didn't finish college. The course got squashed cos of the spending cuts. There weren't enough people turning up to the lessons – micro-electronics at City and East *(College)*. That was the first time, the second time it just went wrong, I didn't like the college – Hackney College. It was too local, I couldn't settle down.

I will be myself, 24–7, I ain't changing for no one. I guarantee that if a black boy been in my situation, in trouble, court and that, where you gonna get the brains from? No one can go to college at my age, if they've been 'working' *(stealing)*. They won't get the clothes they want. You have to go into it from school. You can't go back once you've left.

If you *(they)* want someone to go to college now, you've got to meet them half way by giving them decent money to live on, then everyone would be going to college. We want to go to college, we have to nick. You might as well stay at home and do what you were doing in the first place. Someone might have had the skills and the ability but will never get the chance cos they ain't got the money.

The right amount for someone my age, without a baby, living with their Mum, I reckon something like £80 to £90 every two weeks. Something to give their Mum, and still have a little bit of money for jeans. We don't want to all be the same, we want to be different, and if they give us a little bit more money, we could control it. You'd still get crime, but if people like me who don't want to do crime could live a little bit better, we'd hold it down. But it ain't gonna happen.

They'll say 'you don't need a new pair of jeans' – but we don't want to be without. If they're not willing to help us, why should we help them, go to college, pay for it, and not even get a job? My friend Rudy went to college for four years, he's a fully qualified carpenter; then he got laid off cos of the recession. He's been looking everywhere, Docklands, he hasn't even got a job.

I only buy draw at weekends, £10. That's my luxury, you know. You need something. I'm not a man who takes drugs hard. Weed don't do nothing to you. It don't slow you down like hash. It'll last me till Saturday, and that's it. I don't think that's drugs. The way Holland does *(with cannabis legalised)*, I'd like to live that way. It's better than coke, that's the thing you want to tighten up. I take Es, *(Ecstasy)* that doesn't do much, only if you take it often, it gives you a boost.

People make a big deal out of those things, and I say 'shut up', cos they don't know. I say, 'no one's died from an E. You don't see things, it's not like a trip,' and they say 'rah, rah, this boy's on drugs'. They shouldn't class everything as a drug, you understand?

My friends are the same. If any of my friends were on anything harder, they wouldn't be my friends cos I don't need it. That's when you start stealing hard, cos you need it. They come round and scan your house, know when I'm going out.

I don't trust none of my friends. I trust my Mum and my girl-friend. Not my friends. I talk to them like everything's boney *(bona fide)*, but we're all in the same boat. I could have a brother round here I don't know and two weeks later my house could get broken into.

And certain people have started to gee *(grass)* on their friends. I don't trust no one. A friend could come in with one of his friends when I'm smoking and phone up one of those *(Police Drug Help)* lines where you don't have to give an address, and they're at your door. Certain things you have to keep to yourself.

Everyone wants to step up. I can't trust no one, you just have them as friends, that's it. Certain people will take money if it's in my room. I have about five friends who come round here, hard, hard, who I trust with things.

At first my girl thought I was after her body but I brought her round and introduced her to my friends and they saw I was serious so now they respect that. They have girls too now, a lot of them – they see it's not so bad. If I didn't have a girl I'd be inside, that's no doubt.

My girl Tracey's living at home with her Mum, her sister and the baby. About fifteen minutes' walk from here. I see them every day. I look after it. She's working part-time. She's a sales assistant in Stoke Newington. Her money goes on the youth. Mine goes to my Mum, £30, Tracey, £20, and I'm left with the little change. £12. I paid down on a pair of jeans.

That's how I've been living since day one. That's why I turned to crime, but now I look at it and say 'It's not worth it' though the money is. So that's why I stay in and hold it down, I don't like it but that's how it is. Sometimes you wanna go outside. If I go down the street and I see someone with a lot of money, I'll rob them, simple as that. If I see them spending a lot of money in a shop I'll see where they put their purse and I'll move to them, and that's it, it's gone. If you get catched you get catched, you don't think about it till after.

I used to do it, on and off, for about a year. I was a late starter, I started when I left school. But I've cooled off it. I stopped cos I didn't like all the trouble, it was too much for my Mum. I got caught a couple of times and then the last time they made a big thing out of it and that's when I went to Sherborne House. When I left I stopped altogether.

My girl had her say, she said 'Don't do it, it don't make sense.' We been together three and a half years. She didn't business *(interfere)*. My girlfriend couldn't show me boo *(tell me anything)*. It was when she was having the baby, and I got catched one time, she said 'Don't do it.'

Now when I see a tik *(a prospective victim)*, I think, 'Ah, when I was younger I would have moved to you, but you're lucky today' – and I just carry on walking.

When you walk past you're screwing that you're walking past but when you have, it's too late to go back after she's clocked your face, that's asking to be nicked. But then it's not like you saw the money, and think, 'Rah, I left it.'

But if I had the choice to do it and not get catched for a couple of months I'd probably do it cos, boy, things are getting bad, real hard.

I'll be doing it again soon if I don't get some hardcore money for my clothes, cos I've been wearing the same clothes for a couple of months. That's not me, you understand? So soon if I don't get some money, I'm going to get in trouble. But I'm trying to hold it down as much as possible, mostly for the youth. But it hurts sometimes, that's the way it goes.

My girl is only seventeen and she wants something out of life. We plan she'll keep the baby until two years old and then give it to Gran. I don't know how the baby's gonna feel. I haven't come up to that yet. I don't know. But I do know I want to get something out of life.

But after staying inside his flat for a year, Winston is threatened by a new challenge and the ethos of the street.

Now we got the Untouchables up from Brixton. They only six-teen but bigger than me. They hung around with us and challenged the Tottenham boys. The Tottenham boys cut my friend cos they thought we were one of the Untouchables. They cut one of them *(Tottenham)* boys so bad he nearly conked out from a punctured lung, so the local boys called the police. The Untouchables offered them two grand to drop the charges but they not gonna take it. They want to show the Untouchables they not gonna stand for no more.

That ought to stop it but the sad thing is they *(Tottenham)* probably think they more of a man cos they nearly died. It's rub-bish, man.

I'm trying, man. My friends respect me for not thieving but they don't want to stop. You need determination and good friends to tell you if you look like going off the rails.

All you can do is point someone the right way, you can only let them watch you do the right things. If you've got a youth, say to him if he's doing something good, and point it out if what he's doing is not right. You get him scared by doing it with him. You set up something and show him it's wrong. If he does heroin, tell him he'll end up an idiot, like someone I know. Tell him the truth, things he'll understand. And if that doesn't work you got to leave him, cos you been through it yourself and you know he won't listen.

During the next two months, nothing changed for Winston. All his attempts to get a job led nowhere. His mother was increasingly frustrated. So was Winston. It seemed only a matter of time before he went back to crime. I spoke to him again ten weeks after my first visit.

I'm alright man, alright, but I'm back in court on 23 December for attempted burglary. I just got pissed off, man. No money for the son, and my girl got laid off just coming up to Christmas, just like that – after she worked for them for four years! I just got pissed off with having no money and the kid needs nappies. So when a friend say he going to do a burglary, and ask me to come along, I say I want no part of it. But I'll come along and watch, and keep a lookout for him, if he give me some of the money.

Must be someone was in the flat who heard and called the police. They took us down to the station and was alright, man.

We said we did it, and they just took statements and we left in a couple of hours.

My mother was so angry just didn't know what to do for a long time – she calmed down a bit now.

It was the first thing I tried *(since leaving Sherborne House a year ago)*, and I got caught.

In court, Winston appeared with his friend Spence, who had proposed the burglary. They both had thin moustaches, very short haircuts, and gold caps on their teeth. They wore identical black leather jackets, and baggy jeans and trainers. Spence looked several years older than Winston but was only nineteen, a year younger. He had a much longer criminal record than Winston, but Winston's mother and sister told me he was a good influence on him.

Winston's girl, Tracey, also appeared. She was pretty, henna-haired, and wore fancy Turkish slippers despite the bitter cold. She also had little patience with their predicament but clearly cared for Winston very much. As they lit a succession of cigarettes, they seemed like flies caught in aspic, as though they could do nothing to influence their fate.

Their solicitor warned Winston and Spence that as they were both in breach of a probation order, they had a fifty-fifty chance of going to prison. It emerged that Spence hadn't seen his probation officer more than once in a year because she had been ill, and then transferred offices. No one had given him any supervision or support. He had fallen through the system.

The prosecution described the facts: Winston and Spence had gone to a council flat nearby, broken the window of the bathroom, and were discussing how to climb in when the tenant heard voices and called the police. They had been found crouching behind a stairwell. Spence claimed to be looking first for a friend, then for a squat; Winston said he had nothing to do with any of it. But then they confessed. The solicitor used this as proof of their remorse. I testified as a character witness for Winston, and supported the fine report he had from Sherborne House.

After a severe reprimand for terrifying the potential victim, and a warning that they deserved to go to prison, the magistrate gave them both one hundred and fifty hours of Community Service, with a warning that if they appeared again they would certainly go down.

The next day I organised jobs for them in the warehouse at

Book Aid. They started out working well and apparently enjoying doing something other than hanging around their estate. But after a few days Spence stopped coming, leaving Winston to make the trip on his own. The next day, he produced yet another street friend, known as Silk Cut, who was by ill chance told there was no work for him that day. Silk Cut left early. Soon afterwards, a camera was discovered to be missing. When I asked Winston to deal with this, he promised to try, but never came back, or made contact. When tracked down again three months later, Winston apologised but claimed he could not handle the suspicion. He was now applying for several jobs, and seeking to resume his life. He was still stuck at home, but at least he had kept out of trouble.

Probation officers and many sociologists avoid using the term criminal except to describe criminal careers, for those who have committed themselves to a life of crime. Winston was not a criminal, but he had committed several criminal acts. They call him and the others offenders, because they focus on those acts, and what can be done to avoid them being committed in the future.

Now the choice of actions open to Winston seems to be narrowing as the weeks pass, the job market shrinks, and his lethargy grows. His mother worries he is probably on drugs because he has stopped listening to her demands that he go out and get a job. She is more than ready to throw him out but fears this will only lead him straight back to crime.

It seems terribly sad that Winston of all the group should have landed in this predicament. He has the shortest criminal record, the most qualifications, the strength of character to keep clear of the group dynamics at Sherborne House if not in Hackney – and a child in a stable relationship with a bright, hard working young woman who supports his keeping out of trouble.

Now Winston is in the limbo familiar to so many young men – black and white – with criminal records. It is worse for blacks because of the extra handicap of prejudice they face when trying for jobs. It is as though facing the reality of being Winston in Hackney has proved too much for him.

CHAPTER EIGHT

LUKE

Prison is an apprenticeship in scrubbing floors

Luke is a shadowy figure: white, aged nineteen, quiet, acutely shy, with a caved-in chest that hides his real height — nearly six feet. Although bright and unexpectedly athletic, he holds himself to himself. I'd spotted Luke early on, hunched silently in his track suit bottoms and trainers, often wrapped up in his anorak. He called it his thieving coat, and wore it even indoors in the swelter-ing heat. Luke was watchful, alert, paying more attention than the others, keeping out of trouble while showing an almost secret desire to be approved of, or at least to do well. He reminded me of the dormouse in Alice in Wonderland. I liked Luke from the start. With his sallow, pock-marked face and wispy fringe he looked so tentative that he seemed about to go up in smoke.

I came to know Luke better than any of the others at Sherborne House, beginning on the very first day. He was virtually silent during the first morning session in which the young men began to talk about themselves, and feel their way towards the pecking order of the group. In the break, they all gathered in the 'dining room', the large area that includes ping-pong and pool tables.

The white boys — Luke, Stan, Joel, Johnnie, Sam and a few others — mostly sat apart, watchful and silent, while the blacks moved together, chatting cheerfully around the pool table. As in prison, the new arrivals scanned each other and the scene to get their bearings and establish alliances. Luke chose to make one with me. Having learned I work in television, he asked straight away in an intimate whisper if I could help him to become a video tape editor. I'd expected that towards the end of the programme I would be hustled for work and/or money, but not right at the beginning.

Luke put me on the line within two hours of my arrival. I knew nothing about him yet, but admired his having moved in on me so quickly. Hoping I wouldn't come to regret it, I promised to introduce him, at the end of the course, to a video editor friend from the East End who could help him. Luke was excited at the prospect. He had already been given photographic training at the Battersea Basement, a project for young people in trouble. In this, my first conversation with one of the people I was at Sherborne House to get to know better, I felt shy. As Luke talked, I realised how little I shared with a working-class youth who had spent most of his life in and out of institutions and who was now in one because he was expert at burglary and theft.

When I asked him what offence had brought him to Sherborne House, Luke opened up suddenly, as though awakened from a trance. Instead of his cautious, halting whisper, Luke was brusque and angry: he had been prosecuted for Taking and Driving Away which he admitted he had done, but he was nevertheless very aggrieved at the police for lying to him during his interrogation:

They said they had fingerprints, footprints, loads of evidence, so I might as well confess. So I did. But they had no evidence at all! I'd have got off!

We were driving around in my friend's Golf GTi – nicked, of course – and came to this Renault showroom. All the keys were in the cars. So we took this gold Renault 5 GTi Special – only one in the country! The showroom wasn't alarmed. The keys were in the car. Sweet! Only the gates were locked. So we drove the car straight at the gates. It was a write-off. Complete write-off. Pushed up totally front and back. But we got away.

The old Bill stopped us later cos we were the only ones about at three in the morning. These coppers didn't know us but they took us to Wandsworth where they'd stopped us loads of times for TDAs and burglaries. That's when they done us up, the lying bastards!

Luke's sense of injustice was real enough, but it did not seem to extend to his own actions. He had already been on the Wheels project for compulsive car thieves, where young people have access to fix and drive bangers under controlled conditions. Luke liked it but he wanted his own car.

(Matter-of-fact) My friend would have come to Sherborne House too but he's inside for Aggravated Burglary. That's where you hit or tie up someone who's inside the drum you're spinning *(the house you are searching).*

My friend broke into a house where there were drug dealers

and took £2000 in drugs! *(He smiles at the irony.)* Course they told the police he took cash. Anyway he got done for it cos their uncles are coppers! *(This feeds his cynicism about the police.)*

I was pleased to have established a rapport with Luke. He had already shown me how little I knew about the lives of those at Sherborne House, or their way of thinking. I wondered, listening to his tirade against the police, whether I would be able to suggest to him that not all coppers are like the ones he's met, or even persuade him that in their shoes, faced with the correct suspect and no evidence, he would be tempted to do as they did to trick a confession from him. I was aware that Luke – and I suspected the others too – had a stereotyped view of all coppers as lying bastards, just as most policemen I know see these youngsters as 'toerags', always guilty of something when they're stopped on the street. At the end of the first day, as I headed back to the comfort of my house and happy family, I was all too aware of the difference between my life and his.

Luke's family background is yet another painful saga. He is the eldest of three children. His father disappeared when he was very young. His mother soon remarried a large, strict West Indian with whom she quickly had two children. He consumed her attention, leaving Luke jealous and resentful. Luke's step-father beat him regularly for any misbehaviour. Feeling she couldn't cope, his mother put Luke into care at the age of seven. He had a care order with a social worker to last until he was seventeen. Luke's step-uncle is a 'raga', a black street villain who lives in Brixton, and is currently in Wandsworth Prison.

Luke said he was abused by his step-father – physically rather than sexually, from what I can gather. He began thieving at eight, under his uncle's tutelage. Then he ran away from home, and began sniffing glue. He believes his Mum blames him for the breakup of her marriage to his real father.

Nevertheless, he retained a real desire to be part of what was left of the new family. He called them 'half-caste', and was very close to them all, particularly his step-grandmother and half-brothers. In the session on race at Sherborne House, whites and blacks met separately. Among the whites, although Joel and several others had black step-fathers, Luke was the only one to show sympathy and knowledge of black experience – which he imparted in whispers to one of the group leaders while the rest of the group egged each other on with racist remarks.

Whenever Luke mentioned his mother – which he only did privately to me – it was with barely suppressed feelings. They quarrelled whenever they saw each other. When, a year after he left Sherborne House, I dropped Luke off near his mother's flat and asked Luke if I might meet her, he made clear she was averse to having contact with any outsider involved with him. She has refused to meet his probation officer and his housing officer as well. Their relationship is still highly charged because of the past.

Mum put me into care cos she couldn't cope financially or emotionally. She's never said sorry or anything. I don't want an apology but I want her to see she was wrong. Each time I go home she blames me for everything. It's always my fault, never hers. We have terrible rows. I'd never do that to my kid. I'd starve first.

Drove me mad *(going into care)*. They *(social workers)* probe right into your life but they don't listen, they just want to get their point across. I didn't know what a care order was, but I was taken to my first children's home – a shithole. The others were there for worse things – one kid for killing his sister! He pushed her face down into the mud – and got an indefinite sentence.

Luke was then sent to more children's homes, ending up at a regional assessment centre for problem children, with some secure places, one of which, Luke told the group proudly, was allocated to him.

I ran away from children's home and burgled rich people's houses. They had tennis courts – huge drums. I did it more than before. I didn't realise the seriousness. Just took what I wanted. Did it with the same guy, or with my uncle, or on my own.

My uncle would say 'I want six or twelve expensive carriage clocks.' I'd go into British Home Stores with a Sainsbury's bag, pop them in and walk out. We'd drive to his *(council housing)* estate to sell them. I was ten years old.

My uncle's in Brixton *(prison)* now. He's only three or four years older. He's escaped from everywhere. He did the Punch and Judy robbery – had a smaller kid on his shoulders and wore a long coat. It was never solved.

Contrary to some notions that parental influence is always good, many young offenders have Fagin-like relationships to older relatives. Stu, one of the other group members who didn't finish the course, was taken regularly to Switzerland by his uncle to steal jewellery, which was then fenced by his parents. Children are

useful accomplices because they receive much lighter penalties if
they are caught and prosecuted.

I was nearly eleven when I finally got caught for shoplifting and
went Guilty though there was no evidence against me. They tricked
me. But there's a lot of stuff I got rid of before they caught me.

I went to an approved school for a year in Herne Hill. The only
school I liked. But I kept doing a runner. Police arrested me all the
time – they came and arrested me in my bed. They warned me.

At the assessment centre I was banged up there too and warned
I'd be kicked out and I was. I used to be done for going onto the
(railway) tracks at Brixton.

Luke recounted these experiences to the group at Sherborne
House as part of the review of his criminal record. He spoke with
a mixture of resignation at their inevitability, and a still vivid
sense of their unfairness. But like the others who described their
treatment by the authorities, he seems unaware that he had done
anything to deserve punishment, no matter how perverse the pen-
alties were.

I got no convictions from twelve to sixteen. They sent me to
Special School in the country. They pick you up at home and weekends they keep you inside. If you run away they put you in pyjamas
all day. If you keep doing it, they put you in the isolation block, they
strip you to pants, and then naked. I had to go to class naked.

As most of the group had themselves been in children's homes,
no one deemed this even worthy of comment. I thought it extra-
ordinary, but shortly afterwards the newspapers broke revelations
of similar punishments – such as Pin-down, in which children were
kept in solitary confinement for days in their underwear, or naked
– taking place in children's homes elsewhere in the country. These
revelations explained the group's reaction.

Didn't see my Mum for a year. She used to come eighty miles
with things for me but they turned her away. They took my privileges away. If you behave, you get moved to the extension, the
two independent units and you could go home from there. As I
got older, I calmed down, got more privileges, went to town and
got girls. But I got worse at the end. They had a lot of stupid rules
– like no smoking in the dorms.

In the end I got a stitch-up *(was framed)*. I was growing a huge
amount of grass in the backyard, but they got two little kids to
say I was pressuring them to get me drugs. But that's ridiculous –

I come from London, man. I could just step out the door and get them.

Special School could be rough, very rough. I remember one older kid raping a younger one. I never would do that but I heard it going on next door and shouted at him to stop. But he locked the younger one in the cupboard and padlocked him. I remember some kid sniffing lighter fuel threw it at the social worker, and set her alight. *(The other group members laughed at this.)*

Every time anyone escaped they'd call the police who came with dogs. But it was a piece of piss to get into the town, nick a car and drive to London. I never got caught. I turned myself in after some days in London. I'd gone to my mates, done burglaries, and then ended up at my Mum's. She went hysterical. 'What're you doing here?' she'd scream at me, and make me go to the police.

I finally got kicked out of boarding school because I said they could keep me in isolation but it wouldn't make no difference. Then got sent to Chiswick, a Christian Fellowship. They're a right bunch of plums – no sex, no violence, no drugs, no drink. But I got a girl pregnant there. Spent every penny I could steal on drugs and drink – acid, Es, a couple of lines *(of cocaine)*.

I preferred to do creepers – burglaries when people are in the house. It's great – you listen for the breathing. It's the risk of getting caught that makes it exciting.

If no one was there, I'd sleep in the house I burgled over and over again – they were always on holiday, and they left the dough in the same place. I did it with fourteen, fifteen, sixteen year-olds. I'd go in and then let them in the house, then we'd come out and sort out the money. The police would catch them but think it was only the three of them, and they never grassed me up.

It was so easy. You walk into any big shop and just take what you want – video, telly. I'd go into the Arndale Centre *(a local shopping centre in South London)* all the time and take lots of things, but it's not the easiest place – they got hidden cameras. I got caught once and they took me to the office and showed me a tape of me stealing.

One time I nicked a whole lot of centre punches *(a tool used to punch holes in glass, popular with burglars)*. I cleared out the shop. I went back to school and handed them out but someone grassed me up. But one thing that bugs me – if the school says they care about me, what's the point of taking me to court?

Anyway, he *(the head teacher)* defended me in court saying I was doing well. But the second time, when I was bringing machetes and knuckle-dusters back to school, he took them to the police instead of putting them in the safe, and said I needed a custodial sentence. It doesn't make sense. They say they care but they beat you too.

Many of the group shared Luke's indignation and affirmed that they too had been beaten in children's home. No one commented on the weapons he had brought back to school. Throughout this account, Luke spoke quickly and breathlessly, looking down at the floor, or occasionally at one of the group leaders as if hoping for her agreement. His gentle persona had slipped, revealing a degree of violence that was all the more shocking for being expressed in low tones of injured reasonableness.

In magistrates' court you got to stand up, while in juvenile you sit down. I don't see why you got to stand. It wasn't that serious, cos the solicitors tell you what's gonna happen. The police say you're going down for donkey's years to try to get you to go Queen's Evidence, to grass up the other guy. Even when my co-d *(co-defendant)* wasn't a mate I wouldn't do it.

Most things I got nicked for I didn't do. I was stoned on weed and drink. Whisky, lager, beer. There was drugs on me last charge but the police smoked the lot.

In one police cell, they banged me up with the guy I drove with who'd grassed me up. I started kicking him until they opened the cell and had to move him. *(He's very wound up about all this still.)* They'd have had to kill me to get me to stop.

Police in Chiswick fit you up. They get you for one TDA and do you for three, for shoplifting in two or three cases. Or loads of burglaries. They charged me with thirty burglaries, but I'd only done twelve of them. They stitch you up!

Like the others who committed hundreds of undiscovered crimes, Luke said this with venom and without any sense that he had escaped justice so often before.

When I went to court I was buzzing *(stoned)*. I didn't want go in there in a straight frame of mind. Just wanted to get it over and done with. I was living at home then – me Mum went mad, just had hysterics.

My social worker said she'd write me the best report ever but I'd done too much. I got that Asian judge in Court Three at Lavender

Hill – the one they call Idi Amin. He's had everything done to him, to his family, to his car, his house, everything. But he don't give no one bail.

He says even before the trial starts 'No way you're walking out the normal door. You going out that prison door. I tell you that right now.' He'd taken one look at my previous *(convictions)*. The trial hadn't even started! He did it to me mate too. My mate would have paid £400 in fines – he had a posh job. But the judge wouldn't play. Anyway I was buzzing again, so I said 'You fucking cunt!' and gave him the finger.

During the exercise which involved the group members looking at moral dilemmas, Luke described the predicament young people face when they are caught up in the criminal justice system. They operate from their own code of ethics:

> Luke: *(reading)* A mate is arrested for affray. He denies it and says he was with you. He wasn't. Do you lie or tell the truth to the police? *(straight away)* I'd protect my mate. You've got to – there's too much pressure. *(thinking it through as he leans towards the group)* Anyway, if you don't you'll get hassled or beaten up. I'd lie all the way to court.
> *(proud)* I was offered a chance to get off if I grassed up all my mates so I said 'fuck off' and went to court. I know my mates wouldn't grass either.
> *(The others all agree.)*
> Lenore: *(in the face of such solidarity among thieves)* So who is grassing? Some people are going down.
> *(Silence)*.

During the session on alcohol, Luke admitted to the group that once he starts drinking, he can't stop. He began both thieving and drinking when he was eight.

> Luke: Now I can't allow myself a drink at all. Gone twelve months without offending. But when I'm drinking I don't care. I'll even thieve when people are watching. Whisky, vodka, brandy, Southern Comfort, spirits, Holsten Pils.
> Lenore: Did you consider going to a group to kick it?
> Luke: I laughed it off.

Lenore: Did you practise going to a pub and order orange
      juice?
Luke: Some coppers suggested AA. They said, 'Have you
      got a drink problem? Ring this number.' It was an
      off-licence!
         I hate the police. And the fucking law – there's
      one for the poor and one for the victim. There
      should be a sentence for each offence no matter what
      the other circumstances. No one should go to prison,
      it does nothing for you.

*Interestingly, this policy, where each offence has a standard tariff
no matter what the circumstances or the background of the
offender is known as 'Just deserts'. It has just become law in the
Criminal Justice Act. It is seen by reformers as a way of reducing
the prison population, as custody is only meant to be used for
serious offences. But conservatives like it because it stops sentencers being swayed by social deprivation. It leaves open judicial
interpretation of what crimes are considered serious, and may lead
to heavier sentences, as well as to more people going to prison for
longer. In the exercises in which real cases were presented to group
members for their views of what the sentence should be, most of
them were more punitive than the courts.*

Mark: If bank-robbers didn't go to prison, then everyone
      would run around robbing banks.*
Luke: There should be punishment, just no prison. Prison
      costs £550 per week. *(The latest estimates actually
      hold it to be just under £400 per week.)* It'd be better
      to give the money for a house or mortgage so they
      wouldn't have to commit crimes to get the money.
      Why not send him here?

*In one sense, such a compliment to Sherborne House was less sur-
prising coming from Luke than from any of the others. His performance on the programme could not have been more different from
the destructive pattern of his previous activities and experiences. He
attended virtually every day, achieving far and away the highest
number of attendance points. Others with far fewer points took an
increasing amount of time off. They risked a return to court if they*

---

* See Mark's own comments on prison in his chapter, pp. 75–91.

ran out of points entirely – and relied on the willingness of the staff to give them another chance. Yet, apart from a few remarks like that quoted above, Luke never conceded that he came because he wanted to, because he liked it there, that the company and the various activities were a good deal more stimulating than the wasteland of empty time which was his normal life otherwise.

On the various outings, Luke showed surprising aptitude as an athlete: in the go-karting, he won several heats and came very close to winning the trophy against the ace joyriders. He skied well on both the dry slope and on water, he was comfortable on a horse, and in the rock climbing showed skill and confidence. He also helped me in my struggle to overcome my fear of heights, and offered to hold the rope which I had to use to scale a rock face. At such moments, his whole expression and posture changed: he moved around the rocks quickly and with authority, and wore an open, friendly smile that made him seem like any other young man happily engaged on a sporting adventure.

It was a marked contrast to the guarded crouch Luke maintained in the early groups. He began quite silently, but as he gained confidence, he contributed more often. His comments were consistently interesting. They revealed an elaborate moral framework possessed of its own, often surreal, logic. Its structure, like an Escher drawing, was full of perpetual staircases leading nowhere.

The group did one exercise called 'How far would you go?', using a list of offences and crimes from double parking to murder. Each person had to tick how far he or she would go in committing these offences. Luke was especially amused by the idea. Although they all agreed it was wrong to commit sex offences or mug old ladies, many distinctions between offences were made in more pragmatic terms: whether they were worth the risk of being caught and prosecuted.

Luke: Wouldn't park on a double yellow line, wouldn't
    steal a few items worth less than £20. But would
    steal goods worth £200. I steal cars to make money.
    You sell the wheels, the engine, the frame, or the
    whole car and change the number plates, change the
    engine and ask someone if they want to buy it.
    Someone I know and can trust not to grass me up.
    My uncle's got a garage in Battersea. I leave the car

far out of London for two months, and then do it.
*(I was surprised. Such arrangements involve more
long-term effort than is normally associated with
youthful crimes.)*

Wouldn't rape/rob a bank at gunpoint/commit
murder/armed robbery/shoot someone on contract/
beat up old age pensioner. Would deal in cannabis
but not in heroin.

Wouldn't stab someone. *(His denial was
undermined by his admission that he carries an
offensive weapon.)*

Lenore: What? Why?

Luke: It's a knife. But only for self-protection when I go
out to 'do things'. If someone finds you in their house
they'll shout for the police or kill you.

Lenore: Not many burglars are killed.

Luke: *(urgently)* Lots of people are. If you burgle the
wrong house they'll use a knife or gun to get you.

Lenore: Do any of you know any burglars who've been
killed?

*(No one did, but all the group shared Luke's view
that many people keep knives or guns by their beds.)*

Luke: One time I was under somebody's bed looking for
money – and my mate was downstairs when the
bloke came back and went berserk. I had to jump
out the window to get away three storeys up. I
messed up my leg real bad.

Next question: would you assault a police officer?

Luke: I'd kick a copper if he was doing it to me. I've done
it before.

Many of the offences are things I already done:
(laughs) I punched someone/been drunk under age/
smashed a window of a house/burgled a house/
driven under age/passed false cheques/given a false
name/used abusive language/driven without
insurance.

Deb: Would you do them again?

Luke: I'd thieve again if I needed the money. If I go back
to prison, what's the point in stopping?

Lenore: *(shocked)* But you're doing well. Why should
you?
Luke: *(suddenly very serious: this is his sense of himself)*
But if I start missing sessions or being late – I've
been late twice – I could be breached and sent back
to court, and they'd send me to prison. So what's
the point?
Deb: But –
Luke: Listen, I really want to get through this, and
straighten myself out. But if I fail there'll be no point.
I worked for a year, came in on time every day, and
then got nicked for stealing a car to sell its tyres. I
was in a training scheme but got no money so I had
to get some somehow.

*In expressing a desire to go straight, Luke might have been saying
what he thought the probation officers wanted to hear. I was
inclined to believe him if only because he was so ambivalent about
it.*

*Luke explained his commitment to crime as if it were his only
means of sustenance. Yet in the other activities, he continued to
show abilities that could be gainfully employed in the outside
world. In the workshop, Luke embarked on a seriously ambitious
project, a circular side table with a glass top sitting on a single leg
that was round and curved upwards in a spiral. He worked with
complete concentration, making a series of circular plywood plates
to build up his pedestal. In the art classes he made chess pieces
with the same care and attention. His photography was still more
interesting – he chose unusual subjects in the local area, which he
printed and developed in the darkroom. In each pursuit, he
showed flair and dedication. Yet at every school he has attended
he has failed.*

*At the end of the first four weeks, it was time for Luke's mid-way
assessment. His probation officer, Rex, did not turn up, so he met
with Lenore alone. When she asked Luke about how much help
he'd received from his probation officer, it emerged that Rex had
not seen him since last year. Someone else wrote the report to
send him to Sherborne House. He said Rex had since missed two
meetings. Luke was clearly disappointed, apparently with good
reason:*

I walked for four hours to the last one, so I'm not interested in more.

This was typical of Luke – an almost heroic willingness to observe some rules, and a defiant resistance to others.

He was very keen to get a flat of his own, away from the shared accommodation in Balham in which he lived now. It was run by the council's Independent Living Scheme, which provides half-way housing for troubled young people not ready to live on their own. Apart from the teenage volunteer supervisor who shared the flat, there was also Laura, a young girl, who was driving Luke mad:

She's a religious fanatic. Always praying. And she's an idiot and a liar. She's always stealing my stamps and then shouting 'Who's got my stamps!' And I'm hassled by the neighbours.

Like many of the young offenders with fragmented family backgrounds, his vision of a place of his own was almost his sole practical goal. Having been in care since he was seven, he was entitled to a flat when was eighteen. He was now nineteen.

The flat shit is crap. I been told by social workers since I was sixteen I'd get my own flat. It was in the contract! Otherwise I wouldn't've agreed to live in the shithole I've got now. I been in care all my life.

I was told I'd get it in ten weeks, then six to nine months. I got to put up with it. It's in the contract that if I want a better flat, I got to live first in a poxy flat in an anti-social area. They're all anti-social there. It must be in the water. You talk about sexism – every woman that walks by is whistled at – never geezers. It pisses me off. And every time I go into a shop they think I'm gonna steal from them. It's prejudice!! Just cos some people thieve doesn't mean everyone will.

If they said they'd give me a flat in Balham or the middle of nowhere, I'd choose nowhere! It's fucking crap! I hate the place! They *(the Independent Living Scheme)* want to come over and have group meetings and stick their fucking nose in my affairs. I don't want them sticking their nose in.

When later I visited Luke there, I found the flat was reasonable but shabby because he and his co-tenant did not clean it. It would not have taken much effort with a dustpan, a cloth and a paint-brush, to rescue it from its miserable state. The estate itself was a mid-rise set of council blocks with grass and trees in a mixed but not especially unpleasant part of South London. It gradually

emerged that Luke loathed it largely because he was intimidated
by his neighbours, but the place became synonymous in his mind
with how he was feeling about life in general.

Balham's the worst area I've ever lived in. I used to live in
Wandsworth, Brixton, Wandsworth, then the fucking countryside,
then Wandsworth, and then Balham.

Listening to this unsettling catalogue of movement around
South London, I wondered how, given that he's never had a
family, Luke managed the simple things like laundry and food. At
sixteen, would I have wanted my own flat or would my daughter?
And would either of us have managed alone?

The housing workers were rightly worried that Luke may not
be ready to live on his own, hence their desire to visit and support
him. But Luke's experience of authority has made him deeply
mistrustful even of those patently trying to help. Yet he also wants
support and contact badly. He asked Lenore to help him change
flats, but even field probation officers have no such powers. They
can only refer their clients to the appropriate agencies.

Lenore showed Luke the staff report on his progress. It was
very positive, but he jumped on a reference to possible dependency
on alcohol:

Luke: I'm not dependent on drink. I can go for ages
    without one. Then when I have one I want more.
Lenore: It's like a weakness.
Luke: Yeah – I can not drink, I can not go to pubs but
    when I do I keep going. It's better I should give it up
    altogether.
Lenore: But you're doing so well at Sherborne House! Is
    it because you're doing something – you're busy
    here? *(Luke agreed)*
Luke: On the dole I couldn't do anything that cost money
    so I'd spend my little cash on drink.
    (reads from the sheet with the staff comments:)
    Quiet/thoughtful/don't doubt yourself so much/
    could speak up more/serious/hard working in
    groups/lacking in confidence. *(Since the start of the*
    session Luke had been looking down, drawing and
    doodling. He continued to do so while talking,
    avoiding looking Lenore in the face.)

Luke: Fair comment. It's hard cos you have to get up in
the morning. You need someone else to help you do
it. Specially after I've been drinking.
Lenore: Why can't you control it when you can control
other things?
Luke: Dunno. It's like you start getting drunk and can't
remember what it does to you. I'd rather get drunk
and be able to remember. It's just a feeling. You
can't walk straight. The room's going round and if
it's cold you don't feel cold.
Lenore: Drink makes you feel better?
Luke: Yes.
Lenore: When you're angry, ashamed?
Luke: Yeah. Why do I do it when I'm angry with myself?
*(He was open now. This was a major issue for
him. But we all sensed that Luke had been handled
badly by a host of agencies and social workers
already.)*
Lenore: You could talk to someone.
Luke: Like a rehab centre?
Lenore: Counselling.
Luke: Don't like counselling.
Lenore: You could get into a drink group – like AA.
Luke: I'm frightened of what I might do.
Lenore: Maybe we can help you with that.
*(But this touched another key limitation on the
work at Sherborne House: the probation officers may
not delve into psychological background. They must
concern themselves only with behaviour and ethics.)*
Luke: *(still drawing)* I know why I smoke. And drink too.
Boredom. I don't even like the taste. All that
money, just rolling up joints.
*(Lenore tells him about a photography course and
also a plan to improve his spelling.)*
Lenore: It might make you more secure than cigs and
drink.
Luke: When I'm working, I can get a drink on Friday and
be drunk all weekend, then not have anything on
Monday.
I'm keen on boxing. Been looking for classes. But

haven't gone to the Balham leisure centre because everyone in the area are wankers.

Lenore encouraged him to go for evening classes – to keep himself occupied. But he said that last time he tried he couldn't sustain it. He was a curious mix of optimism, determination and unshakeable defeatism, presumably all born of his experience. His hatred of Balham was vivid, utterly disproportionate to the realities of the area. To escape, Luke returned regularly to his old stamping ground in Putney, 'hanging loose' in the pubs, waiting and hoping to see friends who now were working, in prison, or had their own homes.

Lenore: What do you think of the programme here?
Luke: It's OK. I expected worse. I been to Wayside
     programme when I was ten.
Lenore: Can you get anything out of it?
Luke: Yeah. Education. For me and for them.

This was the sort of positive answer which suggests the value of the course – the participants know how much they need education, and seemed to want it. Luke might have said what he knew Lenore wanted to hear, but nothing else fell into that category. She told him he should be very confident, and finish the programme.

I am confident. I just don't like being loud.

(*suddenly looks up at her*) Why do most people lose their points in the first week? It nearly gutted me to see so many people drop out. I could carry on being late but I'd have very few points left by now. Two (*group members*) already been sent back to court! Not worth risking a few days off.

Luke had more than enough points to relax, but he was genuinely frightened his regime would fall apart if he eased off at all. Moreover, the routine at Sherborne House of early rising for a start at ten in the morning was a complete reversal of the young people's normal hours: sleeping until noon and starting the day then.

Luke: I was late this morning because of the puppy. He
     shat all over the place.
Lenore: You're good! Some people can't control their
     drinking. They can't just splash their face and come
     in the next morning and do the work.
Luke: When I stay drinking I like the feeling and the

drinking. But when I finish, I feel like stopping.

Lenore: *(tries to reassure him)* There will always be things happening, always be fuck-ups. But remember you can handle them. You can start again.

Luke: I've tried to so many times before. It's not like – I wanted to carry on but I didn't know how – it's like reversed. I had to see what the bad side looked like as well as the good one.

Lenore: I think you're doing really well.

Luke: *(quietly pleased, he returns to drawing)* I don't care what other people say to me, like I'm a 'goody-goody'.

Lenore: Some people live their lives that way. You don't. You're strong. You can afford to take a day off from the programme, but you get what you want from it.

Luke: Yeah. A couple of the others in the group – they're almost out – like Bobby, he's got only nine points.

Lenore: We all have our weaknesses. Bobby's is punctuality.*(Luke remembers that Bobby's Giro cheque was stolen too. It brings him back to his flat in Balham, and how much he hates Laura, who shares his flat.)*

Luke: *(suddenly alarmingly angry)* I hate her, but I didn't steal her Giro! I couldn't use it – take a girl's cheque and go in and say 'I'm a boy, here's a girl's cheque!' I'd love to beat her up!

Lenore: Don't.

In this session Lenore revealed Luke to himself as a conscientious young man, who really wanted to do well, but who was always close to violence, drink, and petty crime.

Reflecting on the sadness at the loss of so many group members so soon, I felt those that remained like Luke had such obvious potential, their rescue should be more straightforward. Yet their criminal records spoke for themselves. It wasn't straightforward at all.

Their session ended with a male voice shouting from the women's lavatory. Lenore was furious. Luke discovered who was in there, and that he had no lavatory paper!

Lenore: *(angrily)* Who is it?

Luke: *(smiling)* Won't say! I never grass! *(It was Bobby)*.

Things were not all smooth between Luke and the group leaders. His willingness to talk about his thieving was underpinned by his private definitions of morality. In the exercise that asked if they would steal from family, friends, acquaintances and teachers, it emerged that despite his claim to steal only from rich strangers, Luke had stolen from neighbours. He saw them in the pub afterwards and bought them a drink, or gave them a cigarette. Lenore was contemptuous of this hypocrisy as she saw it, but Luke was unable to take her point. He bitterly resented being criticised as amoral and sulked for days afterwards. On another occasion he accused her of calling them 'lower class' on the strength of a conversation he claimed to have overhead in the lavatory. She was furious, and denied ever using such a term – all the probation officers were ultra-sensitive about the political correctness of their language. Again, he stuck to his point that she looked down on them and went silent for the rest of the day.

As the arrangements were made for Project Week, Lenore asked Luke to come on the sailing trip, and so did I. We both agreed he had been the outstanding member of the group, and the voyage would be an exhilarating change for him – both as an escape from Balham, and an introduction to new experiences. But Luke seemed surprisingly unwilling even to entertain the idea. He said no firmly, twice: 'My girlfriend is scared to be left alone.' He meant, rather, that he was scared to leave her alone. Luke had bruises on his neck that could have been love bites. They suggested a degree of passion – or violence – that went along with his anxiety about whether she would be there when he came back.

I was genuinely disappointed not to have his company on the boat, but we continued to have contact in other ways. Friday afternoon football began with a coaching session led by a member of the local professional team, Millwall. Luke shared the group's general impatience with the drill, and often kicked practice balls far out of the fenced asphalt playing area. They all wanted to play a proper game. I was hopeless in goal on Luke's team. He showed great tolerance, considering how competitive he proved himself to be.

In the photography workshop, Luke decided to make portraits using me as a model. It was an awkward, comic occasion (I'd been delighted to be awarded the card 'Most Willing to Make A Fool of Himself' in a previous exercise). I found myself perched on a ladder, and in various other (unconscious) parodies of record album covers. But among a spectrum of largely useless pictures, Luke took one very good photograph indeed. His work in photography suggested he could make a career in some audio-visual field. He was serious about this, and planned to go to college to study electronics and video in January.

The last week of the Sherborne House programme was at the end of September. In his final assessment, Luke was asked how he saw the best and worst outcomes in the future:

Six months: best would be no court cases, no offending, college. Worst: dunno, if I stopped going to college, messed that up and carried on doing burglaries. Might do that if I lost interest. But I hope not. Don't want to go back to what I been doing. I know if I carry on I'll just get locked away. So I don't want to unless I change my life and start taking risks again – like if I lose a job and feel so bad I'll just want to go out and get money.

(Luke described his hopes for the long term future:) A house with my girl Donna – bought outright, no mortgage, for £75,000. Worst would be to split up with her and lose me flat.

Lenore correctly observed that his most vulnerable period would be the three months between the end of Sherborne House and the start of college in January. But she declared his outlook positive.

Lenore: It's a really hopeful future. No reason why you
    shouldn't do it.
Luke: (with his characteristic mix of hope and bitterness)
    I wanted to go to college before. I'd be there now
    if this place hadn't happened.

In the final awards, Luke won the most points for attendance, and also made the best piece of work in the tech workshop, the splendid circular wooden table with glass inset and spiral leg. It showed that if his ambitions in video failed, Luke also had the makings not just of a carpenter but of a craftsman.

With all his talents, Luke was like a racing car stuck in first gear with the handbrake on. On the last day, the crafts instructor, Tom, arranged to deliver each person's work to his home in the van. For the very first time in ten weeks Luke turned up several hours late, breathless and furious. The van had gone. Lenore appeared

*from the staff room and tried to calm him down. She even offered
to deliver the table herself on her way home which would take her
near to Luke's flat. He would have none of it:*

You can keep the fucking thing. I don't want it no more.

*Shocked and hurt by Luke's vitriolic tone, Lenore told him
he'd deliberately created this row because he hated leaving. It is a
familiar but serious problem for many young people with no place
to go and nothing to do after ten crowded weeks. She left the offer
open if he changed his mind. Without another word, without
saying goodbye to any of us, Luke stormed off. Later, he rang
Lenore and accepted her offer.*

*I worried about what would happen to Luke now, without the
structured routine to rouse him from bed. Hopefully, he'd find work
until he started college. Prior to Sherborne House, he already had
one job, as a photographer's apprentice. His potential was obvious,
yet so far it seemed to have been put only to negative use.*

*I arranged for Luke to meet the video tape editor for a possible
job, as he'd asked of me at the start. It took three appointments
for Luke to show up. On the first two occasions I waited an hour,
and never heard from him afterwards. A message was later passed
via his probation officer Rex. The third time, we were to meet by
the turnstiles in the Piccadilly Circus tube station. Luke turned up
five minutes late, saying he'd been waiting upstairs on the street
and was about to give up if I'd not been where he found me.*

*As we walked along Oxford Street, Luke admired the archi-
tecture:*

Reminds me of Knightsbridge, these old buildings with ledges
and balconies high up. Me and a mate got a long ladder and
reached up to those ledges and climbed over the bars and barbed
wire on the balconies and into the flats. It was scary but sweet.

*We went for a cup of coffee in one of the stores where Luke
had been active. Seeing it through his eyes was a revelation for
me. Every cranny was a place to hide either himself or the goods
he was lifting. He knew all the exits, and the staff doors:*

We'd hide in a corner till the shop shut and everyone left, then
nick our gear and nip out the back way.

*The job interview went well. My friend liked Luke. Having grown
up in the East End, he knew about life on the street. He happened
to be editing a religious series whose producers liked the idea of*

giving a break to someone who had been in trouble. They offered Luke a week's observation to learn how video editing works, to be followed by a job as a runner at £70 a week, with the likely prospect of a training as an assistant editor if he did well. It was just the way ahead that Luke might dream of, with real money and security at the end of it. He was due to start the next day as an observer. Luke never turned up, nor called my friend.

Instead, a week later, he rang me from a call box and said he hadn't gone to the video place or called because he was too broke to pay the tube fare or even make a telephone call until his Giro cheque came through.

Luke: Listen, Rog, you know you said you liked the table.
RG: I did, very much.
Luke: How about buying it from me for £90? It's not for me.
    I gotta buy my girlfriend Donna a diamond engagement ring at £120. She's gonna leave me otherwise. She's gonna go home to her sister. I'm desperate, Rog.

We were cut off because his money run out.

This rang all sorts of warning bells for me. I called him back at the phone box and argued that Donna was only seventeen, and even if they wanted to become engaged, they had to find a ring more suitable to his current finances. I also felt strongly that it would not be the basis of a good friendship or even a working relationship between us if I were to subsidise him, even by the device of buying his table. But I agreed to think more about it. I recalled being warned early in the programme at Sherborne House by Jack, the Senior Probation Officer, about the dangers of trying to help Luke or any of the others: 'Expect to be disappointed. And whatever you do, don't give them any money.'

I was torn between not wanting to lose our contact and Luke's trust, and my strong sense that Jack was right; providing the money would be more likely to damage our relationship than my refusal. I had no way of reaching Luke except by going to his flat. He was not there. I left a note explaining my decision and asking him to call. He never did.

The next time I saw Luke was eight months later, in court.

I learned about the trial from Rex, his probation officer. It seems Luke never started college at all. Since April, he had been in prison. He was in Feltham Young Offenders' Institution, on remand for a burglary committed in Paddington. Almost a year after he left Sherborne House, Luke went up to Knightsbridge Crown court to stand trial.

When I arrived at the court, I offered to be a character witness for him. Luke's woman barrister was reviewing his previous convictions with the detective who had arrested him:

Detective: He's a real cat burglar. Despite all he's done
   before, when he's locked up, he's convinced
   society's against him.
Barrister: *(encouragingly)* There's a gap after Sherborne
   House. He didn't offend for six months!
Detective: *(with obvious disdain)* You mean he wasn't
   caught. He was very arrogant in his interview,
   treated us like shit, the little toerag.

The barrister told me Luke seemed delighted to learn I was there. In the dock he looked very stern, then smiled at me broadly after pleading Guilty.

But it emerged this was not his first offence since leaving Sherborne House. Luke was arrested in Paddington while on bail awaiting trial in Kingston for a previous burglary in March, three months earlier. Although he now pleaded guilty to both offences, Luke could not be sentenced in Knightsbridge because the other court had failed to get him out of prison to be committed for trial. They thought he was still out on bail.

The Knightsbridge judge was furious that he could not deal with both cases immediately. Luke, looking miserable, listened from the dock while the arguments went on about legal technicalities.

In the end, the judge looked at the probation report and granted Luke bail for the Paddington offence as well – for twenty-eight days – while the other case was dealt with. It was a sudden bonus for Luke. He was fully expecting to go straight back to prison for two to three years. When released by the judge, he was almost in a daze. Eventually he emerged onto the street with me, to enjoy his first free moments in two and a half months. He was astonished to be outside.

I went Guilty cos I wanted a sentence – get the waiting and uncertainty over with.

Luke was speeding with excitement, and very embarrassed about his baggy khaki trousers, all-white flat police trainers and his smelly blue short sleeved shirt. It was July, and very warm, but as at Sherborne House in a hot August, he wore an anorak. This one, dark blue and lightweight – was '£70 from America'. I offered to buy Luke a celebration lunch but he didn't want it even in a modest pasta place:

No snobby joint where you have to leave a tip.

As we walked down the Old Brompton Road, I wondered at the figure we cut – Luke, long, thin and pasty, and extremely scruffy, and me middle-aged and grey in my dark suit and tie, worn, as most young offenders do, in case I was needed to go in the witness box. As the prosperous passers-by streamed past us, Luke casually informed me that he'd been on Charlie, crack and heroin for the past two years. This was a shock to me in the light of his sterling work at Sherborne House. But it did explain his lethargy and difficulty in getting started afterwards. It also explained why he wore his anorak in the hot summer – addicts are always cold when not high.

It's what got me into trouble. I been burgling and dealing in acid tabs to earn £100 a night for the Charlie and £50 for the H *(heroin)* – all through Sherborne House. After I came out I went to Camden Town to sell acid tabs in large numbers.

Never told anyone except me *(step-)*Dad. Me *(step-)*uncle took up Charlie bad when he came out of prison last time. He's in Wandsworth *(Prison)* now.

I don't tell no one, not even my girl Donna knows. Cos they learn you use drugs and they label you for life, they dismiss you. *(He showed the same outrage about this as about being fitted up, and other examples of unfairness.)*

Feltham was unpleasant because they treat you like fucking kids. The screws try to stitch you up all the time. Nothing to do banged up for twenty-two hours a day. No training, just an apprenticeship in scrubbing floors. No wonder people go mad and hang themselves.

I was banged up with a real nutter, in for murder. His mate came back and found his wife in bed with someone else so his mate beat him up and strangled him. This bloke was just watching,

too stupid to run away. When it was over he said he was leaving.
The other bloke said 'You got to stay and help me or else I'll kill
you too.' So they dragged the body to a building site and buried
it. Now he's looking at twenty-five years. But he can't stand being
in for five months.

I mean I'm ready to just do my bird, put my head down and do
my bird, and if I got six or seven years, then I'd be going mad
about getting out after that time. Six months is nothing. But he
never stopped shouting and mouthing about it.

I couldn't sleep, not for a long time. I went in and did my cold
turkey *(coming off heroin)*, but couldn't sleep more than one or
two hours a night. I asked the prison doctor for something to help
me sleep. It just dried out my mouth but didn't help me sleep.

I was dreaming of freedom, and of having sex with Donna and
then of her having sex with other people. It was driving me mad.

*In a coffee shop Luke had a cheese salad sandwich and a coffee.
No sweet or pudding. He never eats meat, it seems. It was a very
simple cafe compared to most of those on Knightsbridge but Luke
still found it 'too snobby'. He was keen on a cigarette but waited
patiently until the meal was over before getting them. Later he
was generous with his cigarettes to the various people we met in
the housing trust.*

The DC *(detective constable)* from Paddington was a wanker.
He asked me to tell him all the jobs I'd done in the area. But he
wouldn't do any deals, so he just got the one – though I'd done
dozens of others *(smiles)*. I told him I was with this bloke called
Jason – course it ain't his real name – and we were in this Spanish
bloke's flat when we got caught. My defence barrister got the
idea that Jason knew these Spanish people and the dumb copper
thought it was true. He's a wanker.

The ones in my local nick who done me for the burglaries beat
me up when they nailed me. After, when they searched my flat.
But they picked up my girlfriend's knickers and said 'Whose are
these?' I said, 'Leave them alone, none of your business, cunt.'
And they started on me and said 'What's her name? What's she
like?' and I blew up and said 'You leave her fucking pants alone
you cunts!' But they just went on about it. They're real bastards.

He expects to be arrested in the next few days for another job:
They'll be screwing when they hear I'm out and dying to get me
for something else.

They're corrupt too. On the take from the drug dealers. They tip them off before the raids and can't arrest them. Now the dealers are moved on, they've busted up the place but the dealers are laughing.

You can get any drugs you want round South London. Any weapon too if you got the cash. I don't use H out of proportion, but I did it four times a day, chasing the dragon, freebasing crack or heroin *(lighting it in a paper, and smoking it, or snorting it)*. I'd do it first thing when I woke up, and then in the afternoon, and the evening, and when I did a job, I'd sit down in the place I'd burgled and light up. I'd get a great rush and maybe fall over. It made me *(feel)* very good, but also forgetful.

In Paddington, I was caught inside this flat, and I heard people coming so I had this great rush of adrenalin after the Charlie, and climbed out the window and slid down the drainpipe, but I lost my balance, and they caught me. It's not as bad as if you inject it, so I could manage. But it's over now, definitely finished.

But as the day wore on, Luke became less confident.

I'd really like some Charlie now. But I'm not going to give in. It put me in prison.

It would leave your hands shaking, and you'd start sweating after it wore off until you had some more. But I was smart at Sherborne House. I carried it but never used it there. Not like Alfie *(another group member who lasted less than a week.)* He was stupid and shot up in the toilet. He's in Feltham too doing his bird.

We took the bus to Putney, in which he described the mindless routine in Feltham – bored out of his mind, he began to read: John O'Hara's Mrs Ewing, *'about a lesbian' and several other books.*

When we left the court in the morning, he planned to get a job – any job – the next day, 'on a building site or something' – and to save some money for this month. But by the middle of the afternoon he felt lost:

Wish I could've have stayed inside. I'd be sent to Brixton *(Prison)* for a few days, and then moved back to Feltham. I never expected the squeeze. Brixton is a better place than Feltham, even though it's old. They don't treat you like a kid.

We discussed his turning down the video job.

I really wanted it but there was no bread. I needed at least £150 a week for drugs. Donna said I was an idiot not to take it but I couldn't do without the money *(and it would have kept him too busy to 'earn' it the usual way)*. I also didn't go to college. Same reason.

Near his 'old D's house' (his mother's) *he showed me where he broke in upstairs above the Indian restaurant:*

Found some Charlie in a case but heard the old Bill outside, shoved it back in and under the bed and jumped out the window. Too many old Bill to get away but I landed on this fat one who head-butted me, and the others jumped on me.

His mother wouldn't come out to join me for a drink, so Luke left his anorak at her house, and swapped his detested police trainers for his brother's. We went on to the Independent Living Scheme which has helped Luke through the last two years. He needed to collect his keys, some money, and take the gate off his flat door. The warm welcome he received at the office showed he was not bereft of help. His own Housing Officer, Peter, had taken a keen interest in him and recognised both his value and his limitations.

Despite his gloom, Luke was still capable of charming and smiling at straight people — from the blonde barrister in court, and Charlotte, the motherly court probation officer whose report got him bail, to the Independent Living Project team, and me. But to everyone in his life, he had not been telling the truth about his use of drugs. And for ten weeks at Sherborne House, he had successfully hidden a busy life of crime from all of us.

We then went to see his girl, Donna, surprising her at the counter of the card shop where she worked. Donna is short, plump and pleasant-looking, with light brown hair tied in a ponytail. I'd met her before when visiting Luke; her demure calm seemed a helpful ballast for his mercurial moods. She seemed neither as intense nor as demanding as Luke made out.

Donna coloured when she spotted us, but looked pleased to see Luke unexpectedly free. When we left and walked along the High Street, two pretty girls in a Rover hooted and called to Luke from their car. 'When d' you get out?' they asked. I was surprised on his behalf — he seemed too shy to be at ease with many girls — but Luke took it in his stride. 'Nice girls. Better than Donna.'

We bought two beers, and drank them on the street, dodging through the speeding traffic, rather than waiting for the light.

When I was nicked, Donna's sister came round and tried to get her to go home, and she said it didn't matter cos I was going inside. So I smashed the engagement ring and threw it at her. I said 'Fuck off then, there's your engagement ring. Who needs it.'

Now, three months later, he still seemed angry.

His new flat was in a well-made mid-rise block in a leafy street of Putney, a comfortable suburb in West London that borders on the Thames. The flat was spacious, with large windows looking out onto his neighbours' trees and substantial houses. It was very different from where he lived before. But the rooms were in the same squalid state that seemed to reflect Luke's frame of mind much as his detested Balham flat had. One large room had just a double bed mattress; another a single bed, some sheets and a blanket. Scattered papers from the council showed his rent rebate at £35.56. The only decorations were a few posters for Iron Maiden on the wall of the smaller room, and the odd box or packet. The floor was lightly strewn with clothes – all soiled. The kitchen was dominated by a pile of dirty dishes. No food, no soap, though there was some Flash for the encrusted cooker. Luke looked disgusted at the sight, and said he had been asking for a furniture grant. I think he had been given one which had been spent on drugs.

Earlier in the year, his probation officer, Rex, had explained Luke's failure to get a job or a training course: 'Having the flat was just all that Luke could handle.'

It could easily have been cleaned and tidied up – it wasn't that far gone. But it was clear that no effort had been made at all. Luke's beautiful round table from Sherborne House sat in the middle of the main room, a testament to what he was able to do when he tried.

The power was turned off. Luke needed to call the Electricity Board to fix the wiring that had gone wrong before he went to prison. But he couldn't be bothered yet, and 'didn't mind another weekend in the dark', which sounded like a metaphor for his view of the world. We left to collect his cash from social security, and stopped for 'a drink'. This proved to be a Diet Coke. We'd already consumed a lager each on the way to Wandsworth. Luke finished his on top of the bus before throwing the can out of the window, and smoking opposite a No Smoking sign with a warning of a £400 fine.

Luke's spirits seemed to sink after he saw his flat, although he still talked about keeping off drugs. In the flat he said:

Luke: You know, Rog, I've got the impulse to do
     something crazy.
RG: Have fun?
Luke: No. Go and beat someone's head in.

*We moved on to the office where Luke collected his cash from a
woman official who knew and liked him. As we left he suddenly
announced his plan to dump Donna because, he snarled, 'I'm sure
she's been unfaithful while I been inside.'*

*As an observer, I should have left Luke to break up the relation-
ship that evening. It was further evidence of the self-destructive
nature of Luke and people like him. But I tried to help him think
about it. He had said previously his priorities were: 'A good
woman, a kid and a place to live.'*

*I advised him not to spoil his first freedom, that he had no
evidence Donna had been unfaithful, that even if she had been, he
told her before he went to prison he was ending their relationship,
so she would have thought she was on her own. His preoccupation
– which he'd thought a lot about in prison – was that Donna had
written and told him during her prison visits that she had indeed
been faithful. But it seemed her reassurances only made Luke more
anxious:*

But in sixteen months, after she's had my kid *(she was not
pregnant yet)*, she says 'remember the time you were inside and I
said I was faithful? Well, I wasn't.'

*It was because he was already experiencing the painful feelings
about this future loss that Luke planned to dump Donna ('Not
hit her,' he says pointedly) that night.*

*Luke also longed to see his grandmother, who was raising three-
year-old Thomas, the son of his imprisoned uncle. Luke called
him 'my Tom'. Luke proudly showed me the photos of two little
black kids who are his step-brothers. One was having his birthday
that same day. Luke spoke of him with rare tenderness. His family
feeling was still strong, despite the battleground of wasted lives
and twisted personalities:*

Me uncle in prison has fallen out with his Dad. Me Mum won't
speak to any social workers or the like after a lifetime of them.
She hates them.

*Anxious to keep up his momentum, I offered to give Luke the
telephone number of a group member who'd found work so he*

*could learn how to find a job on a building site. First Luke said
yes, then 'You call him,' and then 'Don't bother.' Nor did he know
how to get the information himself. It was like watching a balloon
lose air.*

*Luke did say he was going to get in touch with the priest who
came to Feltham and talked about jobs. He would ask him for
help. But his energy returned when he spoke about cars – and the
crime he 'needed' to buy one. Luke said burglary was 'boring' and
that he was giving it up – but this was not quite as encouraging
as it sounded:*

My dream is to buy a BMW, or a Merc. I'd like to work in a
BMW garage, then maybe race the cars competitively. But they'd
never hire someone like me. So I'll do one big job that will set me
up – like a Securicor van.

We planned to rob the £8000 in the Bureau de Change at
Thomas Cook in Putney High Street. Me and some mates worked
it out and watched it for a month. I'd go in as a motorcycle courier,
delivering a package at the back, but with a sawn-off in me pouch.
Collect the cash, leave the bike on the Common, pick up a car,
drive down the M4 to a B & B for three weeks and then return
to London to spend it. Didn't do it because the friends chickened
out. I'd be grassed up if they caught anyone. Not that I'd ever
grass no matter what they offered me.

*I warned him about the long-term consequences of any serious
crime, but his answer reflected standard prison wisdom:*

I know I'd go down for seven or eight or ten years *(said with
equanimity)* – but not if I get away with it.

Got away with the Renault job.* They tried to stick me with
£42,000 in criminal damage! Had to drop the charges for lack of
evidence.

*Not surprisingly, prison had trained Luke only in crime, nothing
else.*

Luke: I really want to move to Canada but I can't, not
     with a prison record.
RG: But it'll be spent *(expunged)* in a couple of years if
     you keep your nose clean.
Luke: Not if you been to prison twice.

* The one he described to me on the first day – see p. 184.

RG: I thought you hadn't been in before.
Luke: Not for very long. But enough to be able to take
      anything they throw at me.
RG: The screws?
Luke: No. The courts.

I suggested he might be able to return to the motor project, and apprentice himself for a job as a racing driver.

I want to wash cars in a BMW showroom. Then I'll ask the salesmen to let me work on the rally cars, and then persuade them to let me drive.

This was a fantasy but a practical one, showing he had some grasp of the present and of possible future outcomes. His ingenuity in burglary suggested still more talents he could use elsewhere.

We passed a Bureau de Change, prompting Luke into another energetic outburst:

That's where I brought all the foreign currencies I'd get from houses. If the fuckers tried to charge too much, I'd have checked at the bank first and quote the bank rate at them and force them down. They're greedy bastards sometimes!

I'd nick a car and go out to the country, places like South Wales, to yuppie villages. It was easy, all those cottages full of videos and antiques and money and whatever I could carry. I'd sell them in London, and use the money straight away to buy me Charlie and H.

We was doing sometimes ten burglaries a night, you'd keep going once you were at it – steal a car, and sell it along with the videos. We'd sell the engine, the wheels, the frame or maybe smash the chassis.

Sometimes we'd just carry it by hand – a bag full of several videos. Once I stole a safe with a mate and we carried it from Chelsea to Putney covered in my jersey. We took a supermarket trolley from Sainsbury's and pushed it along in that, and when the Old Bill came by we just hid it, and then went back for it. It took two hours with a hammer and chisel to open it.

We was always hiding from Old Bill. *(we pass Putney Bridge)* One time I did a shop in Putney High Street and hid from them on the ledge below the bridge.

It's the only way many of us know life in the streets is to live it – most people got no flat, no money, no help.

I went straight for a time after they ordered me to attend

Sherborne House. And I do want to be a video tape editor. But I also got a strong desire to rob a bank.

I got a mate who is facing six or seven years for armed robbery cos he was nicked in the act – all on video. He was still very excited when he saw the tape.

I was making sometimes £2000 in cash, spent it all on food, clothes, and drugs. If I had all the money I've had in my hands altogether, I'd be rich – many, many thousands.

He looked wistful. I was very sad for him, and for us.

Finally, exhausted, we parted. Luke went off to see a mate, but clearly wished he was still in prison so he wouldn't have to cope with the task of managing the day to day details of his life. I was deeply depressed by his revelations, and the thought that he would probably go back to drugs and crime within a few days. He was to see his easy-going probation officer, Rex – who knew nothing about his drugs, or the extent of his crimes – on Monday. We planned to meet again the day after.

On that day, I drove over to see Luke around midday. He didn't answer the door, and I feared he had done a bunk even from his own flat to avoid meeting me, as he'd done so many times before.

But he was only changing his clothes. He answered the door in a smart green sweatshirt top (he called it 'jade' when I compli-mented him on it). He wore blue loose trousers that he insisted on changing again when I persuaded him to make a phone call. It meant going outside, to the phone box across the road.

Luke: They're too baggy.
RG: I thought that was smart.
Luke: Too baggy ain't smart.

He was very depressed, and knew it. He promptly announced that his depression was annoying Donna. Her presence soon became clear from small signs. He asked coyly:

Notice anything different?

There was a tiny teddy bear on the bed, and a little more junk – but otherwise the flat was completely unchanged, the same shambles, with clothes everywhere, nothing tidied. The electricity was still off. He said proudly:

Donna's moved in. I'm trying to get her name on the flat jointly but I don't know how.

Luke's speech was slow, and his eyes hooded. He looked stoned but insisted he was off drugs. He said the bottle of pills on the table was 'antibiotics'.

I tried to talk to him about his depression but he didn't want to. He sat silently on the bed much of the time. I told him about the depressions of some of the world's richest women who couldn't get out of bed, about how depression cuts across all classes.

Can't get out of bed in the mornings. Feel knackered but can't sleep. When Donna leaves, I get up sometime.

Luke was still planning to call the priest he met in prison who promised to help him with a job. I offered to go with him now.

Can't. I'm skint.

It was the same story with the call to the electricity board to sort out the wiring. He declined my repeated offer of enough money to use the phone box. He also refused any food, consuming only his own packet of chocolate biscuits, which he was steadily working his way through.

> Luke: Don't want to borrow money from you.
> RG: I don't mind lending small amounts. It was when you asked for a large amount that I thought it was wrong. And told you.
> Luke: Yeah, you did. *(He said this with emphasis but no other comment. I left the matter alone. I offered my car to take him to his grandmother.)*
> Luke: Didn't go the other day. Still haven't. I don't know what to say to her. *(This was the person he loves most in the world. He also wanted to see his uncle.)*
> Luke: He's in Wandsworth Prison for knifing a copper. The copper was trying to save his life by stopping him from jumping out of a fourth-floor window. He's a real addict, he was out of his skull.
> RG: Do you think Sherborne House is more help than prison?
> Luke: Sherborne House was no use. Before I went I heard people say it tried to get into your head – sounded weird. They did try to do that sometimes. I didn't like it. Don't know what the others thought. They wouldn't admit it if they were helped.

That seemed to apply to Luke even more than to the others.

*

*A few weeks later, I managed to speak to his probation officer,
Rex, to see how Luke was getting on, and what view Rex took of
his prospects:*

I like Luke, he's a likeable lad. Didn't go to college as he
planned. I still think all he can do is cope with his new flat. You
know we've got to be careful not to impose our own expectations
on him – we're career-minded. But even those from stable homes
don't know what to do with their lives at this age. Not until their
mid-twenties do they start to work it out. I think one of the dangers
of Sherborne House – which is also very good – is that they expect
the boys to emerge from there and just get right on with their lives.
But they can't just sail ahead, much as we would like them to.

Luke says he's still sticking to his principles, to his morals, as
he'd decided to before. And I'm cautious not to impose my values
on his.

His main preoccupation seems to be the flat – he says he's got
these plastic bags all over the place and needs money to buy furniture. He got a job in a men's clothing shop, and has been in touch
with the college who said he could have a later electronics course
to study. He's still very much with Donna. He's a likeable lad.

*The next time I saw Luke was a few days later. He had told
Rex about his drugs. It seems Rex was not surprised.*

Luke: *(offhand)* Gave me a long speech about rehab.
  *(This time Luke seemed even more uncertain about
  his future. The job in the clothing shop had not
  materialised.)* I started thinking about giving up crime
  last winter. Do you believe that I want to stop?
RG: Yes and no. *(I quoted back to Luke his reaction to
  seeing the Securicor van, and his willingness to risk
  seven years for one big job. He both agreed and
  denied he was tempted.)*
Luke: I know I'd be caught. Just my luck.
RG: You're lucky to have escaped so often before being
  caught.
Luke: I'm unlucky.
RG: It's your own choice to do things after knowing the
  risk. Not luck.
Luke: I'm unlucky! Everything I do fucks up!
RG: What part do you play in that?

(He reacted with a rush of restless energy, suddenly prowling the flat, and talking about doing it up, and getting a job.)

Luke: How many from our group are inside?

RG: Five.

Luke: Sounds bad. *(more prowling)* Donna thinks I'm paranoid. She wants me to stop. It's driving her mad. I'm sure she'd had it off – she's told me and I don't blame her. *(with impressive calm)* I believe her. *(then, bursting out)* I want to get out of this fucking city, move to Swindon. She's agreed. But I'm sure she doesn't mean it. She won't go. *(Luke was furious again at something that hadn't happened.)*

RG: Don't anticipate trouble. You were bloody lucky to find a woman who'll wait for prison.

When we went outside, I bought two phone cards and gave Luke one to sort out his electricity, and speak to the priest who had offered to help him find a job. He didn't want a drink and didn't ask for cigarettes, despite having only decomposed filters in cigarette papers to smoke in his flat. He was very good about money, drawing the line between us just as I had done earlier.

I took him to Brixton to meet the Reverend Delroy, an extremely engaging young black evangelist, who offered to help. He made a call arranging an interview later in the week for Luke to start a carpentry course.

When I dropped him off near Wandsworth Bridge Luke thanked me for the first time for pushing him to go to see Revd Delroy, and for arranging the visit.

I later learned that his interview had been postponed, as the interviewer hadn't realised the urgency of his situation. That was part of Luke's bad luck. By the end of the month of his unexpected bail, Luke had spent one day at the course.

One year after Sherborne House, Luke went back to court for his trial. I turned up in a smart suit again in case I was needed as a character witness. I was, and told the Judge I had watched Luke perform to a very high standard at Sherborne House over ten weeks. His potential was obvious, as were his problems. He needed both training and drug therapy, neither of which he would get in prison. I said I couldn't guarantee what would come of giving Luke another chance, but that we could safely assume what would happen if he went inside. The Judge agreed, and gave Luke another two-year probation order.

Luke appeared to be both thrilled and astonished to be free, this time for good — unless he went wrong again. His young half-brother Anthony was also there. He was all that Luke wasn't: straightforward, cheerful, focused, certain at the age of thirteen that he wanted to be a professional footballer. Anthony was also absolutely straight.

Throughout our celebration lunch, Anthony lectured Luke about staying off drugs and drink, the need to go for a placement in a training scheme and the like. Luke listened and agreed grudgingly that he would stick to this new regime. It meant attending the carpentry training scheme, which was in Brixton — a long bus ride away — and a drug rehab centre in Richmond.

Sitting at the table, picking at his food in a cheerful Fulham cafe, Luke had the undernourished, deprived look of someone who's been in care, and who has not cared for himself. His temperament was more volatile than it seemed, and it would take careful effort to win his long-term trust. But it would clearly be worthwhile. His intelligence and ability to apply himself were so evident that their abuse was a loss to all, not just to Luke himself.

After lunch I could already sense Luke beginning to be weighed down by the difficulty of being free and responsible again for his own actions. I left them both at their mother's place with a plan to regroup later in the day at the office of the Independent Living Scheme.

Luke never turned up. He also quit the carpentry scheme after two days because the journey was too long. He has never been to the rehab centre. He has split up with Donna, and is presumably slipping deeper into depression. I don't know where he is, nor does Peter, his Housing Officer. He doesn't answer the door.

CHAPTER NINE

BOBBY

I'm the only sane one in the family

Bobby is twenty, white, clean-cut, square-jawed, fair-haired, wiry, short, and noisy, with a South London accent and infectious, garrulous charm. He is a natural extrovert who treats everyone as an audience or as mates or both.

Bobby's normal uniform is a sateen windcheater over a white T-shirt, jeans and trainers. He has the lean, tight physique of a boxer, which he once was. He stopped boxing after becoming partly deaf; his deafness makes him speak a little louder and adds to his general bonhomie. Bobby also has a violent temper and the strength to act on it which has been a major source of his difficulties. But he's endearing for all that because of his directness and his genuine concern for (some) people.

Despite his relentless cheerfulness, it is hard to exaggerate the difficulties in Bobby's family background. One sister tried to stab one of her husbands, and did stab another. Bobby said to me once in passing, 'Me Mum and me sisters all been in mental hospital. I'm the only sane one in the family.'

Despite his disastrous childhood, Bobby's criminal activities started relatively late but included TDAs, drunk driving, driving without insurance, burglary, fighting, non-payment of fines and breach of probation and Community Service Orders. He was actually arrested in November 1988, and then went on the run for a year. He turned himself in, was given the Community Service Order, breached it, and was sent to Sherborne House instead of prison. He had already spent two months in Feltham on remand.

While Bobby was struggling to attend Sherborne House, cope with a host of problems where he was living, and clear his decks with the law, his mother turned up one day and said 'I'm moving to Southend, I can't stand it any more.' She asked Bobby to pack *for her, and didn't say where she would be living. So he packed up her things without knowing her new address or having any prospect of seeing her again.*

His father runs a garage where Bobby occasionally works. But they fall out regularly, so he too is, at best, an erratic source of support.

But for all their problems and his, Bobby has tried to maintain contact in a painful and futile attempt to keep a sense of family alive.

Over lunch one day at Sherborne House, Bobby exchanged painful reminiscences with Luke about their time in care.

Luke recalled the whiteness of the room in which he was put in solitary confinement at his Special School. He hated looking back. Bobby took a different view. He was curious, perhaps because he remembered little:

I want to learn to read properly so I can get me papers back from the Social *(Security)* cos they're mine to read, ain't they? That's my past in them files. Maybe I'll write a book about it. Not a book, just something. Me Mum stopped me, and so did me foster parents. They told me not to read them cause I was just getting upset. But I want to.

I first met Bobby in an interview with Ellen, the education officer, at the start of the Sherborne House course. He told Ellen he was made a ward of court while very young, and put into care. He was in Southdowns Children's Home in Winchester for four years.

(Cheerfully) Never really went to school. Didn't know if I was coming or going. Went from one fucking boarding school to another. So I'd prefer spending the day thieving than going to school. The only place I liked was fixing motorbikes. I loved that. Been in trouble since fourteen. I'm trying to sort myself out. Eighteen months ago I was hopeless. Then I made plans ahead. I got me a place to live through Save the Children. Getting me own flat after I leave Sherborne House! Apex *(a voluntary agency that helps ex-offenders to find work)* found me a carpentry job. I need to spell properly but I can read and write. I made plans.

Bobby didn't present himself as a victim. He was positive in addressing his circumstances. Bouncing around in his chair with nervous energy, Bobby seemed carefree and careless but certainly not evil. He had many debts and outstanding fines to work off but he wanted to study and improve his writing skills. Now that he was trying, he seemed a good prospect to go straight if he could finish the programme.

But it was by no means a certainty. Bobby had a very hard time coming to Sherborne House every day. He had to cross London from Wimbledon to Tower Bridge, a difficult and long journey by tube and bus, to arrive by ten in the morning.

I like this place. I quite enjoy coming. But I ain't a thief no more so I don't see why I come here. I'm a bugger for getting out of bed. Me bed is too fucking comfortable. It's a brilliant mattress. Sleep right through the alarm every day – the sleep of the dead. I'm gonna have to get rid of it. I got to do it. I know I'll go away *(to prison)* if I don't finish the programme.

Bobby took part in the groups with gusto – he loved talking about himself, and his unending saga of domestic and legal problems. Listening was not his strong point, and was not helped by his hearing trouble which he disguised very well.

One of the early groups involved examining real cases of other young offenders, and trying to guess the sentence:

Lenore: Seventeen year-old black male charged with
    affray for hitting an eighteen year-old with a brick.
Bobby: Affray is so easy to be done for. Just shouting can
    get you done for 'starting a riot!' Some get fined £500
    for that!

Stu would give him four to six months in a detention centre. I would give him a fine, say £50 plus compensation. Bobby would give him a fine and compensation and a Probation Order of two to three years. His real sentence was 240 hours of Community Service and a £500 fine. Very, very heavy in my view, though not as heavy as Stu's sentence of custody. I'd be surprised if either the fine was paid, or the huge number of Community Service hours actually completed. Bobby commented:

I had a CS order like that, but I couldn't get out of bed on Sundays – I'd sleep till the afternoon. *(Saturday night is a heavy clubbing night, always until the small hours of Sunday. That's part of the CS punishment.)* I'd wake up and think 'Oh Christ, I should be at CS.' That's why they sent me here.

Well-intentioned as it may be, having avoided the use of custody, such a sentence is a recipe for further offending. If the offender fails to do his sentence and pay the fine, he goes back to

court facing a still 'higher tariff' sentence: custody, or its equiva-
lent like Sherborne House. That is just what happened to Bobby.
Yet how much of that next stage will be his own fault, rather than
a court 'teaching him a lesson' he could not realistically learn? If
'affray' stands for a fight, then he is unlikely to feel guilty about
what he has done, just aggrieved at being caught and victimised
by such a heavy sentence. And how is a seventeen year-old youth
expected to find £500 on top of his normal living costs? The only
easy way is criminal.

As if to prove the point, Bobby described his recent life:

Wake up in the afternoon, have a bath, and go down to the
bookies. Used to gamble a lot: horses, dogs, fruit machines.

Bobby thought nothing of losing £50 in a visit to an arcade or
pub. He used to thieve for the money:

But I gave up gambling when I lost £250 in an accumulator on
the last race at Wimbledon *(dog track).*

Shows I've got will-power. Now I can sit in a pub and look at
a bloke hooked on the machines and it don't bother me.

But Bobby had a long way to go to put his life in order. He was
waiting for a flat, to which he was entitled having lived in care all
his life. He knew the grant system well but was vague about the law:

I only open me telegram or the solicitor's letter that tell me to
be in court in the afternoon of the day I'm supposed to be there!

As with the others, money for Bobby was more than just a matter
of survival, though the mundane matters of bills were a permanent
headache as he emerged into independence. As a ward of court until
he was eighteen, Bobby was due to be housed by the council. To
prepare him, they gave him a place in the Independent Living Scheme,
just as they did for Luke. It is a half-way project involving some
supervision for teenagers in trouble to learn how to cope on their
own. Having his own flat was something Bobby looked forward to
enormously, though how he would fare was seriously open to doubt.

It's this thing about London, see – everything costs money. You
can't live on £27.50 a week. You got rent, electricity, fags too –
it can't be done.

When young offenders speak about their dole money, they see
themselves as victims. To them it is patently unfair and unrealistic
to expect them to live on that sum – chicken feed by their previous
standards – without being tempted to resort to theft.

Although bad at managing his domestic finances, Bobby was a

natural wheeler-dealer. On one occasion he steamed into Sher-
borne House out of breath halfway through the morning, and
appeared in the staff room (off-limits to group members) with a
small hand-held television: 'Cost me £50. Worth £130!' The day
before he had brought in a portable telephone. During his time at
Sherborne House he bought and sold two cars and a motorbike.
But that day he had come to talk to the staff about his giro prob-
lems and his need for more money to live.

I've been to the DSS to report me Giro's been stolen probably
by some of the wicked cunts that live in my house. *(Lenore told*
him off for his language. He didn't mind, and barely drew breath.)
The woman at the DSS was Chinese and told me I should be an
MP cos I'm so good at arguing. But it takes three weeks at least
to get a new cheque if you report it stolen. You get a new one
straight away if you just say it's gone missing.

Bobby seemed to live on the edge of disaster: his door was
kicked in several times and the council wouldn't fix it more than
twice. The gas and electricity were always about to be switched
off. The bailiffs were after him for unpaid fines, and each of their
visits increased his debt by the cost of their fee. This drove him
wild, and led to a hilarious attempt by Bobby to renegotiate his
fine over the telephone. The first time he rang the wrong court
office. When he found the correct one, the clerk had gone home.
Bobby planned to threaten to burn down the courthouse but
instead proved persuasive on his own behalf. He doesn't give up.
Like so many young offenders, Bobby has a highly developed if
idiosyncratic sense of personal rights.

After I got busted, they took all my stuff and records and Teas-
made, all that stuff. The CID said 'all of it came from burglaries.
You claim it and we'll nick you!' The records didn't belong to the
people they returned them to so I rang Customer Complaints at
Scotland Yard and got a letter saying I could claim them after all.
So CID said again that they'd nick me if I took them, but I did
and they couldn't do nothing. I got it all back with a receipt that
makes it yours.

In the exercises, Bobby showed a skewed sense of moral recti-
tude that could be useful to him if he manages to keep out of
trouble as he now intends to do. Much of the Sherborne House
work is based on awakening, or rebuilding the group members'
own innate sense of right and wrong.

This was the purpose of the exercise on moral dilemmas:

Bobby: *(reads)* Would you accept a lift from a girlfriend who's over the limit? In the past, I'd never leave a car behind no matter how drunk either of us was. Now I'd take a cab. I think. Maybe.

Mark: I don't trust my friends sober, let alone drunk. *(He doesn't laugh. A nastier side of Mark was emerging today.)*

Bobby: Over three pints and it slows your reactions, affects your driving – I got done for drink driving so I know.

Deb: *(reads)* You find something in your bag you haven't paid for. Would you go back?

Bobby: Depends on what it is. I used to pick up something every time I went shopping. I had to take something every time – for the bath, or whatever.

Luke: *(leans in towards Deb with nervous contempt)* If anyone says they'd go back and pay for it they're mugs. It's a business, man. *(He leans back, having delivered himself of this verdict.)*

Deb: *(honestly thinking about it)* I'm not sure what I'd do. It depends on if I'm still in the shop or on my way home. *(It was crucial to their credibility within the group for the leaders to be open about their own albeit modest past misdemeanours. I was too.)*

Bobby: *(to no one in particular)* I was last done by the manager of a shop who rushed out and grabbed me – I'd had a fight with him before. He asked me to come back and I said 'No! I ain't done nothing,' and hit him. So he pulled me back and tore off my coat and we had a tussle. There was this lock on the floor which he reckoned I took.

    Nothing on camera, no alarm went off. No evidence but he took me to court. They said they was going to Crown Court for Assault. I could've gone down so I went Guilty at the Magistrates. Got fined £200. It was a bike shop in Clapham.

Luke: *(his sallow, sad face lights up with their shared secret)* I know the guy. He's a plonk. The place is easy to get into – every weekend it's done. You just open the door a bit – the police come, check nothing's gone – then you cane it. Everything's there at the back – stereo radios, motorbikes. *(Luke was delighted by the memory, as if recalling a bountiful Christmas, which he will never have had.)*

Lenore: *(dryly)* No wonder the guy is twitchy. *(Luke had objected to being followed whenever he went into a shop. Her remark is lost on them.)*

Mark: *(reads)* Would you leave a window open on a weekend training scheme so a friend could burgle the place? *(matter-of-fact)* Not if they would know you.

Lenore: *(astonished)* But you'd be a suspect if you had a record.

Bobby: But you're sweet if no one grasses. Most people are done through grassing. I'd never grass. I've been done for other people's jobs and knew who done it. I went remand for it but still wouldn't grass. They came to my prison but they didn't admit it themselves because they thought I'd grass them up. *(He tells this story without bitterness. It's clear this ethos is very strong as a code of honour, but it is reinforced by the threat of violence to those who break it.)*

Sunny: *(clever)* I'd leave the window open and do it myself.

This frankness has disclosed all of their ethical styles. They have done things like this before, some of them often. But the probation officers' evident disapproval makes some of them – like Bobby – uncomfortable. They press the group leaders to admit they'd be tempted if broke and facing a £400 fine. Lenore says: 'I couldn't do it. No matter how hard up I was.'

During Project Week, Bobby came on the sailing trip. He showed how and why he has trouble sustaining relationships and jobs. His conversation flowed nonstop, day and night. Lying in his bunk, Bobby kept us awake with a stream of consciousness of random thoughts, comments and jokes about the mattress, the food, and his sleeping habits. When others remonstrated they

wanted to sleep, he'd say 'Good night John Boy' – quoting the
Waltons – and then, after a minute or two of silence, resume his
monologue.

Like Johnnie, Sam and Joel, Bobby slept heavily between his
rostered duties, which he seldom did without being pushed extra-
ordinarily hard. During one strenuous landing when all hands
were needed on deck, Bobby was threatened with punishments
unless he came to help the others. He was completing his toilette,
preparing for a night ashore. Ignoring the angry calls from above,
Bobby simply carried on singing to himself 'No can do-zy'. He
finally arrived on deck as if coming on stage – when the work had
finished. He was unabashed, and hurt that he failed to receive his
usual welcome.

On the last day, Bobby and I were given the task of cleaning the
cabin. While I did the work, Bobby was again grooming himself
happily. He ignored my friendly and then impatient requests for
his help to the point where our usual good relations broke down
entirely: I was cross, and that made him cross. I could see how he
contributed to some of the family arguments he described, how
his foster father lost patience with him over mundane matters like
the music from his stereo and finally cut the ends off the plugs.
Bobby was immovable, and unrepentant about the way he went
about his business no matter how it affected others. (Long after I
had forgotten the incident, he came up to me at Sherborne House
and said, 'You've gone off me, Rog, haven't you.' I hadn't felt
that, though I was less charmed by him. But his form of apology
served to clear the air.)

During the voyage, he told a constant stream of dirty jokes ('The
Irishman fucking the Jewish woman: "I thought all you Jews were
tight." Jewish woman: "I thought all you Irish were thick!" '),
and exploded when we failed to laugh at the worst of them: 'You
lot are the most boring bunch of fuckers I've ever met.'

Onshore, Bobby showed a trader's interest in a wide variety of
things, not just cars and motorbikes: we passed old houses and he
admired the antiques in the window, always in terms of their price.
But he also had a sense of the pleasure in things – whether merely
a delicious French bread sandwich, or the seafood laid out splen-
didly on the harbour stalls, or the elaborate variety of trainers –
and girls – on display in the shops and the discos we visited one
by one like pilgrims in Dunquerque and Ostend. Bobby was par-

ticularly keen on exotic drinks, and discussed the subject at length. He was determined to buy the strongest rum available – which he did – with a view to getting blasted on his return.

In Ostend, we encountered an exceptionally pretty girl outside her shop, and at the collective request of Bobby, Johnnie and Joel, I started up a conversation with her. As soon as she smiled at them, they moved on, speculating on what she was probably like. Bobby decided she was so special, he would return to Ostend after Sherborne House to 'collect her'.

On the way back to London in the van, Bobby joked about finding a rich older woman to look after him. For an athletic, good-looking young man with a lot of charm, this seemed a not altogether unrealistic prospect. He told me later that from the age of fourteen he had never sustained a relationship with a girl for more than a few weeks, and it was always based entirely on sex. But his recent experience with one woman in her twenties had made him realise that women wanted and could give more than that. In the session on relationships, another group member, Stu, had insisted women were only interested in sex, and if any girl asked him back for coffee that was what she had in mind. Bobby scoffed at that view, and said he now knew several girls 'just as friends'. Although several young men in the group were already fathers, Bobby was the only one to express anything but a purely macho view of women.

Bobby struggled to complete his time at Sherborne House and to make the most of it while he was there. In the last session of weight training, Stan, Mark and Winston decided jointly not to take part, despite the threats of warnings by Molly, the probation officer, and the exhortations of the dynamic black instructor. While they chose to hang around outside the gym and smoke cannabis, Bobby seized the chance to have what became a private coaching session. He did all the strenuous exercises with zeal.

The problems of his family always threatened to overwhelm him. Bobby missed so many sessions he ran out of points and was technically in breach of his probation order. The staff were sympathetic to his predicament and gave him another chance.

But Lenore and Deb were concerned that all his absences had deprived him of much of the benefit of the group work, and that Bobby had not really looked at the things which led him into trouble – like his temper, and his tortuous relations with his family.

The degree of his involvement with his sisters' problems emerged
most vividly in the exercise that asked each member from whom
they would steal – family, friends, acquaintances, teachers. The
group leaders worked hard to make him test his answers against
his experience:

Bobby: My sister Ellen – wouldn't steal from her at all.
 I got too much respect.
Deb: Even when you're angry and not thinking straight?
Bobby: Been into those situations loads of times – I've
 even broken up the flat – but you don't steal from
 your family. I did once at thirteen, I robbed the gas
 meter – that was that.
Lenore: Loads of people do that, even in this room.
 You're the only one who's admitted it.
Deb: You respect Ellen too much to steal from her. What
 about the other sisters?
Bobby: They're really crazy. They've done things to me –
 Katie's stolen off me. But I wouldn't hit her. I'm not
 that way inclined.
Deb: You wouldn't be entitled to!
Bobby: *(perplexed at this idea)* Sometimes you got to
 show you're really annoyed.
Lenore: They can't listen to you when you're hitting
 them.
Bobby: You don't understand my view – Katie sitting
 there drunk on a bottle of rum going on and on at
 me – I said 'if you weren't my sister I'd bash you,'
 so I poured the drink down the drain and she went
 mad. I hit Katie and Louise.
Lenore: *(appalled)* Why?
Bobby: Louise stabbed me. Katie I don't get on with at
 all. She's a bitch, never sorted her life out, always
 poncing off other people. But I wouldn't steal off
 her. If I asked for an ornament I liked in one of their
 flats and they said no, I'd accept it.
Lenore: But you always quarrel. You might smash it.
Bobby: You're twisting my words. I break up my flat
 when I'm angry, not theirs. Well, the other day I
 rammed a scraper through the wall cos Pauline just

went too far. I don't like seeing my sisters fight. I try
to separate them. Unless Katie deserves it. Every
time I see my family they're having arguments. Me
sisters. Their boyfriends. Louise's crazy – she
stabbed a girl to death when she was very young.
They put her away for years. Stabbed her bloke the
other day and nearly killed him. Her first husband
she stabbed in the knee. She's just fucking crazy,
man.

Lenore: *(reeling – we all are)* Are you all alike?

Bobby: No. Me and Ellen are the only sensible ones. I
said to Pauline she had a fucking hard life – I'm
going to do what I can to help her when I got me
life sorted out.

Lenore: You're the sensible one yet you do things
impulsively.

Bobby: What's 'impulsively'?

Lenore: Spur of the moment – like bashing in the TV set
the other day, smashing your flat . . .

Bobby: *(hurt)* You say that like I'm bad but me sisters
get things really going and I get really wound up.

Lenore: You could walk away. You could walk away
and put some distance between you and her or
them.

Bobby: *(getting angry)* Don't make me out to be a fucking
woman beater. I did that in the past and I don't
look to the past.

Lenore: You've done some things for yourself but you
need to get things in order.

Bobby: I got a split decision temper.

Deb: You've got to look ahead, make plans.

Bobby: *(still cross with the image he feels they have of
him)* I don't go down the road and just lose my
temper. I'm not a fucking maniac.

Lenore: *(on surer ground now)* You could spoil things
for yourself – like your flat.

Bobby: I take my aggression out on other things. It just
comes like adrenalin.

Lenore: It just comes? Or it's triggered off.

Bobby: It's triggered off. By arguments.

Lenore: There were no arguments on the boat, yet you
   got the hump.

Bobby: Sometimes I get the hump first thing in the
   morning. *(trying to express something new for him)*
   I'm not an aggressive person, but things just bundle
   together by the end of the week and I just get the
   hump – but people think it's for no reason. I do feel
   bad afterwards.

Lenore: You have to stop yourself before it's too late.
   You didn't want to smash the TV set and now you
   can't put it together. You say you feel good about
   yourself but last week you got drunk by yourself,
   smashed the flat and now you're having to tell
   someone it was burgled – you're having to lie.

Bobby: The way I feel now I'm going to knock my family
   on the head *(drop them)* and get me flat sorted now
   and then get in touch later. Cos every time I go there
   I get wound up. I leave as annoyed as what they are.

Deb: Have you ever left your family alone for a while?
   *(This is the obvious solution, and the group leaders
   have been hinting at it for some time.)*

Bobby: They're me family! I like to know how they're
   getting on.

Lenore: If you weren't there, they'd have to sort things
   out themselves. Have you ever thought that maybe
   you're not helping them? That they could sort things
   out but they're not if you're there – you're the
   scapegoat, always to blame.

*Slowly grasping the point, Bobby argued that Pauline was in need
of help – her boyfriend was in prison and she's pregnant again.
But he realised that Ellen no longer got involved with the other
sisters, and that maybe the reason his mother had left was to get
away from them all. So he agreed to try the idea of looking after
himself for a while.*

Lenore: It's an important stage for you – starting college,
   a new flat. You can't take on everyone's problems
   as well. You won't be able to keep your flat or your
   place at college. You only got through the programme
   here by your fingertips. You had several squeezes.

(*Bobby nods gratefully. Deb returns to the original exercise.*)

Deb: Would you steal from us?

Bobby: Wouldn't steal from anyone I know.

Deb: Have you ever?

Bobby: (*honest now*) That depends on if I like them.

Deb: Is that the same as respect?

Bobby: (*cross again*) Listen, most of my friends are thieves and I don't see them no more.

Lenore: (*keeping on now*) Who do you know that you would steal from?

Bobby: People at school.

Lenore: Do they know you've stolen from them?

Bobby: Course they do. Listen, I'm not a fucking archangel that's gone wrong. I got beaten up loads of times.

On leaving Sherborne House, Bobby more or less stuck to his plan. He worked for his father for a while at his garage, learning to sand down and repaint cars, with a view to taking over the business one day: 'Much better to work for yourself. No hassle about a criminal record.' On the strength of his performance on the boat, I felt Bobby was temperamentally better off as his own boss as well.

Several months later, I visited Bobby in his new flat, on the fifth floor of a mid-rise council block in Streatham, with a balcony and a nice view. The place had two large rooms and a kitchen, and was sparsely furnished but clean. The sitting room had nowhere to sit down but sported a good stereo system, a television set and video – 'all bought for a song, not stolen Rog, honest!' – a noisy little mongrel dog, whose energy reminded me of Bobby, and a python curled up in a large fish tank. Bobby was very proud of the flat, and looked forward to doing it up properly. He had lots of plans for it, and was determined this time to keep out of trouble.

He had a date to go dancing that evening with two Latin American girls he'd picked up on the bus the day before. He was taking both of them out because he fancied the one who couldn't speak English. But first he had to drop the video at his sister Ellen's house. Ellen was the one of his sisters who was, by his account, normal. Hoping to meet her, I gave him a lift.

In the car, Bobby told me he had fallen out with his father who he said had short-changed him on a car.

I started dealing in cars and bikes very young. I just bought an Alfa Romeo Sprint for £180 and sold it for £400. Then I sold me Dad a Metro for £580, cos he needed money. I said to me Dad I'd sell it to him if I could get me cash back. Then I learned he sold it on for £800, and made another swap for which he made £700. I got nothing.

Bobby felt very bitter about it. In fact it seems to have been a breaking point between them. Bobby had a row with his father and lost his job.

To Bobby's credit, rather than return to crime, he found a job on a building site which required that he be at work at 7.30am! Getting out of bed at six in the morning to go to (almost) legitimate hard work was the best proof that Bobby had really changed.

We arrived at the high-rise council estate where Ellen lived with Eddie, who, according to Bobby, was a tough South London character. They had two small children and a ferocious guard dog. As we parked Ellen spotted us through the window, and was furious. Opening the door to the noise of the dog and the children, she snatched the video recorder from Bobby without a greeting or thanks, and said 'Didn't you know he never likes me to see any-body – any man – unless he's around?' Bobby took this welcome in his stride.

Back in the car park, we ran into several of Bobby's old mates, all of whom had been in prison, and some of whom now had families while remaining active criminals. Bobby made an excuse and we left. He seemed determined to keep away from crime.

Some days later one of his friends was rearrested. Bobby sus-pected me of having tipped off the police. I only learned this many months later, when I visited him again to do the interview one year after he had left Sherborne House.

Bobby looked really well, his spirits were up. He said he would not go back to crime. The situation was quite extraordinary. I was met at the door by Anna, a vivacious Costa Rican girl who was the non-English-speaking sister he'd picked up on the bus when I'd last seen him. They were now married! They looked a sweet happy couple in the framed wedding photograph – Bobby was even wearing a fawn coloured suit and tie. This change to domes-

ticity was reflected in the flat – now utterly transformed. It was decorated nicely, with flowers, a low grey sofa, a black smoked glass coffee table, a Christmas candle, and a fancy sound system with huge speakers. There was also a larger television set and video. The black bookcase against the wall Bobby had made at Sherborne House. The walls were also painted grey and white, and adorned with smart posters and photographs: pictures of a child, and another of a scowling bulldog, with the caption 'Make my day!' What began as a bare bachelor's pad with nothing more than a bed, a stereo, a TV and some pets was now a home. The snake had gone, though. ('Had to get rid of it Rog, Anna didn't like it. Made a bit on the sale.')

The noisy dog was still very much around, but so too were Anna's whole family, who gradually emerged one by one from the adjoining bedroom rather like clowns from a circus car. Her parents are straight middle-class professionals: her mother is a physiotherapist and her father an engineer. They had been to England twice, first to check Bobby out, and then for the wedding and stayed. They were shocked at her choice of husband. But they were apparently content to stay for weeks in his tiny council flat when their other arrangements fell through. It had become a nice place to be. It was the flat of someone living what looked like a normal life. To gain a measure of his progress I began by trying to delve further into the past Bobby had alluded to at Sherborne House.

I'm twenty-one on 20 December, in two weeks' time. It's alright. Tell you the truth, I'd like to be sixteen again and start all over again, cos I left my education a bit too late you know. Now I've got to go to college for three years, I won't be qualified till I'm twenty-four. If I'd started when I was sixteen I'd be fully qualified now.

I was born in Roehampton Hospital, Queen Mary's. I can't really remember hardly anything about my family from early on. Only from ten onwards. My Mum and Dad split up when I was very young, and I was shifted around children's homes and my Mum's family and things like that. I just can't remember much before I was ten.

First of all we all went into individual children's homes, that was me and my four sisters – Louise, Ellen, Pauline and Katie. Then they put us all back together again. After I was about five I stayed with Pauline till I was about thirteen, and Ellen stayed with

Katie. Then we all got put into one in Wiltshire, and we stayed there for about four and a half years. But Louise stayed in the boarding school all the time cos she was a bit gone in the head – she weren't all there, you know? She had some problems *(she had, of course, stabbed another girl to death)* and they wouldn't let her out – they put her in a secure unit.

We stayed in the home; the first to go was Ellen. She fell pregnant at sixteen. She moved back in with my Mum. Next was Pauline, then Katie. Then they asked me if I'd like to go back home and I said 'yeh'. After I went back home to my Mum's in Balham, she'd married again to a bloke called John. That didn't last very long, a couple of months. Then my Mum fell ill again and went back into hospital.

She'd been ill before. That was the main reason why we all went back into the children's home, cos my Mum had – I don't know what they call it – a lot of nervous breakdowns, when I was very young. All the time we were in children's homes she was in hospital, sometimes for two years at a time.

I was so young it never used to bother me – I was always very confused about what was happening around me so I never paid much attention to anything. I took what was coming to me and accepted it. But it's different now, I seem to think a lot more about it than what I did then.

I'm upset at seeing how things have turned out. None of my family got anything good out of being in children's homes – three of them got children now, they're all still on the social security. None of them's got jobs. I don't see much of my Mum. She's moved to Southend with a bloke called Freddie she was with for a couple of years. Then she split up with him when she was in Southend.

To her it was making a new start. She wanted to get away. She said the family were giving her a lot of problems, but then she split up with him *(Freddie)*, and she's just stayed there and don't contact anyone any more. Last I heard she was a bit ill, so my Mum never did get well again. She stayed ill.

As for my Dad, when I was a kid I used to respect my Dad. I used to think a lot of him. But to me now he's just a person, he's not even my Dad, cos I tried to get in contact with him to help me out in certain things and he just don't want to know. I realise that now about the way he feels about us, while when I was a kid I was very confused and didn't know what was happening. I didn't pay much attention as to why he didn't stay with us, but now I realise – to him when he got remarried, his second family was all that he had. He forgot the first family. That hurts. Sometimes I feel angry, like I want to go and hurt him. But it ain't going to change anything. Things are what they are in the long run. All I can do is just try and make a future for myself.

I've stopped thieving, I ain't thieved in a year, since I went to Sherborne House.

I just did burglaries, never did anything else. I assaulted a policeman, but that was just fabricated. He was saying I done that cos I got hit by the police and he was saying it was a form of defence, but that was a load of rubbish.

I stole a car, drove to Lewisham, and police tried to stop me by jumping out in front of the car. I drove on, up a one way street, and went into a wall. The police ran after me. I ran round the car, a policeman hit me with a truncheon and gave me a good kicking. Then on the way to the station they was hitting me in the riot van. When I went to the station the copper said I hit them first and they hit me to restrain me. I didn't touch anyone.

I'm not a violent person but I do get into fights. I've fought before but not for a long time. To me it's just a form of defence. If somebody hits you, you don't just stand there – you hit them back.

I used to have a very bad temper, I still have. I react to things on the spur of the moment. If I fight with someone, I'll do anything I can to stop the fight to hit them so they'll stop.

I'm not a fighter but I used to go to night-clubs and see someone I didn't like and fight them. I'd look at their girl, and eye them up, just to provoke them. If someone eyed my girl, I'd do it to them. It's either my girl, or the geezer's girl. I'd kick someone who asked for it, or was going to do it to me.

I went to buy a motorbike and I had the cash. I got there first and this bloke comes and wants to fight cause he wanted to buy it too. So I went outside and beat him up in front of his girl and his friends. I felt good about that because I showed him up as not as tough as he thinks he is.

You can't let them take liberties. If you don't fight, they'll do it again. (*Like many young offenders, Bobby was willing to lose his liberty to stop someone else taking what they call 'liberties'.*)

I was in a friend's house and this bloke, the one who wanted to buy the bike, came into the bathroom and said he wanted to fight me, so I said 'Fair enough', and we went outside. As I was going out the door he threw a punch in my face. I grabbed hold of him and hit his head on the balcony. I picked him up and I was going to throw him over, but then I thought I better not. I beat him, and I said we better stop and leave it at that. He said okay.

I didn't throw him over the balcony cos he'd have bloody died – it was on the fifth floor! I'm not that stupid. It was just my anger, I thought to myself, 'No don't do it.' I wouldn't have done it. I'm not like that. When I saw him again, he was nice.

Stopped all me burglaries. Don't want to risk it. But if it comes, it comes – I got to fight. Saw a fight last night. It started with someone being sarcastic: 'What are you doing?' 'Sitting here. What's it look like?' That was enough.

When I used to fight I used to switch off. If I find someone's being funny, I can't talk about things, my only way out is by fighting them. After that the majority of the time they seem to respect you for what happened. The other week I was working and this black bloke kept being funny with me. I had a fight with him and after that he was alright with me.

I'm not one to fight with knives or anything. My idea of fighting is not stabbing someone or hitting them with a lump of wood, it's just throwing punches.

Knives are a way of feeling more secure in yourself. I used to carry one but I never used it. I used to carry a switch blade – spring loaded – where the knife comes out of the top and goes back in again. I never felt the need to pull it.

Loads of people have pulled knives on me. One geezer came at me after a fight about speakers and was going to stab me in the back. What I say to them is 'just put the knife away and I'll fight you.' They get scared and think 'Bloody Hell! He can beat me if I didn't have the knife!'

When I have a fight I don't really think about it after. That's my way of getting out of things – by fighting someone. Nothing ever happens. I have a fight and that's it.

I been in prison. I was in Rochester for four months for a burglary. I've also been in Feltham on remand for eight months. It's funny because you wake up in the cell, and you think you're indoors and then you realise you've been nicked again. You think, 'Ah what if I was in a different place, I wouldn't have got arrested

in the first place. If only I'd had been doing something different.'
My Mum used to say 'it's not what you've been nicked for now
– think of what you got away with in the past.'

Funnily enough, I quite enjoyed prison cos they had so much
sport. I'd missed out on it at school and I really enjoyed it. The day
I left prison I thought 'I won't be playing football, or basketball or
stuff like that any more.' I don't know, some people come out and
they feel really institutionalised, but I was only in for a few months.

I didn't get friendly with any of the staff. Prison officers are all
much the same – trying to find something wrong so they can get
you in front of the governor. I was always in trouble. When I
was in Feltham I was saying unconvicted prisoners should be out
working like convicted ones are. They said I'd refused to obey any
of the rules which I suppose was true. When you're in there on
remand you're always waiting for the day you go to court. Until
then you never know what you're doing, how long you're going
to be in prison for.

I was deliberately bad cos I wanted to go in front of the governor
to explain my situation. By then I'd pleaded Guilty in court and
was just awaiting sentence, while they did a Social Inquiry Report.
So I wasn't an unconvicted prisoner. *(But Bobby's plea didn't
work, and he was stuck in his cell.)* When you're there it makes
you think a lot, in your cell twenty-three hours a day, you got to
occupy your mind in some way. When you're there all you hear
is 'I ain't ever thieving again, things are going to change.' But it
never turns out like that, cos the first day you're out, you're back
in the situation you was in when you went in.

I don't think you can change the way people are. If you've got
someone who enjoys robbing banks that's just the person they are
– they can only change themselves. I took that upon myself. I
stopped hanging around with the people that was doing it. The
most important thing to stop you thieving is to stop going round
with the people doing it.

I've got a couple of outstanding things at the moment, but that's
from things that happened a long time ago. It's not things that
I've done since I've left. Things like fines. Apparently I've got a
warrant out for my arrest, something like TDA, but I'll have to
find out about that when I get arrested.

*This is a classic predicament both for the young men and for
the probation officers. The justice system moves so slowly that the*

offences catch up with them long after they can remember why or what they did – making the punishment utterly cut off from the act itself. Moreover, they may well have grown out of crime, or been through a learning experience such as Sherborne House or both. The fear of old offences catching up can undermine their progress to straight living.

One of my sisters got arrested about a year and a half ago, and the police said 'Have you seen your brother Bobby? Tell him there's a warrant out for his arrest.' So when I phoned them up they said it was to do with a TDA. But I think he was just saying that to get me to go down to the station. *(It happened while he was at Sherborne House and soon after he'd given up thieving.)* It'll do my head if it just hangs over me.

I don't know why they don't just come and get me here, to tell you the truth. The other day I accidentally knocked a woman over while I was driving a motorbike – I was working delivering pizzas. It was raining, the geezer in front of me had no brake lights, so when he slammed on the brakes to avoid the woman, I skidded past him, and hit her. The copper who came CRO'd me *(checked his name with the police computer in the Criminal Record Office)*, and nothing come back, so maybe it's got dropped. Probably just another of those fucking fines.*

I don't think they should fine people on the dole. They just can't afford it. They should give them a Community Service for a day, or something like that. I would rather go to prison for non-payment of fines. I been fined twice. Once for £15, but I didn't pay it. I think they only give them to cover some of the court costs. I don't like paying them. They *(the bailiffs)* came round the other day and someone let them in to show them I was living there. I'll have to see to that. *(This casual threat itself showed how close he was to more trouble, despite his clear commitment to avoiding it.)*

They should've taken them round the back, shown them some empty room and said I'd moved on. I haven't got the money, and I've got better things to spend it on, things like clothes that I really do need. I've got an outstanding fine of £250 and I haven't got a pound that I could give the court at the moment.

All the group members seemed to ignore fines, no matter what

---

* The accident led to a charge of Driving Without Due Care and Attention which is now hanging over Bobby as we go to press.

the consequences. They obtained money in various ways – usually illegal – but used none of it on fines, and then claimed absolute penury in court to have their fines reduced to nothing. They were right in that they had no jobs or legitimate income. But I was surprised they did not prefer to pay off their fines quickly simply to get shot of the problem. The probation officers did not delve into their reasons, being concerned only with changing behaviour. I suspect they can't let go, and that being in trouble is part of their own self-image. Like Bobby, they presented their refusal to pay off their fines as in a sense virtuous. But it's not – they simply see fines as unwarranted and unjust, furthering their image of themselves as victims of circumstances beyond their control. In Bobby's case, that would be an accurate description of his child-hood, but it was remarkable how cheerfully he described it.

The children's home gives you everything a kid needs. They give you a school, more or less they give you everything you'd have in a family except you've got a lot of different people looking after you. But the thing is, once you've turned eighteen and you've finished being a ward of court then you just leave there. I don't think there's much you can do except find yourself a place to live, and most kids that do that find themselves on the dole and getting them paying the rent.

I went from children's homes and eventually I went into a boarding school in Middlesex. They had a built-in school as well as living accommodation, athletics, a big football pitch, motorbikes you could drive two times a week, that was quite good there. But then it closed down. A lot of the kids there were going out thieving. There were bad things happening.

It's not the place they were in, it's that when you've got a lot of problems with your family and things like that it's another form of getting away from it, forgetting it when you've got money in your pocket.

It's like that for some kids but with me it was different, cos I never did thieve at the time, I only started when I was about . . . I can't even remember. The majority of them ended up going to prison. Serious things started happening. A couple of them nicked a car and got chased by the police in front of the boarding school and then crashed into another car and killed the bloke who was driving it. Then there was a lot of glue sniffing. Everyone ended up addicted to it.

The staff weren't really bothered about it, all they was concerned about was that no one got harmed. But everyone used to go off to a field and sniff glue and they said 'If it happens again you'll get booted out!' The same thing would happen the next day, and it went on continuously like that, until a couple of kids got kicked out. I left soon after that.

Most of the time when they're tough about things it makes it worse, cos it makes you feel as if you're being pushed, and it makes you want to do it even more in places like that. You do it just to annoy them.

What might have worked better than just to let you do it is to find out why they're doing it, sniffing and thieving and stuff. It's no good talking to people after they've done it, you have to speak to them and give them counselling before. It might make them think twice about it.

What it is, the majority of kids that have family problems do turn to crime; they find a way of getting away from the other problems that surround them. That's all I used to do. If I used to feel bad, I used to go out and sniff glue.

When I was sixteen I just stopped, decided it weren't for me anymore.

I was sniffing glue in my Mum's flat and I went unconscious and fell asleep. I woke up the following afternoon on the landing. Maybe it scared me, I don't know, but I stopped after that. But other kids can't. They feel they can't go without it.

I haven't touched hash for about six months. I found I could get along a lot better without puffing. If I was puffing it would be harder to get out of bed the next day. And you get in moods when you haven't got it. What it was, if you've got money you buy it. The more you've got, the more you buy.

I've taken speed, Ecstasy and acid. I haven't taken anything else other than that. I took speed three times, Es twice and acid I took twice. I didn't feel good after taking any of them, so I didn't bother taking them again. I only done that cos I was going out to a rave.

I carried on raving without them. It's good when you're on them, it's when you come off them the next day you just don't feel your normal self. That's when you get addicted to things cos you feel you've got to take it again. But I can take something, and if I don't like it I can stop.

One of my sisters is addicted to sulphate, but to me I could never understand why she couldn't stop. It's a downer.

When I take speed *(amphetamines)* I go out and feel on top of the world and everything is very good. But when you wake up the next morning, you're back where you started. So to me it's not worth taking.

I hardly drink anymore. If I go out to a pub, I'll have a drink, but that's once every couple of weeks. I used to like drinking, but now I've slowed down, just like everything else.

It all comes down to money: if you've got money then you can do anything you like. To get money if you're not working you go out to thieve. Most of the time it's when you're in a group of people. If there's four of you, and three are thieving or puffing, the odd one out always seems to go in with the group and do it, cos if you don't you feel out of place.

I stopped thieving. If I met one of my mates, and he said 'I'm gonna do this or that,' I'll say 'I don't do it no more.' It does make you feel bad doing it. But it's lucky, cos the majority of my friends are in prison now, doing three or five years! They're the people I used to hang about with. I figure if I'd stayed with them, I'd be inside as well. Instead I'm still here, and I'm trying to make a go for things for myself.

I never really do think about what's happened to me in the past. Sometimes I think if I'd been in a position to go to college when I was sixteen things might have been different. But I wasn't. There were a lot of problems going on with my family. I was living with my Mum and she was ill.

You can be forced into things. It used to make me feel I had the opportunity to go out and thieve and things like that. I'd say the majority of people who end up starting thieving have either been in children's homes or had family problems. Those are the two main categories. Someone who's lived with their parents, had a good family life, a good education. It's very rare someone like that turns into a thief.

I had a good foster home at one point and I wasn't doing anything serious when I was with them. I was with them two and a half years. I think I moved to my foster home when I was about fifteen. It was good, normal family life. But I always had my music on too loud. Finally Ron, my foster father, came in and cut my plugs off the hi-fi. I didn't want to fight with them any more so I moved out.

Then I moved on and started thieving. I got arrested a few times, I was on remand in Feltham, then came out, and got arrested for TDA. I got in touch with my foster mum and she came to court to say I could live with her again. That was the only reason I got bail. Anyway, seven months later, it went to Crown Court – two assaults, reckless driving, TDA stuff like that. I got found guilty. The judge asked for Social Inquiry Reports and I got bailed again. Then nobody saw me for a year!

I had another argument with my foster mother and moved out of her address – which meant I broke my bail automatically. So I went on the run cos I didn't want to go back to prison. I was working on a demolition crew and buying and selling motorbikes, sleeping on the floors of me friends and sisters.

I couldn't drive legally, got stopped a couple of times, and couldn't use my real name. So, after a year, I just said 'Fuck it! I'll go to court and face it,' and I handed myself in. Then they give me Community Service. I went a couple of times but I fell out with the bloke I was working with. I was moving furniture and I started chucking it about. So I went back to court again and that was when they referred me to Sherborne House. I got a place to live in the Independent Living Scheme.

The courts've been very lenient with me. But that's only owing to my circumstances. If I'd gone to court and I hadn't had things going for me – a flat and a training course – then I would have been sent straight to prison. If they put me back in, I'd only go back to stage one where I was in the first place. When they give you alternatives to prison they're giving you another chance.

Maybe I've got a good face in court and I know how to be. Some people go in with a cocky attitude and the judge thinks 'Ah you're the funny one,' and puts them straight in prison. If you go in and put all your cards on the table then you've got a good chance of getting a placement like Sherborne House. They only give it to the people they think will get something out of it.

I've got a friend who's been in and out since he was fourteen. When he went to court the other week for fracturing someone's face, the judge said, 'If you can do that with one punch, you ought to be a boxer.' He sent him to AA, three days a week. He's given him another chance. He's still thieving. He won't change. What can you do but send him to prison? He hasn't got no sense. He hasn't got the brains to change.

It's a very hard position to be in the judge's seat – half the time they don't know if they're wrong or right. Like the judge with me – he asked for Social Inquiry Reports every three months for two years cos he wants to know what's going on with me. Maybe reference to my case helps him to deal with other cases like mine.

The one hard thing for me is work – cos I've never had to get out of bed in the morning. A couple of weeks for me is great. I can stick with it cos I'm getting money but after that I get bored as I'm doing the same thing again and again. But I've got to learn to live with that – to adapt. You know, learn to change. I don't take drugs any more, I don't thieve. The next step is working and studying.

I've started college, I've got myself married, I feel a lot better in myself now. I've got a nice flat. All I really need is to finish college, get a placement. Once I've got my education, I'll never be out of work. Motor vehicle repair – to repair crashed cars.

I used to go joyriding. Stole a few cars you know, crashed a few. With joyriding, I just used to nick a car to get round in. Nick it, change the number plates on it, and just drive it. To me it was a form of transport. Other kids will nick it to deliberately smash it up. I used to drive it for my own personal use. When I got fed up with it I used to get another one. But then I got nicked for TDA and got a driving ban and stopped altogether.

I used to love it, driving cars and motorbikes and all that. When they set up courses for kids, banger racing or speedway for ex-offenders who've only been nicked for TDAs that's a good idea. Once they go out there and start doing it, they haven't got the urge to go out and steal cars cos they're doing it a couple of days a week, going there, repairing and driving the cars. You find that the majority will stop nicking cars if that's all they're doing, as they don't have the urge to do it anymore.

Motor projects of the kind Bobby described are few and far between, an absurd state of affairs considering how widespread is the joyriding problem. They lack financial, legal and political support, but cost a fraction of the price of prison cells for joyriders put away under new legislation which makes it an imprisonable offence. Moreover, unlike fines or prison, motor projects provide training and a positive source of the excitement that teenagers seek in crime.

I like driving at high speeds. When we was in boarding school, they bought bikes and we used to repair them and drive them round a field for a couple of hours. It was really good. You feel you'd achieved something when you've won, but once I came out of boarding school I didn't have that any more so I turned to nicking cars. It's hard to explain why you actually do it. But the reason most people do it is that any type of car you want – a high powered one, a convertible – you can steal it. You haven't paid for it yet you feel it's yours, cos you're driving it. Driving your own car if something goes wrong you have to pay for it, but if it's not yours you can tear it, you can do three sixties *(three hundred and sixty degree turns)* in it, you can do what you like.

I've never gone over the top like that, going crazy. People who do things like that are just stupid. If I was to steal a car I'd only drive it about for my own personal use.

There was a road in Wimbledon where we used to go fast, but it wasn't a public highway and there weren't any people about. I used to love taking a bike to its maximum speed, about a hundred and ten, something like that. I've got a nice bike now. I'm just repairing it, a 650 Turbo. I'm off my ban now and I've got my Stage Three driving test in January. Once I've got that then I'm legal, all I need is insurance.

It's all in my own interests. If I didn't stop I would have just carried on going in and out of prison, in and out of prison. That's no future for me. There's other people enjoy going in and out, they think it's great. They come out and say 'I've just done three years.' To me that's just a waste of three years of your life – you can't get it back again.

But another thing is, say they got nicked for a job they could have got £1000 out of, in the three years they was in there. If they had a job at £100 a week they would have tripled their money anyway, cos they wouldn't be earning while they were still in prison.

I used to love going to discos, buying a car and nice clothes, stuff like that, and to do that you go out to thieve. It's an easy way of getting money. The alternative is to go out and work, but it takes you a long time, while if you're thieving you can get it all in a day.

It never occurred to me it was wrong. All I was thinking about was the money I was earning. In a way you could say I got – not obsessed – but I used to feel very happy cos I had money in my pocket.

I never used to think of the people I used to thieve off. It never used to occur to me. Sometimes I used to get into someone's house and think 'Cor this is beautiful.'

I was only there to get some money – it was just an everyday occurrence, break into a house. Once I'd got the cash I'd stop. If I didn't get any I'd go out the next day. To me it was actually like a job. I was just there to get some money.

I used to have one bloke who bought everything off me, and sold it on. Or a friend would say, 'I want this' or 'I want that' and you'd go out and get it. But everyone wants gold, it's so easy to get rid of. I used to sell stuff to jewellers as well. One day the guy went in the back and called the police.

I used to get a girl to go into a jewellers to ask how much stuff was worth. All jewellers will buy stuff off you.

You just give them a story, they're not particularly bothered about you. If they're funny towards you the first time, you don't go back to them.

I got caught purely from being too greedy, I took too many chances. I jumped over a fence to get over the back of a house in Southfields, and on the way back out again I got into the car and the police pulled up next to us, a man had seen me jumping over the fence.

Another time I got nicked coming out of a jewellers with some gold. It was valued at £26,000. We done three that day.

It all went back to the woman who owned it. Except for a ring that was worth about £1200.

Funny enough I've never had any problems with dogs – I just pat them – I even fed one once to stop it barking! You can switch alarms off, and most front doors are not secure, but the majority of time I used to get through a window. If it's got a special security lock, you can just take the window out. I'd stop at a Rottweiler at the front door. Or a person – I'm not one for doing aggravated burglary – automatic three years.

There was one that I felt bad about: I got into a house and it turned out to be an old woman's house and I always felt bad about it. I don't know why. I didn't take anything. I just left it as it was. It didn't seem right stealing off an old person. Young people, they can work and get things back but old people can't. But I never used to really think about things like that. If you've got a conscience you wouldn't do it. Now I have got a bit of a conscience.

The reason why I started stealing in the first place is that I got in with a group of people that were already thieves. I'd never really thieved before. Stupidly enough I started thieving with people who knew nothing about it, even though they was thieves, so I ended up getting nicked a lot of times. The majority of times I got nicked cos I was grassed up. Other than that I wouldn't have got caught.

Sometimes I look at my friends and I feel sorry for some of them. I had a good friend called Ray. We used to hang about together, nicking cars and bikes, having a great time. Now I've stopped thieving, and he's carried on and now he's in Wormwood Scrubs. He was one of my best mates. But the reason he's always been thieving is he's never had the chance to do anything else, he's never had his own flat, anything to make a go of things. As much as what he'd like to stop thieving, the position he's in stops him. He's got no money, nowhere to live. He feels as if he's forced to go out and do it.

What changed me was that I had too much going for me at the time – I got my flat, I felt as if I had something to live for. When I was thieving I was going from one place to another, but once you get your own flat, I dunno, it gives you the intent to go out to find yourself a job and go to college. But some people are not like that, I've got other friends who've got flats, girlfriends, babies and they still go out thieving every day. It's just a way of life for them. I've got everything to go for at the moment. My flat, college, my wife.

Probation is good in one sense. You talk to people while you go there and it makes you realise what you're doing – they're talking to you about future plans; and I had a good probation officer, I still have. She listens a lot and then gives you advice, while some of them are idiots and are just there for the job.

Community Service I didn't really like and didn't bother going. Sherborne House is a better way of avoiding prison than Community Service. When I was on CS, every time I went there someone was talking about what crime they'd committed that week. It didn't make any difference to them.

Sherborne House is different in a sense that because of the counselling it makes you think. There were some people there that weren't bothered but I'd say they'd be back in prison now. (*He was right. At least five of the fourteen who actually started the course have already been incarcerated.*)

In the groups and after, you went through all the aspects of why you started thieving, family life, everything. But I'd say a year before I went to Sherborne House I'd nearly stopped, I'd only go out occasionally. Since I finished there I haven't been out thieving once. I just got to leave it behind me. I don't miss the thieving. I miss the money.

Sherborne House did stop me. But you can't change someone just by putting them in Sherborne House. They've got to want to stop, and for some thieving is just a way of life. Thieving is like a ladder. You start nicking cars, then doing burglaries, then robbing a bank. It's the same as drugs, sniffing glue, hash – then onto one thing and another.

I quite enjoyed Sherborne House. I'd go back to Sherborne House for another ten weeks. Then three months after I finished I got this flat, and since then things have been on the up for me. Everything has changed since I got married seven months ago. I can't say I'm a goody goody, it's just that I've stopped doing things.

I've broken away from family. I don't really see them now. Most of the time I feel regret when I see my sisters. One has had a baby, she's on the social *(security)*, and I don't see that she has much of a future. It's nice to have a baby, but she's tied herself down. She hasn't got any qualifications, she can't get a nanny and go out and work. Her boyfriend's gone down *(in prison)* for a long time.

Louise, I don't know what she's doing. Her husband is in prison too. Apparently the police went to his house cos they were having domestic problems. He pulled all the gas pipes out the wall and stood there with a lighter threatening that if they came in he'd blow them up. *(laughing)* I thought he was very lucky. They sent him to the Old Bailey cos there were old people about living downstairs, and he got twelve months. What a stupid thing to do. Louise was on TV the other week! Daytime. She was talking about prison officers and coppers.

To me, every policeman has got an attitude. They feel as if they're a different person to you just cos they're with the police. None of them listen to you. I've met one good copper, and that was a sergeant in Clapham. I thought he was good and then I had a fight and told him to fuck off, and he and another copper came in the cell and gave me a good kicking. He turned out to be one of the bastards as well.

I had a warrant out for my arrest, so I gave a different name when I was brought in for fighting. He recognised me, that's why I told him to fuck off. One came in and started hitting me. I was laying on the bed. He jumped on me and held my arm behind my back and the other one hit me. They said 'You're not as hard as you think you are.' I said I could hit them back if I wanted to. They said: 'Why don't you?' I said 'I'm in enough trouble as it is without getting in any more.' Then after that I went to see the doctor. When I went in front of him he said 'What the hell happened to you?' cos I had so many bruises all over me. But I didn't say anything.

In Peckham nick I was knocked unconscious. When I saw the doctor I deliberately wanted to go to hospital to show there was nothing wrong with my hands, cos the police were saying I'd hit them. The doctor made a report saying there were no cuts or bruises on them which was good. The judge took that into account. But I couldn't prosecute them as I got a Guilty for assaulting them. Always the police say they were hit first.

Bobby has been at the mercy of one authority or another since he was first put into care at the age of two.

I was interfered with once by the head of the children's home. I've never told anyone this before but I was too young to realise what was happening. I used to come in from school and I used to be really bad, and he used to make me pull my trousers down and used to threaten me with a belt that he was going to hit me, till I started crying. Then he'd say to me to sit on his lap and say 'Give me a kiss.' I never realised what was happening but I realise now. He said, 'Would you like to go home?' and within two weeks I was back with my Mum, I think because of what had happened. I was about eleven or twelve. It don't really bother me now, but he was the actual head of the children's home. I don't know if he's still there. *(The head of the children's home in question has now been sent to prison for five years for interfering with three other young people in his charge.)*

When I was about fourteen, the first girlfriend I had was a girl called Sharon. I wasn't one for relationships. I used to meet a girl for sex, stay with her for a couple of days, and that was it. Before I met Anna the longest I'd stayed with anyone was three months.

I didn't like to feel tied down. I used to like doing my own thing. Not anyone to tell me to do otherwise, say like a mother or father figure. I didn't want any of that. A girlfriend or wife is the same – *(with mild disgust)* they always want the best for you. *(Bobby had described his time with his foster parents in positive terms, but when his foster father told him to turn the sound of his stereo down, they had a row that led to Bobby leaving the house for good.)*

It has changed with Anna, definitely. I think about her as well as me. I've surprised myself since I got married. I don't go out to discos, I ain't got the money, but I also think about my responsibilities.

I'm gonna be faithful to her. I'm not like that. She's funny, she goes on about it, but I've had chances and haven't done anything.

Anna was a virgin when I met her. I wasn't worried about her (*having AIDS*), but I'd had a few affairs before I met her so I went and had a test before I'd done anything with her. I got a negative and things went from there.

One of the reasons I stayed with her was purely cos she was a virgin, cos that's what I'd always wanted for so long. I did, and that's one of the reasons why I stayed with her.

It means a lot. You find someone that's a virgin, they give you all the respect in the world. Whereas if you find a girl that's been with different boys, they're not one to stay with you too long.

But there's a lot of family problems. When I first met her, everyone was saying it was cos of her visa that we were getting married but it weren't. She fell out with my family. The only one who came to the wedding was Pauline.

Anna's Mum came over from Costa Rica and met me, and stayed for a week. She went back and then the father consented, as she was only seventeen. She is eighteen now. We married in a registry office, but we're getting married in a Catholic church as well. Never been religious but I am a bit now, cos Anna and her family all believe in it. God, God, God, everything is God.

I told the Mum I used to be a bad boy. I think she thinks badly about it. Before Anna came over she used to model shampoo and things like that. She had a good education and all the rest of it. Anna told me her Mum was saying, 'Look at all the nice boys you had and what you ended up with.'

But it annoyed me a bit. She just has to accept me the way I am. I'm just a normal, everyday person. Even if I was still thieving.

Don't trust no one other than Anna, I don't even trust you, Rog. (*This hinged on the arrest of the friend that we had seen while taking the video recorder to his sister. Bobby thought I might have turned him in. Hopefully, I persuaded him otherwise. But Bobby had not mentioned it before I asked the question – a sign that he expects other people to be unreliable.*) I never have trusted anyone. If you put your trust in someone – say you go out thieving with someone, I've trusted them. When we get arrested they grass me up, it's happened to me a couple of times.

Having abandoned thieving, Bobby lived on the dole and attended a training college one day a week. He also had a part-time job. When he fell out with the manager and lost the job, he tried to go to college full time. But there were no places available, so he was at a loose end in the daytime, between his weekly journeys to the dole office.

Dole is a very good idea, though some people don't bother looking for work. Dole for me is good cos I wouldn't be able to study without it as I wouldn't be able to pay my rent. I do the Employment Training scheme – it's government funded, and they pay an extra £10 a week on your dole money. It enables you to go to work, learn a trade, go to college, and they pay your rent.

Some people can't live on it but for me it's good cos I don't smoke. I get £32 a week. If you spend £10 a week on fags you can't. I can personally survive on the dole, but I've had to give up everything in the way of discos. You just have to go down to the extreme basics of life. I have to pay £10 a week on electricity. Then travel, £5 a week, food £15, gas bill, £3 a week rent. If you haven't got all the things in your flat already, you'll never be able to buy it.

For three or four months it was really hard, but now Anna is going to college, and has got a job things are looking up. Once she learns English she's going into fashion and design. She's really good at drawing clothes and stuff.

She keeps telling me Spanish words but they go in one ear and out the other. I can't put much interest into it. I pay attention but I can't remember it. But we're going to Costa Rica, we're moving there permanently. A big change in my life, but I won't until I finish college.

I used to have a friend who spoke really good English, he sounded right upper-class. He was an alcoholic and he used to go knocking on doors. He'd say 'I live in so and so house down the road, and I've locked myself out – can I borrow some money.' He once went into a house and this woman took him upstairs. She turned out to be a prostitute. She lent him £50. People always lent him money cos of the way he spoke. But I never took money off people.

Kids start stealing younger and younger these days. I was in Peckham last week when kids did a sports shop through a hole in the roof: just dropped in. They're only eleven but they're all walking around in track suits and trainers *(Bobby seems genuinely appalled at their behaviour)*. It's not just the way kids are brought up that does it. Fathers who been in trouble with the law slap their kids around and say 'Don't do it again!' *(laughs)* I might be a social worker. One of my friends used to thieve and he's a social worker now.

This is not a fantasy. In many other countries, ex-offenders often become probation officers and social workers. But it is rare in Britain, where many white middle-class probation officers deal with people and situations alien to their experience. Bobby has the energy and compassion to help others. But he lacks patience, discipline, and training, which he now hopes to obtain.

Everybody's life is built up on their education. Kids don't learn nothing in the National Health *(sic)* schools, you got to send them to a proper school to get a good education. Get a few exams and a nice steady job.

Bobby's ability to hold down a steady job clearly depends on his learning to control his temper. Perhaps living with Anna will help him.

Anna is a sunbeam, a natural optimist, who seems a good complement to Bobby's volatility. She has been utterly devoted to him, while standing up for herself. Despite the comfort of her background in Costa Rica, she has been willing to take menial jobs – cleaning, waiting on tables – while also taking English classes and finding a place in college. She sets Bobby a fine example.

Bobby wants to move to Costa Rica, to start his own car repair business. There was no better evidence that his new family have affected his life for the better.

Nothing would make me go back to thieving now. I've got too many responsibilities. Don't want kids, not at the moment; it would put me in a bad financial situation, worse than I'm already in.

Since then, they have had a turbulent time. Just before Christmas, Anna thought she was pregnant. Bobby was desperate. The situation was all the more awkward because her parents were still living with them at the time, with no common language between them. The pregnancy proved to be a false alarm, but the tension was such that in a row with Anna he struck her. She left with her parents and stayed away for weeks. Her parents were furious and wanted

*Anna to return with them to Costa Rica. Bobby finally won her
back – though the breach with the parents was never closed.*

*In the spring, I arranged for Bobby to become a volunteer at
the Book Aid warehouse while he looked for a regular job. He
was lively and funny and mucked in with the work in a way he
had not done on the sailing trip at Sherborne House. Showing real
commitment to producing money for his marriage, he put in full
days shifting books and then went off to do an evening cleaning
job. He showed a growing interest in the books, and asked if he
might have the odd book of poems, and How to Teach Yourself
Spanish. Everyone came to like Bobby, and missed him when he
left. He had managed to find a regular job in another warehouse.
But he feared to tell the truth about his criminal record and so
gave a false name. When they pressed him for his national
insurance number, Bobby panicked and left. He is now looking
for legitimate work, or full-time study to be a qualified mechanic.*

*The last time I spoke to Bobby, he was keeping his spirits up
but was worried. For all his good intentions, his situation – legally,
emotionally and physically – is fragile: he bought a damaged car,
fixed it up, sold it for a profit, and then bought a motorbike.
Unluckily, he hit an oil slick that had caused several previous
accidents and wrecked both the bike and his leg.*

Just my luck. Got to find a job, Rog. Ain't no full-time places
on the college course until September – that's five months away.
I want a job on the cards now – all proper, cos I think the Social's
(Security) watching the flat *(looking for evidence of illegal working)*. I made it up with me Dad, that's good. But he ain't got no
work for me cos of the recession.

Anna's pregnant. It's definite – she's three months gone already.
She's scared of the pain. I'm happy about it, but don't want her
working now cos of the baby. It'll be alright if I only get a job.

Me Mum's back in London. She split from the man she was
living with in Southend. But I ain't seen her. I decided to get me
own life together first. Ain't seen her. Ain't spoken to her. But I
know she's back. We got an answering machine now. Came back
and heard her voice on the machine. She was crying, just sobbing
into the machine. Didn't leave no message. But I knew it was her.

CONCLUSION

Interview with a prospective candidate for Sherborne House:

Jack: What was your childhood like?
Young offender: *(pauses)* My childhood. *(pauses again)*
   My childhood wasn't.

*These young men have described their own criminality. It needs
no elaboration from me. But readers may be tempted to rush to
judgement, and distance themselves from these young people – if
only to compensate for their disappointment. It is tempting to say:
they only get what they deserve; many young people with similar
problems do not resort to crime; and, they have put themselves
beyond the pale. But as much as they may seem so at first, these
accounts are not a cause for such dismissal or despair. They challenge us to ask uncomfortable questions of ourselves and our
values. In many ways, our lives and theirs are mirror images.*

*Throughout my time with these young men, I kept looking back
on my own teenage years, on the support and tolerance I had for
my misdemeanours at school and university: I lived in a protected
time zone until the age of twenty-one. I looked at my own children
– a son aged twelve and a daughter nineteen – and those of my
friends – some of whom were and are lost or in trouble and on
drugs. Many of my son's better off school mates carry Swiss army
knives for fun, not self-defence – and indulge in the dangerous
pastime of setting light to aerosol deodorants. They are all fashion
victims. They all watch television and are excited by the style
conveyed in advertisements. They seek to define themselves
through what clothes they wear, the cars they crave, and how they
furnish their rooms. In an echo of the streets, they listen to the
same music, wear the same trainers, baseball jackets, track suits*

and jeans and have people around them that drink too much and use drugs. But for them it is only an uncertain foreground in a picture which has a more secure perspective in the background, unlike the street culture from which their music and body language comes. Our children know that when they finish school, if they cannot support themselves, we will look after them. Being middle class is in part defined by this possession of the freedom to explore the world around you in your teens, or even on into your twenties. We, their parents, are their safety net. This security allows them to find themselves, to rebel in less socially disruptive ways.

But these young offenders have no such future: they are testing their masculinity when the usual outlets for their rites of passage are gone. Apprenticeships for honourable blue-collar jobs like mining and the docks, and national service were all routes that channelled teenage testosterone productively. However brutalising in other ways, the army at least offered an escape and sometimes useful training in a contained environment – like a residential college. Both offered a safe haven from family politics while preparing for life as an independent adult.

Now these young men leave school and home early and hit the streets aimlessly. We expect them not to react as young males have always done through the ages: to establish their own territory, to fight when they feel insulted or threatened by their peers, or the police, to assert a sense of self, albeit a self under siege. Yet these reactions are normal. Such wayward behaviour is usually indulged in the armed services and in university sports clubs. They legitimise the use of force to test one's masculinity, a crucial part of the rite of passage.

What positive examples do they have of the restraint demanded of them? They have been bombarded since birth with macho imagery from Rambo to Margaret Thatcher. These young men are video veterans not just of violent fiction but of the Falklands and the Gulf War. George Bush won universal applause for drawing a line in the sand to prove he is not a wimp. Can we expect young men on the street, to whom face and respect are all-important, not to do the same?

We expect them to respect the system of justice which has condemned them. But on what basis do we command their respect? They read about huge rises for businessmen while ordinary workers' jobs are shed, about insider trading, about insurance frauds, about tycoons getting away with millions from pension funds, or claiming to have senile dementia and walking out of

*open prison and into a pension for life. They know that if they
are caught shoplifting or joyriding or assaulting someone in a pub,
they will have no such protection.*

*We judge these young offenders as if they had the same opportu-
nities, protection, and values – and had somehow turned their
back on them – and us. We call them evil, and 'try to teach them
a lesson' as if we were all playing the same game on a level playing
field and they had cheated. Perhaps we have cheated them.*

*We label their actions according to different measures than those
we apply to our own. Their self-aggrandisement is declared criminal
whereas ours is not. How many of us do not work at reducing our
taxes, have never fiddled expenses, driven over the limit, or worked
for or paid cash rather than declare the income to the tax man? We
condemn their public violence while failing to tackle the private
abuse of wives and children which cuts across all class lines.*

*We expect them to stop their addictions when we do not control
ours – as if cocaine were not a major middle class problem and serious drinking the bane of all classes' social life. They must live with
disastrous emotional problems without therapy or counselling –
even in prison. Yet both are available to us under less stressful circumstances. We focus only on their behaviour: whatever is going on
inside them, they must stop breaking the law – at once.*

*Surveying the battered landscape of these young men's lives, it
would be comforting to draw simple conclusions: that prison, or
parental supervision, or intensive probation like Sherborne House
is the means to stop their offending. Each of those solutions emerges
as an influence, but by no means the answer to the problem.*

*Many of them had been to prison and carried on offending.
However much they resolve to avoid it while inside, three-quarters
of young inmates are rearrested within two years of leaving. Most
young offenders see prison as part of their blooding, just another
badge of honour. Many have friends and can get drugs inside.
Prison can also be a positive relief from the pressures of life on
the street. At the end of their sentence, few are met at the gate by
a father-figure with a pat on the back. Most come out to nothing.*

*Parental ineffectiveness and frustration shone through the inter-
views. Most had disastrous home lives but a few did not, and were
the only ones in their family to have gone wrong. Their parents'
behaviour ranged from collusion and tolerance, to harsh disapproval and outright rejection – all too extreme. But how can*

we legislate for greater parental responsibility, as the government hopes to do, when one in three of all marriages ends in divorce?

Sherborne House made an impact on most of the group members, but the extent of its influence is impossible to measure. That many of them carried on offending while attending the course was disappointing, and is an indication that their habits would take time to change.

In judging their progress, and the work of Sherborne House, we must compare it to the three years of college or university offered to young people who want to be there. Many students waste their first years on drink and drugs and have difficulty getting out of bed: if Sherborne House rules applied, they would not last a term.

Ten weeks for damaged young people ordered there by the court is a hopelessly short time to reverse the momentum of years of social pressure. Yet hard-core persistent young offenders addicted to crime, who have committed hundreds of offences worth thousands of pounds, are expected to remake their lives entirely on their own from ten weeks and day one. Sherborne House does all it can – and remarkably well in such a short time. I'm pleased to learn they have focused the latest courses more towards the practical skills needed for finding jobs. Education is now built into the programme for everyone, and Friday mornings are spent preparing for the time after they leave – compiling CVs for job and school-grant applications.

But afterwards, like prison, there is no parachute for those that leave, no soft landing, no support system other than the occasional half hour with their field probation officer, who may or may not know anything about them and the intensive work they have just been through. It is not enough.

If we listen to their complaints, and do not treat them merely as excuses, the common demand is for jobs and training, and a better arrangement for the dole. It makes common sense: if we want them to give up activities which provide them with excitement, cash, respect from their peers, and the means to acquire the material things which our culture values, we must do more than punish them. For most criminals, punishment is simply a professional hazard. The average earnings of a busy thief – even allowing for time spent in prison – offer a standard of living untrained ex-offenders would find very hard to match in the straight world. We speak about 'teaching them a lesson' but the lesson they learn in prison is not the one we want – as George Bernard Shaw said, we punish people not for their crimes, but for getting caught.

We want them to believe in the system, and join it at the bottom, with the promise of greater rewards on the way up. But they have no access to the ladder at all. We want them to change, but offer only sticks and no carrots. There are currently 800,000 unemployed youths aged between seventeen and twenty. Yet provision of training for all youth is being cut back. The few agencies – NACRO, APEX, NEW BRIDGE, SOVA – that help young offenders to find jobs are voluntary, hang on by their fingernails, and waste most of their precious time raising money. Yet we spend millions on publicity urging people to lock their doors, and literally billions of pounds on the War on Crime. In 1990–91, prisons alone accounted for £1.5 billion – an increase in real terms of thirteen per cent on the previous year.

Prisons are asylums, with high walls to shut people away from our thoughts and sight in the name of protecting us from their actions. But when they come out, bitter and vengeful, and with no other prospects, they may threaten us more. Remember, only five per cent of all young offenders commit seventy per cent of their generation's crimes: theirs is still the peak age for committing burglary.

With the rate of crime doubling every ten years, we can expect to reach ten million recorded crimes per annum by the year 2000. The so-called Dark Figure of unreported crime is estimated at three times that number by the British Crime Survey. We cannot afford to carry on as we have done if only for our own protection and peace of mind.

Rather than throw more money at the consequences of crime, we need to reallocate resources more purposefully to attack the roots of criminality. This is beyond the brief of the criminal justice system, but it is not a fantasy. In other countries, national and local government departments work together with employers to achieve it.

Most young offenders start much earlier than the first time they are caught. It is now received wisdom that the first years are the most formative in a child's development. In France, universal child care is seen as a vital part of crime prevention as well as a general social good in itself. Children in Britain are first entitled to support at school at the age of five.

A study by the Cambridge Institute of Criminology suggests

that persistent young offenders share a complex of indicators that can be seen by the age of seven. They include one or both parents unemployed, domestic violence, excessive drinking, parents split from one another, poor housing conditions, and learning problems. Only domestic violence falls within the purview of the criminal justice system. The Home Office has expressed concern to help young people at risk, but the will is not yet there to pay for the scale of social programme this involves. Must they wait for their moment in court to merit our attention?

In seven hundred French cities and towns, tri-partite efforts between the government, local authorities and the business community offer programmes for all youth, not just those in trouble. Juvenile judges there have the power to order the provision of housing and/or training if they believe either is necessary. Moreover, they do not measure their success in terms of reoffending rates as we do. They believe that the momentum towards creating good citizens out of bad ones has its own obvious value.

In Britain, we remain fixated on punishment and invest almost nothing in alternatives. Each time there is another outburst of trouble with joyriders or rioters the response is the same: complaints of social deprivation or police aggression are drowned by the calls for stronger punishment, more police, and outrage about the leniency of the courts. We react instinctively when we should take a step back and ask ourselves what is in our best interests as a society. Those interests coincide with those of the young offenders more closely than we realise.

Jeremy Bentham designed the first penitentiary in the hopes it would serve to return prisoners to society as positive citizens. Now, more than one and a half centuries later, we can be sure he was wrong. In England, the prison population is already the highest in Europe and rising, as is the number of suicides among young inmates. But in Scotland, the reduction in the use of custody for young offenders has been matched by a fall in the crime rate. In parts of Germany, where they have abolished the use of custody for young offenders, the crime rate has also fallen. It is time we devoted our energies to exploring other ways of dealing with offenders.

Luke: Nothing to do banged up for twenty-two hours a
     day. No training, just an apprenticeship in scrubbing

floors. No wonder people go mad and hang
themselves.

*Since the urban riots of the early eighties, there has been a public
disagreement between those who hold young offenders individu-
ally responsible for their criminal acts – the police, most sentencers, and the government – and others who blame their
environment and upbringing. Among probation officers, interestingly, attitudes are split. Sherborne House, seen as a radical instru-
ment within the probation service, is designed to make offenders
realise that, despite their background, they have a choice.*

Sam: When I'm working, I don't burgle. Simple as.

*The interviews show that though temptations remain, most can
turn their back on the friends that steal. You can almost hear them
growing up.*

*Does that mean the conservatives are correct – that social fac-
tors are less important than personal morality? It must be a combi-
nation of the two: our society is based on the notion of free will
within social contracts. These young people reflect the values and
assumptions of their street culture as clearly as their mirror image
equivalents in public schools and Oxbridge. If we seriously expect
young offenders to adopt a new set of values, we must offer a
solid and reliable context for this transformation, with the same
protection from the outside world that boarding school provides.
It costs £12,000 to keep a boy at Eton for a year. It costs £8000
over the year for a place at Sherborne House. A year's place in
prison costs £20,000.*

*There are fifteen thousand young offenders currently in custody
in England and Wales. Sherborne House can only accommodate
twenty-eight young men at any time, for a maximum of ten weeks.
It is the only full-time programme in the whole of Greater London.
The Home Office estimates that there are no more than a hundred
intensive probation programmes in all of England and Wales, of
which only a handful are as rigorous as that at Sherborne House.*

*Of our total expenditure on police, courts, and prisons, we
spend less than one per cent on all forms of crime prevention. If
we really want to achieve law and order and maintain the Queen's
peace, our spending priorities are upside down.*

It is long since time that we asked ourselves what we expect from the criminal justice system as well as from those who pass through it. If we expect it to reduce the levels of crime, it has failed lamentably. If we want the offenders it deals with to give up crime, are we providing the means for them to do so? We are still trapped in the puritan notion that anything positive done in response to negative actions is a kind of reward – rather than the more pragmatic view that we must repair the damage. Canadian Indians call it 'closing the circle'. If that is our shared objective, we must look at more than the actions of the criminals.

It was striking that at Sherborne House, the hapless victims of the boys' actions – who at the moment of the crime absorb the impact of the young offenders' resentment against all of us – were largely ignored, until several group members became victims themselves. Both Sunny and Mark, two of the most violent and amoral offenders, said being burgled themselves made them give up burglary.

Our criminal justice system virtually ignores the victim. It is a theatre of punishment – a kind of state revenge conducted in the name of the victims and society. The victim is merely the excuse that sets the whole ritual in motion. Their only role in court is as a witness, and they are often not told of the outcome. Mediation brings offenders face to face with their victims and often leads them to pay compensation or to work in some form as reparation to make good the damage they have caused. It deals with the victims' need to understand why they were picked on for the crime, and to be reassured that it will not happen again – at least at the hands of the same offender. Research has shown these are far more important concerns than the revenge which sentencers feel is uppermost in the public mind.

Such encounters also bring offenders far closer to their crime in its physical and emotional impact. Under the current arrangement, the few offences they are caught for are punished sometimes years later, with a fine or prison sentence that ends up with offenders feeling victimised themselves.

The use of mediation is spreading quickly in civil disputes, such as suits against and between large corporations, like British Rail or BT. In the United States, every state and federal agency has its own mediator to deal with public complaints before they reach a court. In Australia, Canada and New Zealand, mediation is also

effectively deployed in settling disputes between individuals –
between neighbours or spouses or landlords and their tenants,
even between parents and their runaway children – which might
otherwise flare into violence and land the antagonists in criminal
court. Despite its success, criminal justice professionals have been
ultra-cautious about the use of mediation in any but minor cases,
like vandalism.

But on those occasions when victims of violent crime have been
offered the chance to meet their attackers, to explore the reasons
for the crime and express their feelings, a high proportion of both
the victims and the offenders who have submitted to the experience
have declared it beneficial. For cases involving burglary, mediation
offers an ideal forum to bring home to the offenders the unseen
trauma they have caused, and to devise appropriate reparation.
Experience of this in the USA, Canada and Germany suggests that
such reparation is far more likely to be paid or honoured by the
offender than normal fines or compensation orders. As the inter-
views in this book make clear, such impersonal punishments are
normally ignored, as are the feelings of the victims.

To close the circle, we must be willing to deal with offenders as
people in their community, with hearts and minds, and potentially
useful abilities, not just as categories and problems. This involves
facing some uncomfortable truths: we need to see and understand
their logic, their experience, their perspective, if we want to
encourage them to live as we do.

The persistent offenders who pass through Sherborne House –
and the courts – have a disturbingly low image of themselves.
They see themselves as outside society, and therefore excluded
from both its rules and obligations. When they do have contact
with the rest of us, they feel like failures – in their family, at school,
at the job centre, at the dole office, with the police, with potential
employers. They pass among us invisibly, moving in their own
circles, driving in stolen cars, sneaking into houses, spending their
days vegetating at home and their nights hanging out on the streets
or raving in clubs – a self-contained world that gives them their
own sense of achievement and often a lot of pleasure, until they
are caught, and perhaps sent to prison, to be hidden away again.

Shall we ever listen to them, to these young people? They know
even before we tell them that what they do is 'wrong', that drugs
damage their brains, that the pleasures of E and crack and racing

stolen cars are transient. That is part of their appeal. That so many of them share an utterly modest and conventional desire to settle down in their own little house with a good woman and a straight job speaks volumes for their grasp of society's values, despite the fact that they have no stake in it as yet. In spite of the obvious difficulties facing them, their desire to become legitimate stake-holders rather than career criminals is one large reason not to despair of them. These are not, after all, the ambitions of 'evil' people. But, like all of us, they behave according to the treatment they receive. If we condemn them to languish outside the circle, they will react predictably.

Their ideal is virtually identical to ours. But they approach it from the wrong side of the window. Without help, their faces will remain pressed up against the glass. It is not surprising they are occasionally tempted to break it to grasp what is on the other side.

I began this project asking judges and magistrates why they sent so many people to prison who are not obvious dangers to themselves or to the public. I have emerged with greater sympathy for the judicial predicament. If they order these young men to undergo probation or Community Service or pay a fine, they risk being blamed for the next offences, and feel personally insulted when the same people reappear before them.

It is painful to face the disappointment of persistent young offenders taking two steps forward and one step back. Yet there are no easy answers. Graham Smith, the ex-head of the Inner London Probation Service said, 'Persistent offending is often an obsession – sometimes even an addiction, not a series of single rational choices the way the courts see them. For people who habitually offend, it is already an achievement for them to slow down before they stop.' This may not console the victims of their last few offences (my computer was burgled just as I started to write this book), but it does point the way towards that place where these perpetrators become useful, law-abiding citizens – given time.

Not all the people in this book will make that transition. But after watching them closely I feel all of them could – given will-power and resourcefulness on their part, and encouragement, tol-erance and opportunity on the part of those of us they meet along the way. The challenge is theirs, but the consequences if they suc-ceed or fail are chiefly ours. They are, after all, our children too.